MAHAMAYA

Owing to the antiquity and rarity of this book, certain pages are regrettably absent, and readability is compromised due to the blurring of the original text. If you possess any insights regarding the availability of these missing sections, kindly inform us. Your assistance is crucial in ensuring the completion of this significant work for the benefit of future generations.

MAHAMAYA

THE WORLD AS POWER: POWER AS CONSCIOUSNESS

(CHIT-SHAKTI)

BY

SIR JOHN WOODROFFE

AND

PRAMATHA NATHA MUKHYOPADHYAYA

GYAN

Published by

Gyan Publishing House
5, Ansari Road
Daryaganj, New Delhi-110002
Phone: 011-47034999, 9811692060
E-mail: books@gyanbooks.com

Distribution Network
gyanbooks.com
India, USA, Canada, UK, Australia

ISBN: 978-93-6280-200-2 (PB)
First Published, 1929

2nd Impression 2024

Printed at: Gyan Press, Delhi.

MAHAMAYA
Author: JOHN WOODROFFE AND PRAMATHA NATHA MUKHYOPADHYAYA

MAHĀMĀYĀ

THE WORLD AS POWER: POWER AS CONSCIOUSNESS

(CHIT-SHAKTI)

BY

SIR JOHN WOODROFFE

AND

PRAMATHA NĀTHA MUKHYOPĀDHYĀYA

PUBLISHERS:

GANESH & CO., (MADRAS) LTD., MADRAS—17

1954

BY THE SAME AUTHOR

Introduction to Tantra Shastra
(*Key to Tantrik literature*)

Principles of Tantra
(*Tantra Tattva*)

The Serpent Power
(*Kundalini Shakti*)

Shakti and Shakta
(*Essays on the Shakta Tantra*)

The World as Power
(*Mahā Shakti in various aspects*)

Garland of Letters
(*Studies in Mantra Shāstra*)

The Great Liberation
(*Mahānirvāna Tantra*)

Wave of Bliss
(*Ānandalaharī*)

Greatness of Shiva
(*Mahimnastava*)

Isopanisad
(*A Tantrik interpretation*)

Hymns to the Goddess
(*Stotras of Shankaracharya etc.*)

Hymn to Kali
(*Karpuradistotra*)

Kamakalavilasa
(*An important work in Sri-vidya*)

Printed by D. V. Syamala Rau, at the Vasanta Press,
The Theosophical Society, Adyar, Madras

PREFACE

THE English reader is recommended to have recourse to the authors' previously published books (set out in the advertisement) for a better understanding of the present volume. Its subject is an exposition of some aspects only of the Indian doctrine of the "World as Power" (Shakti-vāda), as also a comparison between this and the better known Vedānta system called Māyāvāda. Both systems speak of Māyā, but understand the term differently as explained in the first and following Chapters. Consequences of prime importance follow therefrom.

All the known ancient religions of the world including those of what are called "lower culture" have believed in a universal fund of Power which cannot be defined and circumscribed. All imply a universal, indefinable, all-pervading Power, not necessarily in itself "personal," but of which personality is an expression. So Dr. Carpenter (Comparative Religion, p. 81) speaking of the concept *Orenda* "of the North American Indians" says that it expresses an incalculable Energy manifesting in and as the sun, moon, and stars, waters, plants and animals, and all other objects of nature, breathing in the winds and heard in the thunder. This belief commonly called Animism is a crude form of the doctrine of an *Anima Mundi* held by some of the greatest thinkers. It is the universal background of the doctrine of Power on which ancient faiths, higher or lower, have rested and out of which they have evolved. When all such faiths and conceptions are reduced to a common denominator, we find a doctrine of Cosmic Power itself unmeasured and undefined, but which "measures" out (the root meaning of *Māyā*), or makes finite forms in the formless infinite which together (form and formlessness) constitute one alogical Whole (*Pūrna*). That Power was called the *Magna Mater* in the antique West, and in India is named *Māyā* when it finitizes and *Mahāmāyā* when it liberates from the finite. The finite is conditioned Being, and that is the universe or *Sangsāra*. *Nirvāna* is Being unconditioned. The two are at base one, since the finite beings spring from the infinite and re-enter it, the latter yet remaining unaffected.

The "World as Power" doctrine has grown from simple origins to which expression is given in sexual imagery. It, like all else, has been sublimated by the Vedānta of which as Shrīvidyā it is a form. Sex is here both the symbol and sensuous manifestation of a fundamental dichotomy or diremption evolving in Consciousness and of a fundamental polarity appearing in its Power. It is with the doctrine thus philosophically developed that we deal.

In this exposition of Consciousness-Power (Shaktivāda) reference is made to western philosophy and science. To anticipate criticism it may be said at once that it is not intended by the authors to assert that all the conclusions of such science and philosophy here mentioned were in the mind of the Indian sages. What is affirmed is that much of modern Western scientific teaching is consonant with and follows logically from the principles laid down in Indian Scriptures dealing with Power or *Shakti*. These general principles implicitly contain more than the Indian texts explicitly state. Nothing, however, is here said which is not warranted by these texts and general Indian beliefs. Western philosophy and science may therefore be used to illustrate the Indian Principles and their applicability to many problems both ancient and modern. They do so illustrate precisely because the principles implicitly contain the scientific and metaphysical conclusions which are here found in them. This might seem to be too obvious for statement were it not our experience that mention of Western doctrine made by modern exponents of Indian Scriptures, frequently leads to the charge that an attempt has been made to read something into such Scriptures which is not there. On occasions this "something" is to be found expressly stated. In other cases it is the legitimate deduction from first principles which these scriptures do affirm. Whether the Vedânta in this or any other form, or for the matter of that, Western Science, shifting its position from time to time, are in all respects or at all true is another question. This book is written according to Indian practice from the point of view of an adherent of the system of the World as Power. Its object, whatever be its effect, is not to prove the truth of this or any other system but to give an exposition of Consciousness as conceived in the doctrine of Power (*Shakti*)—a hitherto little known system—and in such exposition to show that it is not a mere fossil in a museum of antique thought, but has practical utility to-day. It offers to Western philosophy a new conception of Consciousness and Mind, and brings to the controversies within the Vedântic schools a profoundly conceived contribution, in its theory of Power and in its doctrine of the unity of conditioned and unconditioned Being, of the state of worldly experience which is *Samsāra* and of that superwordly experience which is *Moksha*.

OXFORD J. W.

20th April, 1929 P. N. M.

CONTENTS

By Sir John Woodroffe (Arthur Avalon)

CONTENTS

I. Vāk or the Word—II. Artha, Pratyaya and Shabda—III. Ashabda and Parashabda—IV. Parashabda, Causal Shabda—V. Shakti as Stress—VI. Eternality of Shabda—VII. Shabda as Language—VIII. Natural Name—IX. Vaidika Shabda—X. The Tattvas—XI. Shakti—Potency to Create—XII. Nāda—the First Produced Movement—XIII. Bindu or Shakti—Ready to Create—XIV. Māyā Tattva—XV. The Kanchukas—XVI. Hangsa—XVII. Kāma-kalā—XVIII. The Gross Tattvas and their Lords—XIX. Causal Shaktis of the Pranava—XX. The Kalās—XXI. The Garland of Letters or Varnamālā—XXII. "Om"—XXIII. The Necklace of Kālī—XXIV. Dhvani XXV. Sun, Moon and Fire—XXVI. Bīja Mantra—XXVII. Shadadhvās—XXVIII. Mantra-Sādhanā—XXIX. Gāyatrī Mantra—XXX. The Gāyatrī Mantra as an Exercise of Reasoning—XXXI. Ātma-Sādhanā.

MAHĀMĀYĀ:
POWER AS CONSCIOUSNESS

INTRODUCTION

As later and further explained, the Universe of Experience is said to be analysable into five aspects, namely, Being,[1] Consciousness,[2] Bliss,[3] Name[4] and Form.[5] These are called the Five Predicables.[6] For any object *is*, is *known*, is *pleasant* to some experiencer or another, in some relation or another, and has a *Name* and a *Form* or a defining set of qualities. Form is the defined object denoted by Name which is the idea of it expressed in word[7] of which the thing spoken of is the meaning.[8]

Of these five Predicables the first three are common to all object experiences. The last two terms, Name and Form, differ from object to object; the Name and Form of one are not those of another.

All five Predicables taken together stand for the Reducible Real or World-Order,[9] that is, Being-Consciousness-Bliss appearing as Name and Form, or the psycho-physical Universe of limited Selves. The Universe as the psycho-physical is the Reducible Real because it derives from, and

---

[1] Sat.

[2] Chit, Samvid for which however no English term is an equivalent.

[3] Ānanda. These three terms make the compound Sachchidānanda.

[4] Nāma. [5] Rūpa. [6] Asti, Bhāti, Priyam, Nāma, Rūpa.

[7] Shabda. See J. W.'s "Garland of Letters".

[8] Artha. See *Ibid.* [9] Vishvarūpa-Brahman.

on dissolution is resolved into, the Irreducible Real as God. The Universe is thus imaged as the super-imposition of Name and Form on the basis of Being-Consciousness-Bliss. In the words of one of the Tantras the Lord paints the World-Picture on this basis with the "Brush" which is His Will and with which He as the great Artist, the Poet or Maker, expresses Himself to be well pleased. If we abstract Name and Form, the three first Predicables, or Being-Consciousness-Bliss, stand for the Irreducible Real[1] whether as the thinkable Supreme Self or God,[2] or as the alogical Godhead.[3] The Irreducible Real as Power to evolve as the Reducible Real and involve it again (Itself remaining unreduced) is the Reality-Whole or *Pūrna.* It has an infinity of aspects of which 'irreducible' and 'reducible' are two, logically appreciated.

Being is Consciousness and Consciousness is Bliss. The Selves[4] are pragmatically limited Being-Consciousness-Bliss. The Irreducible Real is Being-Consciousness-Bliss unlimited by Name and Form whether as Supreme Self or as alogical Godhead, and is thus free of all limitations which characterise its manifestation, the Reducible Real. "Unlimited by Name and Form" may mean, as later explained, two things: (1) *excluding* Name and Form; and (2) *exceeding* Name and Form. The *Pūrna* or Reality-Whole, logically appreciated, involves three aspects: (*a*) a universe limited by Name and Form; (*b*) Being-Consciousness-Bliss

---

[1] Brahman-Svarūpa. It is said;

Asti, bhāti, priyam, rūpam, nāma, chetyangsha panchakam.
Ādyam trayang brahmarūpam, jagadrūpam, tato dvayam.

[2] Sakala-Shiva, Sakriya-Shiva, Shiva-Shakti Tattvas, Īshvara or Īshvarī, Saguna or Apara-Brahman, the logical Paramātmā.

[3] Paramashiva Tattvātīta, Nishkala Shiva, Nishkriya Shiva, or Nirguna or Para-Brahman, the alogical Paramātmā.

[4] Jīvātmā or Purusha.

unlimited by Name and Form; and of this latter we have two forms in the two senses of the term "unlimited".

There is no non-being as such. By 'nothing' is meant no thing, that is, no psycho-physical name and form. Such appearances or concrete forms may be thought away, but not being as such. Is-ness is never negatived. 'Nothing' then means only lack of form and name. These vary, but Being is everywhere and is always given, either as the alogical Real or God-head or as God, who is the highest logical construction placed upon the alogical, or as the limited beings or selves. Being is then both experience itself and the unalienable basis of all modes of experience.

The term Being, however, does not tell us what Being is, which is learnt from introspection. Man then becomes aware that he not only *is* but that *to be* is to be *conscious*, and function as such. For his being is indistinguishable from his consciousness. All forms or modes of consciousness may be thought away, but not consciousness as such, for it is the changeless basis of such modes.

What is called 'subconsciousness' or 'unconsciousness' does not imply Being functioning apart from Consciousness as such, but (as later explained) apart from certain degrees and tones of consciousness which are pragmatically accepted as constituting consciousness.

There is no equivalent in English or any other language for the Sanskrit term *Chit*. The nearest rendering of "Chit" is consciousness because it is revealed as the empirical conscious self. But the term is not altogether apt, because consciousness in the English sense of the term requires an 'I,' and a 'This,' which is other than the self which has experience of it. Consciousness as God or Supreme Self is a consciousness of the unity of 'I' and 'This,' and alogical consciousness or God-head being above all dualities, cannot be called a self. There is, however, no more appropriate term available. If we abstract from empirical consciousness all limitations, we have pure, that is, unlimited consciousness or *Chit*. As these limitations arise from the association of consciousness with mind and matter, we can say that pure consciousness is that which is dissociated from mind and matter and is mindless,[1] bodiless,[2] consciousness. Empirical consciousness is that which is associated with a psycho-physical body and is the consciousness of the individual centre or finite self.[3]

This (*i.e.*, Pure Consciousness dissociated from Name and Form) is the special sense in which the term *Chit* is sometimes used in Vedānta. But *Chit* is also the Reality-Whole or *Pūrna*.[4] In this extended sense It is Consciousness functioning as Perfect Power *to be* and *become* a Universe of Name and Form. In this sense the World is *Chit* in essence, in power and in manifestation.

Bliss is implied in Being-Consciousness. Wholeness and fullness as perfect Being-Consciousness, is perfect Bliss. As Shruti says[5] "the great and limitless is bliss, not littleness and limitation." Pleasure and pain indicate expansion and diminution of being respectively. Bliss proceeds from the expansion of conscious life towards freedom and fullness of being. The ultimate real is then that which cannot be conceived as other than Being-Consciousness-Bliss, or fullness of being which is the essence of all the existents which have the attributes of happiness and unhappiness according as, and to the degree that, essential Bliss[6] is revealed or veiled.

To the concept of Being-Consciousness-Bliss, we must add that of Power (*Shakti*). The former is Power-holder.

---

[1] Amanah. Unmanī Bhāva. [2] Videha. [3] Jīvātmā, Purusha.

[4] See *post*. [5] Chhāndogya-Up., VII, 23.

[6] The Sanskrit term is "Ānanda," which like "Chit" is untranslatable. See *post*, however, for explanation.

Power and Power-holder are never separate from one another. Could *Shiva* as motionless Being be bereft of His Power, he would be but a corpse (*Shava*). The two (Power-holder and Power) are as such one, though the transformations of Power are many. We speak of transformation or evolution, because Power and its holder is held to be both efficient and material cause of the world. Power as the material cause is thus transformed in, and as, its effects, though the cause remains what it was. The cause contains its effect, and the latter is the cause modified as effect. The rule is pragmatically different in the evolved universe, where it is said "milk when it becomes curd ceases to be milk".

It has been said that, strictly speaking, creation (*ex-nihilo*) is not taught by any system of Hinduism, each system presupposing some "potential matter" out of which the world is evolved in recurring cycles, from eternity to eternity, and that the essence of that "prime matter" and its dependence on spirit or spirits at whose call or presence it evolves, varies according to the different systems. By "potential matter" in this statement must be understood that which in itself is not matter, prime or otherwise, but is the cause of the becoming, amongst other things, of the material world. That cause is the Power of Consciousness which, as the individual Centre, establishes a dichotomy of self and not-self in itself, as the Consciousness-Whole.

Moreover there is no first creation. The Universes come and go eternally. The present Universe, therefore, is not something entirely new, for it is the outcome of past worlds and their activities or *karma*. Not only "conscious" entities but *all* individual centres in the world have their *Karma* which is here conceived as essentially Play[1] out of Joy[2]—therefore, essentially free action, though pragmatically restricted.

[1] Lilā.   [2] Ānanda.

Man in his essence is the Ātman or Being-Consciousness-Bliss, and in and as his bodies, he is a Power of the Ātman or Brahman. There is thus no impassable gulf between Divinity and Man, for he is already divine in his essence even though he may not have realised it. This Essence as Power works through mind and matter its forms, until that Supreme Experience which is the formless[1] Essence is reached.

Reality may be regarded from three aspects. The Universe is the reducible real since it derives from, and on dissolution is resolved into, the Irreducible Real as God. God or the Lord (Īshvara) or Divine Mother (Īshvarī) as the Hindus call Him and Her, is the reducible Real regarded as in relation to the Universe of which It is the Creator, Sustainer and Ruler. It is the Irreducible Real considered as Being-Consciousness-Bliss-Power, and reducible real considered with respect to its own self-limiting Forms (Time, Space, Causality) by which it manifests itself as the Creator, Sustainer and Ruler of the Universe. That aspect of the Irreducible Real in which it is considered as It is in Itself, beyond its aspect as in relation to the Universe, is the alogical Godhead.[2]

The terms "Absolute" and "Transcendental" also should be clearly defined; *the distinction between Māyā-vāda and Shakti-vāda hinges on these definitions.*

Both "Absolute" and "Transcendental" mean "beyond relation". But the term "beyond" may be used in two senses: (*a*) exceeding or wider than relation; (*b*) having no relation at all. The first does not deny or exclude relation, but says that the Absolute, though involving all

---

[1] That is, beyond all limitations.

[2] Both aspects (as also many others) combined give the *Pūrna* (Whole). See *post*.

relations within Itself, is not their sum-total; is not exhausted by them; has Being transcending them. The latter denies every trace of relation to the Absolute; and says that the Absolute must have no intrinsic or extrinsic relation; that relation, therefore, has no place in the Being of the Absolute.

Shakti-vāda adopts the first view, Māyā-vāda the second. From the first point of view, the Absolute is relationless Being *as well as* Manifestation as an infinity of relations. This is the true and complete Alogical Whole. Inasmuch as the Absolute exceeds all relation and thought, we cannot say that It is the Cause; though It is the Root of Creation; and so forth; but inasmuch also as It does involve relation and thought, we can say that It is the First Cause; that there has been a real creation, and so forth.

The Māyāvāda view by negating all relation from the reality of *Brahman* negates from its transcendent standpoint the reality of causation, creation, and so forth.

"Beyond" may, therefore, mean (1) "exceeding," "fuller than," "not exhausted by"; or (2) excluding, negating, expunging. By diagrams:

(1) 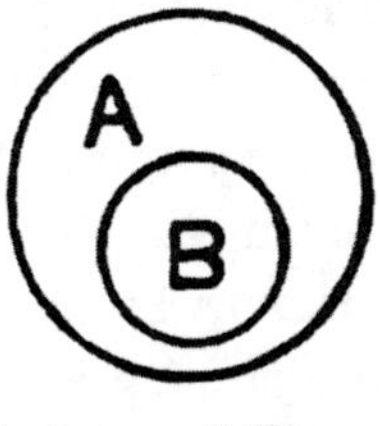

A is beyond B,
i.e., exceeds B

(2) 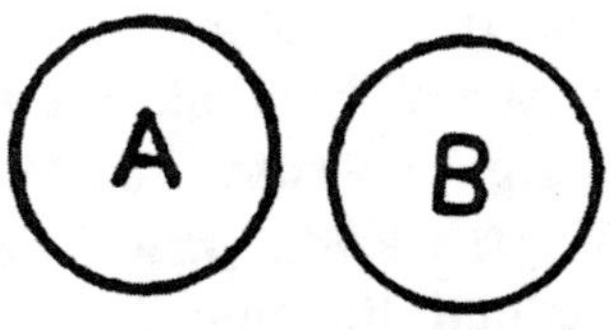

A is beyond B, *i.e., excludes* and is quite outside B.

In Shakti-vāda, the Supreme Reality is fuller than any definition (limitation) which may be proposed. It is even beyond duality and non-duality. It is thus the

Experience-Whole, the Alogical. The Māyā-vāda Pure *Brahman* is an *aspect* of It: but it is not the Whole (*Pūrna*).

The expression "wider than relation" may be thus illustrated. I am related in one way to my wife; in another way to my children; in yet another way to my brothers, friends, and so on. I am not fully expressed by any one of these relations, nor even by their aggregate; for, as a member of an infinite Stress-system I bear an infinity of relations. Pragmatically, most of these are ignored, and it is thought that I am expressed by a certain set of relations which distinguish me from another person who has his own "set". But *Brahman* as Absolute can have no such "set". It is expressed, but not fully expressed, even by the infinite set of relations which the Cosmos is, because relations, finite and infinite, imply a logical, and therefore, segmenting and defining, thought: but *Brahman* as Absolute-Experience-Whole = the Alogical.

Since *Brahman* = Experience-Whole = *Chit* as Power-to-Be-and-Become, it is nothing like the unknown and unknowable being ("Thing-in-Itself") of Western Sceptics and Agnostics.

In all Indian systems the World is real in the sense that it has objective existence for, and is not a projection of, the individual mind. In all such systems Mind and Matter co-exist. And this is so even in that form of *Ekajīva-Vāda* which holds that *Brahman* by Its own veiling and limiting Power makes one Primary Self of Itself, and that all other selves are but reflexes of the Primary Self, having as reflexes no existence apart from that of the Primary one. The world of matter is not a projection of an individual mind, but its reality is co-ordinate with that of the individual mind, both being derived from the Self-veiling and Self-limiting operation of *Brahman* appearing as the one *Jīva* or Primary Self. *Brahman* in appearing as

Primary Self also appears as its (logical) correlate or Pole—the Not-Self; and this Not-Self is the Root-Matter on which the Primary Self is reflected as multiple selves, and their varied relations. Matter, in this fundamental sense, is not, therefore the product of the First or Primary Individual (Self); it is with Self the co-effect (logically speaking) of a common fundamental activity which is the veiling and limiting action of the Supreme Being.

The version commonly given of Ekajīva-Vāda, namely that the one Primary Self is I, and that You, He and the rest, and the world of objects are its projection—is loose and unpsychological. In the first place, "I" cannot be there (logically conceiving) without its Correlate or Pole—the "Not-I," so that, by the very act by which "I" is evolved from *Brahman*, its Correlate is also evolved and this Correlate is Root-Matter. In the second place, projection, reflection, and so forth presuppose not only the projecting or reflecting Being (that which projects or reflects), but also something on which the projection or reflection is cast. Projection out of nothing and projection into nothing will give only nothing.

Where then there is Matter there is Mind. Where there is no Matter (not necessarily gross) there is no Mind. One is meaningless without the other. Each is every whit as real as the other. But there is no Indian system which is Realist in the sense that it holds that Matter as experienced by man exists when there is no Mind of man to perceive it. Such a state is inconceivable. He who alleges it himself supplies the perceiving Mind. In the First Standard[1] Mind[2] and the so-called "Atoms"[3] of Matter are separate, distinct and independent Reals.[4] Matter does not derive from Mind nor the latter from the former. In the Second

[1] Nyāya-Vaisheshika. [2] Manas. [3] Paramānu. [4] Dravya.

Standard[1] both Matter and Mind are equally real but derive from a common source, the Psycho-physical Potential[2] which, as such, is neither. 'Psychic' here means Mind as distinct from Consciousness in the special sense of *Chit.* This Psycho-physical Potential is a Real,[3] independent of Consciousness which is the other Real. In the Third Standard as non-dual Vedānta, the position is the same, except that the Psycho-physical Potential is not an independent Real but is the Power of the One Supreme Real as God. The world is then Real in the sense that it has true objective Reality for the individual Experiencers for the duration of their experience of it. No one denies this.

The next question is the problem of Monism. If ultimate Reality be One, how can it be the cause of, and become the Universe? It is said that Irreducible Reality is of dual aspect, namely, as it is in relation to the World as Īshvara the Lord or God, and as it is in Itself beyond such relation which we may call Godhead or *Brahman.* According to *Māyāvāda, Īshvara* is *Brahman,* for *Īshvara* is *Brahman* as seen through the veil of *Māyā,*[4] that is, by the Psycho-physical Experiencer. But *Brahman* is not *Īshvara,* because *Brahman* is the absolute alogical Real, that is, Reality, not as conceived by Mind, but as it is in Itself beyond (in the sense that it is exclusive of) all relations. The notion of God as the Supreme Self is the highest concept imposed on the Alogical which, as it is in itself, is not a Self either supreme or limited. The Absolute as such is not a Cause. There is, transcendentally speaking, no creation, no Universe. The Absolute is and nothing happens. It is only pragmatically a Cause. There is from

[1] Sāngkhya-yoga.
[2] Prakriti.
[3] In Sāngkhya, one, in Shaiva darshana, many.
[4] Though this veil be of a refined "stuff" (Vimala-Sattva-guna).

this aspect no *nexus* between Brahman as God-head and the World. In the logical order there is.

What then is the Universe? It is said by some to be an "illusion". But this is an inapt term. For to whom is it an "illusion"? Not to the Psycho-physical Experiencer to whom it is admittedly real. Nor is it an illusion for the Experience-Whole. It is only by the importation of the logical notion of a Self to whom an object is real or unreal that we can speak of illusion. But there is in this state of Liberation no Self.[1] More correctly we say that the World is *Māyā*. But what is Māyā in Māyāvāda? It is not real for it is neither Supreme Brahman nor an independent Real. Nor is it altogether unreal for in the logical order it is real. It is neither Brahman nor different from it as an independent reality. It is unexplainable.[2] For this reason some of the scholastics of this System call it the doctrine of the Inscrutable.[3]

In the doctrine of Power (Shaktivāda), Māyā is the Divine Mother Power or *Mahāmāyā*. The two aspects of Reality as *Brahman* and *Īshvara* are each accepted, as real. The Lord is real but that which we call 'Lord' is more than Lord, for the Real is not adequately defined in terms only of its relations to the Universe. In this sense it is alogical, that is "beyond Mind and Speech". As the one ultimate Reality is both *Īshvara* and *Brahman*, in one aspect it is the Cause and in the other it is not. But it is one and the same Reality which is both as *Shiva-Shakti*. As these are real, so is their appearance, the Universe. For the Universe is *Shiva-Shakti*. It is

---

[1] As the Buddhists said—in Nirvāna even the knowledge that the phenomena have ceased to appear and are therefore unreal is not to be found. Das Gupta, Hist. Phil. 142.

[2] Anirvachanīya. [3] Anirvachanīya-khyāti-vāda.

their appearance. When we say it is their appearance, we imply that there has been a real becoming issuing from them as Power. Reality has two aspects. First as it is in itself and, secondly, as it exists as Universe. At base the *Sangsāra* or worlds of Birth and Death and *Moksha* or State of Liberation are one. For *Shiva-Shakti* are both the Experience-Whole and the Fact which exists therein as the Universe. Reality is a concrete unity in duality and duality in unity. In practice the One is realised in and as the Many and the Many as the One. So in the Shākta wine-ritual, the worshipper conceives himself to be *Shiva-Shakti* as the Divine Mother. It is She who as and in the person of the worshipper, Her manifestation, consumes the wine which is again Herself the "Saviouress in liquid form".[1] It is not only he who as a separate Self does so. This principle is applied to all Man's functionings and is of cardinal importance from a Monistic standpoint, whatever be its abuse in fact.

Real is again used in the sense of eminence. The Supreme Real is that which is for itself and has the reason for its being in itself. The Real as God is the perfect and changeless. The Universe is dependent on the *Ens Realissimum*, for it proceeds from it and is imperfect as limited and changeful, and in a sense it is that which does not endure, and in this sense is called 'unreal'. Though however, the Universe comes and goes, it does so eternally. The Supreme Cause is eternally creative. The Real is then both infinite Changeless Being as also unbeginning and unending process as the Becoming. In this system the Real both is and becomes. And the essence of is-ness is Activity or Power. It yet becomes without

---

[1] Tārā Dravamayī.

derogation from its own changelessness, as it were a Fountain of Life which pours itself forth incessantly from an infinite and inexhaustible source. Both the infinite and finite are real.

Real is again used in the sense of interest and value and of the 'worth while'. In this sense the worshipper prays to be led from Unreality to Reality, but this does not mean that the World is unreal in itself, but that it is not the supreme worth for him.

In whatever sense then the term Real is used, the Universe is not an illusion. All is real, for as Upanishad says "All this Universe is verily Brahman."[1] The Scriptural Text says "All." It does not say "This, but not That." The whole is an alogical concrete Reality which is Unity in Duality and Duality in Unity. The doctrine does not lose hold of either the One or the Many, and for this reason the Lord Shiva says in the Kulārnava Tantra "There are some who seek dualism and some non-dualism but my doctrine is beyond both." That is, it takes account of and reconciles both Dualism and Non-dualism. The natural and spiritual are one.

Reality is no mere abstraction of the intellect making jettison of all that is concrete and varied. It is the Experience-Whole whose 'object' is Itself as such Whole. It is also Partial Experience within that Whole. This union of Whole and Part is alogical, but not unknowable, for their unity is a fact of actual experience just as we have the unity of Power to Be and Power to Become, of the Conscious and Unconscious, of Mind and Body, of freedom and determination, and of other dualities of Man's experiencing.

What the term *Chit* means is expressed neither fully and adequately, nor univocally, by the English word

[1] Sarvam Khalvidam Brahma.

"Consciousness".[1] Barring the case of the materialist who holds that consciousness is a "by-product" of matter specially organised as brain-substance, Western Idealists, Realists and Pragmatists are not agreed among themselves either as to the nature or as to the function of consciousness. They conceive it differently. None of these conceptions approach the Vedānta concept of *Chit* as the Supreme and Perfect Reality-Power, as regards the depth and amplitude of its import. In fact, in the history of Western Thought, Consciousness as such has been so far permitted to appear in a minor role even in Idealism. The chief part has been assigned to Reason or Thought, to Will, to Imagination, and, as has recently been the more usual practice, to Experience. Commonly in these forms of Idealism, Consciousness is not the substance of Reality—which may be a Cosmic Idea, Reason, Will, and so forth. Commonly too, Consciousness is not a *proprium*, or even an inseparable accident, of Reality. The Cosmic Idea or Will may thus be with consciousness or without it; it may evolve into consciousness only in some places or positions and remain unconscious in others.

Recently there has been a tendency in Idealism to make Experience the basis of Reality instead of a specific aspect of it such as Reason, Will or Imagination. This bases Reality upon "Fact" instead of a "section" and abstraction of Fact. But such approximation to the Vedāntic position has meant but little gain to Consciousness which is still commonly taken to be a separable

[1] Sometimes the substitute is "Intelligence" which is even more inappropriate. *Cf.* Dr. Carpenter, "Comparative Religion," pages 60, 157. Chit="Thought," also "Understanding" and "Intelligence". (p. 158).

See also, R. G. Bhandarkar's "Vaishnavism, Shaivism and minor Religious Systems" (Encyclopædia of Indo-Āryan Research, Vol. III, Part 6), page 78—Chit="Intelligence".

accident of Experience; Experience can be, and often is, it is supposed, sub-conscious and even unconscious.

At the back of this supposition is the taking of Consciousness in a restricted sense making it either abstract "awareness," or else, coincident with normal, "fully awake" "conscious" experience only: the former view showing it as a "torchlight" which makes us aware of the contents of experience; the latter making it the "lighted zone," the cognised contents of experience. In either case, Consciousness is not the equivalent of Experience which is supposed to be the larger fact. The "torch-light" is believed to reveal some of the actual contents of experience, while the rest lie outside the reach of its illumination. In the alternative supposition also, the "lighted up" contents of experience are believed to be a part only of the total content. And Consciousness is thus restricted not merely in individual experience, but also, commonly, in Cosmic Mind and Experience. This latter has been supposed to possess consciousness either as a separable or an inseparable *accident*; but, commonly, it has not been believed that consciousness is the essence and substance of the Cosmic Experience.

There is, however, no warrant for taking Consciousness (*Chit*) in the restricted sense of either a "torch-light" illumination, or as the "illumined zone" of Experience. The first alternative raises four issues: (1) Does the "torch-light" illumine the whole of an individual's experience or only part of it; in other words, does the circle of illumination coincide with that of experience, or is it included in the latter? (2) Does it illumine individual experience always or only occasionally? In other words, is individual experience conscious now, and unconscious then? (3) Does it illumine the whole of cosmic experience or only a part of it? And, (4) Is Cosmic Experience conscious now and unconscious then? Now, taking these four issues together, they may be decided on the principles of the Doctrine in this way: Consciousness as the Illumination[1] illumines and never fails to illumine the whole of Experience, though in the case of individual Centres, the fact of experience being illumined may be ignored, that is unrecognised, pragmatically, often to a degree which reduces such illumination, for practical purposes, to be non-illumination as the subconsciousness or unconsciousness. Really, however, "subconsciousness" and "unconsciousness" are grades of Consciousness itself—that is, if what has been unrecognised and unaccepted for ordinary practical purposes be recognized and accepted. This Perfect Illumination is the Ether of Consciousness[2] which is unbounded and unrestricted. The total content or Object[3] of Experience is so also; and, while both (the Illumination and the Illumined) are infinite, the former is intuited to be even a greater infinity (if infinities can be compared) than the latter;[4] and this reverses the position commonly taken in non-vedāntic views, eastern or western, that the circle of illumination forms a part only of the circle of experience.

Then, as regards the second alternative—making Consciousness, not the Illumination or awareness only, but concrete, conscious experience with a content—the criticism is this: The concrete experience with an object or content is a condition of Consciousness; but Consciousness has a transcendent condition also, which is immanent in the ordinary conditions; and this transcendent condition of Pure Consciousness or Pure Illumination is not an abstraction. It can be intuited in the ordinary experiences, and realised apart from the determinations of content or object, in *Yoga*.

---

[1] Prakāsha. [2] Chidākāsha. [3] Vimarsha.

[4] Antarlīna-vimarsha.

Consciousness, thus, may be with a content or without it;[1] and though, by Rāmānuja amongst others it has been contended that the Illuminator must co-exist with the Illumined as its logical correlate, Consciousness itself is alogical, beyond all antitheses or poles; and yet manifests by its Power all poles and correlations in experience. Pure Consciousness, immanent as the unchanging "ether" in ordinary changing experiences, and realizable as such in *Yoga*, is not, therefore, the Illuminator as distinguished from the Illumined (which as poles must co-exist); but it is Illumination itself which is its own content. The doctrine thus keeps clear of two unwarranted positions: (1) Experience with a content ("modes," "states" or "determinations" as they are called) is the only real, concrete fact, of which contentless, pure consciousness is an abstraction,[2] and is, therefore, unreal; and (2) Experience as contentless consciousness is the real Fact, upon which, the varied content of experience, that is, world-experience, has been laid as an unreal appearance as that of magic. On the contrary, Pure Consciousness is real, its Power to evolve as a world of varied content and to involve it again is real; and the world of varied content, which is the manifestation of Reality-Power, is also real.

Nor again does the Shākta view regard Consciousness as an "accident," separable or inseparable, of the Reality-Experience. Consciousness is not statical only as the "Ether"[3] but is dynamic or stressing; it is not Being only, but it is Becoming also.[4] In fact, the essence of Being is

---

[1] Savishesha or Nirvishesha.

[2] *i.e.*, Chit is savishesha only; it is never nirvishesha chinmātra.

[3] Even this implies the Being-Power of Chit; see ante.

[4] Cf. Fichte, The Science of Knowledge, Preface p. iv, "The facts of Consciousness are not facts of mere being, but facts of activity." Cf. Also Gentile's idea of Being in his Philosophy of the Spirit.

Power and Function to Be. So that Consciousness is the varied world-experience, as also, transcendent, pure Illumination. It is at the same time the Basis, the Evolver and the Content of Experience. This view does not recognise any ultimate duality between Substance and Attribute,[1] between Power and Possessor of Power,[2] between Power as Cause and Power as Effect or Manifestation,[3] however they may in the logical order be so treated. Hence, if Consciousness as Power evolves as the World-Experience, the three terms involved in the process (*i.e.*, Consciousness, Power and World-experience) must be ultimately identified with one another. It is dualism to maintain that Consciousness is one thing and its activity or Power is another; that the Power of Consciousness to be (*i.e.*, existential activity) is one thing, its Power to become or evolve is another. It is not possible in this view to regard Consciousness as an "accident" or even as a "proprium" only of something else—of any substance. Consciousness is the Substance,[4] the Power, and the evolutes and involutes[5] of Power. Philosophies, western or eastern, have often reduced it to an "accident," because they have taken it to mean limited, pragmatic consciousness only—that is, what in ordinary parlance passes as "normal consciousness" distinguished from both "sub-conscious" and "unconscious" and because they have taken it in an abstract way to mean "awareness" or "feeling" or "cognition," and not in a concrete way to mean *Reality functioning to be and yet to evolve as experience of a varied content.* Thus, in this view it has been wrongly supposed that feelings, thinkings and willings, which constitute the actual life of

---

[1] Guna and Gunī.

[2] Shakti and Shaktimān.

[3] Kārana and Kāryya.

[4] Padārtha.

[5] Vyakta and avyakta products.

experience, are the facts of which consciousness makes us aware in part; and that, whether they be thus revealed and "shewn" or not, they happen, go on and change—in fact, the drama of mental life plays itself whether or not the stage be lighted by consciousness.

Limitation of the meaning of *Chit* or *Chaitanya* is responsible for a view like, or more or less similar to, the above not only in Dualistic systems, but also in many Idealistic monisms. The *Nyāya-vaisheshika* makes consciousness a separable feature of individual Selves, though in the case of the Lord, it is regarded by it as an inalienable, that is, permanent[1] feature. But it is a feature only, not the Substance. The *Bhatta* School of *Pūrva Mīmāngsā* makes *Ātman* conscious in one part and unconscious in other, thus anticipating the modern "floating ice-berg" conception of mental life "nine-tenths of which are buried in the depths of sub-consciousness". The *Sāngkhya* System, though it makes *Chit* the essence of *Purusha*, makes the psycho-dynamic Principle evolving "Understanding," Mind and so forth, unconscious, so that Experience is an unconscious process lighted up by consciousness. Consciousness, it is true, is there not merely as a lighter or reflector; its witnessing the process—unconscious in itself and causally a "closed curve"—somehow influences it, in this way that, it goes on with reference to the witnessing, and it stops where such reference ceases. And since, in this view, there are many witnesses, the process goes on with reference to other witnesses, though it may stop in respect of some, that is, those who attain liberation.[2] In this view, Consciousness is recognised as an independent Entity (it is no longer a mere property or accident of something); and the "catalytic action" which it exercises on the evolving

[1] Nitya. [2] Kaivalya.

Psycho-physical dynamic Principle[1] implies its Being-Power, as well as, Power to influence the Becoming of some other Being. This leads a considerable way to the *Shākta* Vedānta position; but it is a halting method in so far as (1) it does not make Consciousness the whole Being and Experience; and (2) it assigns practically the whole realm of dynamism (*i.e.*, evolving power) to a Principle alien to, and independent of, Consciousness, reserving to itself only a vague veiled suggestion of power expressed in its so-called "catalytic action".

Even Idealistic Monisms have sometimes stopped short of the final position here adopted. The attitude of such monisms towards Consciousness has commonly taken four forms: (1) Consciousness as Perfect Knowledge (that is, Knowledge of all generals and particulars) is an element of the Supreme Reality which is also the Supreme Power; but it is not the whole of it, the sum and substance of it; so that, if the Supreme Reality-Power is represented by a circle, Consciousness forms an aspect, part or element of that circle; it is but one attribute of the Supreme Substance which has an infinity of attributes,[2] and there is nothing to warrant the supposition that this one attribute is the basis and root of all others. Furthermore, Consciousness with an infinitely varied content is an aspect of the Supreme Reality; pure, contentless consciousness is not an actual state of experience either in the Supreme or in the individual realities; it is an abstraction and, therefore, unreal. (2) Another position, whilst agreeing with the first

[1] Prakriti.

[2] *Cf.* the doctrine of Spinoza in the West which gives the Substance an infinity of attributes of which we know but two, *viz.*, Thought and Extension. See his Ethics; Proposition XI. read along with Def. VI and Prop. IX.

as regards all other essential points, makes Pure Consciousness not an abstraction and unreality, but the Illumination [1] of the Perfect Being or Lord, which aspirants may actually realise as Pure *Chit* and nothing else at a certain stage of their spiritual approach to their final objective, but pushing beyond that stage, they realise that what was pure, featureless [2] illumination before is really the light radiating from a Perfect Being infinitely rich in power and content. Perception of the Light only—apart from the form and features—is, therefore, ontologically speaking an abstraction, since Perfect Being is not Light [3] only; but psychologically speaking (that is, as an actual, though halting and imperfect, perception by the aspirant of the Supreme Being), it is not an abstraction. The intuition of Pure Light in what is called "non-polar meditation" [4] gives, accordingly, an approximate and subordinate view of Reality, transcending which the aspirant has a truer vision of Reality [5] as the Perfection of power and attributes. The vision of the Pure Ether of Consciousness is thus a stage, and not the goal of realisation.

(3) Next comes the position of *Māyā-vāda* which reverses the above order or relationship between what has to be regarded a stage and what the goal of realization, what must be looked upon as Reality and what as an abstraction. Here, the "Pure Light" alone shines when the goal is reached, forms and features, powers and attributes appear but on the way to it; so that, *Chit* as Pure Light is the Supreme Reality, of which "a varied content" is not, indeed, an abstraction, but upon which is laid as an

---

[1] Jyotih.

[2] Without Nāma and Rūpa.

[3] Nirvishesha Chinmātra.

[4] Nirvikalpa Samādhi.

[5] *Cf.* the conception of the Vaishnava placing the eternal Abode of the Lord (Vaikuntha and Goloka) beyond the Chidākāsha of Vedānta.

ascription or imposition[1] due to *Māyā* which makes Reality appear otherwise than as it is in itself.[2]

The stress in the first position (1) is laid exclusively upon "infinitely rich power and content" nature of Reality, as it leaves no room for the "Pure Light" either in the scheme of Being (*i.e.*, ontologically), or in the actual experiences of Being (*i.e.*, psychologically). Consciousness is ever with content and never without it: this is the position. The stress in the second position (2) is laid as in the first, but Consciousness as Pure Light is recognised as a subordinate and imperfect (though actual) stage in the realisation of Perfect Being. In the third position (3), the stress is shifted on to what has been unreal in the first and subordinate in the second, so that what is the real and ultimate in them (1 and 2), becomes unreal or only pragmatically real[3] in the third. In all these three positions the emphasis is laid now on this and now on that phase or aspect[4] of the Supreme Fact.

Hence (4), it is claimed, that if the Fact is to remain the Fact, no emphasis must be laid upon what is but a section or aspect of it, but it should be laid upon the Whole.[5] Pure Consciousness "without content" and Perfect Consciousness of infinitely rich content, are both logical aspects of the Whole which is alogical. The Whole can be approximately described in terms of its aspects (that is, as Pure and as Perfect), but, in itself it is fuller than such descriptions of it. Thus It is Pure in the above sense, but is not that only; It is Perfect in the above sense, but is not also that only. Again, it is only from a pragmatic and logical standpoint that of these two or other aspects of It, we can regard one as the primary and higher, and the

---

[1] Adhyāsa. [2] Vivartta. [3] Vyavahārika sat.
[4] Kalā. [5] Pūrṇa.

other or others as secondary or lower. In fact, any aspect is as much real as any other: thus Perfect (*i.e.*, infinitely rich) Consciousness is as much real as Pure Consciousness; Consciousness as Power is as much real as Consciousness as such; and the Product or Manifestation of this Power is as much real as the Power itself. We disturb this even balance and co-ordination of the aspects by attempting to thrust them into pragmatic, logical moulds.

It is true that, in having to state an alogical Fact logically and to represent an extra-temporal and extra-spatial process temporally and spatially, the *Shākta* doctrine speaks as if *Chit* as Pure Consciousness[1] were alone "in the beginning," that this Consciousness then evolved into a Consciousness first of latent, then of patent polarisation between Self and Not-Self, between consciousness as Illumination[2] and that as the Illuminated or Object[3] that this Object is then variously evolved; that all this is then involved back into Pure Consciousness; and that while this process of evolution and involution goes on, Pure Consciousness as such changelessly abides. This statement gives, of course, primacy to Pure Consciousness as compared with Its Power to evolve and involve, and also, as compared with the work which that Power does. Pure Consciousness is there whether or not It operates as Power to project out of Itself an Object of varied content, and withdraw that Object back into Itself. This reason coupled with the fact that the most fundamental expression of existence, namely Being[4] and Joy,[5] is given in Consciousness as such[6] as it is given (that is, to the same ultimate degree and in the same fundamental way) in nothing else; the fact that liberation

---

[1] Parā Samvit. [2] Prakāsha. [3] Vimarsha.
[4] Sat. [5] Ānanda. [6] Chit.

is not attained except by realisation of Pure-Being-Consciousness-Bliss, would seem, from a logical point of view, to ensure the primacy given to Pure Consciousness. But really, in the alogical complete Fact itself, in regard to which as the Whole we cannot make any statement in terms of Space, Time and other Categories, Pure *Chit*[1] is co-ordinate with, and not superior or subordinate to, the Power[2] by which It evolves and involves; and this again is co-ordinate with Its manifestation as the total Product or Achievement; and these co-ordinate aspects (*viz. Chit* as Being, *Chit* as Power[3] and *Chit* as Product[4]) embraced by, and in, the mysterious Whole is Fact. Liberation cannot be attained except by realizing *this*; since bondage is due to the non-realization of this—which is but non-recognition, that is ignorance, of what the Fact is. There is, therefore no liberation by realizing what is an aspect only. Liberation is achieved by realizing that *Shiva* as quiescent Being-Consciousness-Bliss[5] (which also is Power-to-be), becoming as dynamic Being-Consciousness-Bliss[6] and evolving and involving infinitely varied Objects, that is, World Experience which, on the whole as also in detail, is Being-Consciousness-Bliss.[7] The World is *Shiva-Shakti*, and the Fact is not realized, and therefore liberation is not had, so long as it is looked upon as a product of *Māyā*, in the sense of that which is neither real nor unreal; as a "mirage," as an order in which there is actual, as distinguished from pragmatic unreality, unconsciousness and

[1] Shiva.

[2] Shakti; Shāstra makes Shakti the consort of Shiva, and they are in inseparable union and alogical unity. *Cf.* Devī Bhāgavata, IX. I, 10, 11, which make Shakti Brahma-Svarūpa nityā (eternal); and She is related to Reality as Being as the heat of fire to fire.

[3] Kārana or Shakti.

[4] Kāryya Brahman.

[5] Sachchidānandamāya.

[6] Shakti Sachchidānandamayī.

[7] Jagat Sachchidānandamāya, which is the Play of Shiva-Shakti.

unhappiness.[1] Not only the World as a sublime whole, but the World in its minutest details (even in the so-called "stocks and stones") must be perceived to be nothing but Being-Consciousness-Bliss in Play.[2] It is the whole Being-Consciousness-Bliss Power (*Shiva-Shakti*, and nothing but that: It seems to be "small" only with reference to the province of Convention in which the particular Centres "consciously" live and move and bargain. Hence even a grain of dust is Perfect *Shiva-Shakti* incarnate, and must be realised as such by an aspirant before liberation can be had. The Perfect Being thus really given in the "infinite" as well as in the "small" is a miracle, and the basis of this commonest of all miracles is laid in the primary act by which the Perfect Being-Becoming Power in order to evolve a world of correlated Centres potentialized Itself as the infinitesimal "Point".[3] And if the Infinite can thus, according to the premises of this doctrine, live and operate in, and as, the Infinitesimal, It also can do so in, and as, the "finite" and "limited" being—which, in the fullness of fact, is not finite and limited at all except with reference to the conditions of the province of inter-central convention. That province begins when, and in so far as, the realm of *Māyā* begins in the evolution of the Thirty-six-Principles, in the form of the so-called "impure" Principles.[4]

In the *Shākta* view, therefore, there is no place for Unconsciousness,[5] except in a pragmatic and conventional way, relating either to Reality as Being, or to Reality as Power, or to Reality as product or Manifestation. The "seeming" consciousness"[6] of *Sāngkhya*, or of *Māyā-vāda*

---

[1] That is, the opposite of Sat-Chit-Ānanda.

[2] Lilā. [3] Bindu.

[4] See Chapter dealing specially with Māyā and the Kanchukas or "Envelopes".

[5] Achit or Jada. [6] Chidābhāsa.

as it is commonly stated, has no place either. If there be any "seeming" in the scheme of world-manifestations, it will be found rather in the other way—Consciousness "seeming" to be unconsciousness, Joy "seeming" to be indifference or pain, free Play "seeming" to be necessity and determination. And yet this "seeming" as an actual element in the Play of the World-Power by which the Divine Mother variously "screens" Herself in the form of interplaying Centres, is no "illusion". This "seeming" is no seeming, since both the Power and Herself—screening Play as interplaying Centres are real. It is seeming in altogether different conditions, *viz.*, (1) when that Power withdraws Her Play as Centres into Herself and plays with Her own Being;[1] or else (2) when to the eyes of a "fortunate" Centre She lets the screens and veils drop, and permits it to realise the identity between Herself and Itself.[2] A block of stone is really unfeeling and unconscious matter to an ordinary Centre whose total assemblage of conditions[3] is of a certain kind relatively to that of the stone; it is no "seeing" in that given tissue of relations; it is then an outcome of the real interplay. But the character of the play—the bearing, impression and import of the one in relation to the other—is bound to change with the change in their total assemblage of conditions;—a circumstance which does not make the first "impression" unreal, and make the later real, but makes each real in its own way and sphere. The term "seeming" as applied to such partial, conditional experiences of correlated Centres may be justified in one sense only—that Power as Being-Consciousness-Bliss never ceases to be such, in

[1] Which is Shiva Sachchidânandamâya, playing with Shakti Sachchidânandamayî. This is Âtmarati.

[2] Expressed in the experience—"Sâ'ham"—She am I.

[3] Karma and Adrishta.

Itself or in Its manifestations, whatever be Its veiling and unveiling play. A block of stone as Perfect Being-Consciousness-Bliss (involving Play) is, therefore, the Standard Experience to which other experiences are more or less near approximations, constituting "grades" and "values," but each real in its way.

The above position keeps clear of both common Realism making things exist outside and independent of Consciousness and Experience, and common Idealism making them "ideas" or "clusters of sensations, actual and possible" only. Things do exist outside and independent of Centre-referred and Centre-owned Consciousness and experience;[1] but Consciousness, without such reference and limitation, is the Fact and the Power to evolve as facts. On the other hand, Consciousness as the root Being-and-Becoming Power becomes real things as also real minds apprehending, judging and otherwise experiencing those things; this combines the truth in Realism and that in Idealism. Thus, a block of stone is not, from this standpoint, "matter" only: it is *Chit* as Joy and as Play—though the fact is veiled to ordinary Centres; on the other hand, it is not an "idea" or "mental construct" only: it is *Chit* as Power constituting it as much and as active a reality as the experiencing and reacting mind is. While pulling down the arbitrary wall erected by "Scientific Realism" between Primary and Secondary qualities of which the former alone are supposed to be real, the doctrine does not go to the other extreme of that "naive" Realism which regards the mental impression as a "copy" of the external thing. Things as "standard" realities exist in, and for, the Supreme Mind, other Centres' perceptions being gradual and partial reproductions of those "standards" or models—a circumstance which does not

[1] Ishvara is not here included in the Order of Centres.

make their perceptions unreal, but approximations to the real; each Centre knows the reality subject to the limitations of its *Karma* and "cosmic situation".[1] There is need, therefore, for the education and development of man's "knowing instruments," giving him progressively higher and larger visions, through science and philosophy, through intuition and meditation, and, finally, "revelation"[2] and realisation. This view supplies what is deficient in naive Idealism also by (1) making Matter and Life every whit as real and active as Mind, and (2) forbidding exclusive emphasis on this or that aspect of Experience, such as Reason or Idea, Will or Imagination. Its *Chit* is not transcendent or empirical consciousness only; it is not being or becoming only; it is not quiescent or dynamic only; it is not undetermined or determined only; and it is not of this feeling-tone or of that only. It comprises all these and other alternatives, and, (from man's viewpoint) contradictory phases. Its fundamental being and expression is Joy[3] pulsating as Will-Power and manifesting Itself in an unspeakably sublime cosmic Play. It is not a mere "abstraction"—a "wilderness" of Pure Being or Pure Nothing as some critics of Vedānta[4] have imagined the abode of Reality to be.

This view concedes also the possession of an element of truth to "Pragmatism," ancient or modern. Philosophies in India have always recognised the Province of Convention,[5] the conditions of inter-Central "behaviour" by which

[1] Adrishta, the result of karma.

[2] Shruti and Āgama. Shiva, in the Kulārnava Tantra, reveals, for example, five "Methods" by His five mouths, and a sixth by an esoteric sixth.

[3] Ānanda.

[4] This refers to the Māyā-vāda Reality, but is not appropriate, since in that system Pure Being = Pure Bliss.

[5] Vyavahāra.

the experiences and realities of the correlated Centres are determined. In Indian Thought, by *Karma* a Centre is what it now is, what it was, and what it will be; by *Karma* it determines not only its "cosmic situation,"[1] but its Cosmos also; since, to each centre the Cosmos and its realities and are, seen, as its Karma[2] has determined them to be for it; to another Centre, they are different more or less, and to the "same" centre also, they change as its *Karma* changes. There can be no more thorough-going "Pragmatism" than this. "Pragmatic consciousness," "Pragmatic reality" has its place, but, in the Shākta view, however, it is not "illusory". Pragmatic consciousness is Consciousness as Power limiting Itself as this or that mode or aspect of Experience for the purpose of *Karma* (*i.e.*, Play) in a particular line and manner;[3] and Pragmatic reality is the Reality-Whole determining and circumscribing Itself with reference to the conditions of action and enjoyment[4] of the Centres and groups of Centres that have evolved or will evolve in It. When, therefore, the modern Pragmatist says that the "fact" or reality for a given Centre, A, is constituted by the behaviour of A, or the "uses" to which A can put that reality, he has the support of non-dual *Vedānta* provided (1) the behaviour is primarily the play of the Reality-Whole to evolve and play as A, and also as B, C, D, and so forth, correlated with it; (2) the behaviour of A and each of the others is also play[5] (as *Karma*) subject to the conditions (*a*) the manner of A's play in the past,[6] and (*b*) the nature of B, C, D and the manner of their play relatively to it is understood;

---

[1] Adrishta.

[2] The Pūrva-Mīmāngsā in particular shews Karma itself as Īshvara or Lord "Karmeti mīmāngsakāh".

[3] See *ante* for examples of "Pragmatic facts".

[4] Karma and Bhoga.

[5] Implying Joy and Freedom.

[6] Constituting its tendencies and adrishta or cosmic situation.

and (3) that by behaviour[1] again of the appropriate kind, A can release itself from being an individual Centre subject to limitations.

The Neo-Pragmatist very often builds his case upon biological besides psychological grounds. A. B. C. D. form a system of Centres (some living, and the rest "non-living") not only co-operating but in conflict with one another—in "the struggle for existence". In relation to A. B. C. D. constitute the "environment"; and A lives, and expects to live, by adjusting itself and the environment each to the other, adjustment meaning the adaptation of A to B. C. D. as much as that of B. C. D. to A. Thus A changes agreeably to a change in the environment, but also changes the environment agreeably to itself. Through Natural Selection and other long-continued processes, A's organism has been so constituted as to be, generally, a suitable "machine" for doing this work of vital adaptation. Generally the machine does its work smoothly and by a pre-established arrangement—represented by its stereotyped sets of reactions—the "automatic" actions—reflex, spontaneous, instinctive and habitual. These are supposed to have their nerve-arrangements in the spinal cord, medulla oblongata, cerebellum—that is, in regions below the cerebral cortex which is the organ and seat of consciousness, either sensory or motor. The automatic actions are, accordingly, not accompanied by consciousness, and are believed by some to have nothing to do with consciousness. Consciousness accompanies those actions which meet with a sort of "deadlock" in the centres of automatic action, and which therefore, cannot "rattle smoothly off". The cortical centres which are the centres of consciousness are the centres of selection (of "deliberation and choice") by which deadlocks

[1] As Sādhanā.

are removed. All actions, whether automatic or deliberative, are "behaviour" framed with reference to what is of use and value to the individual or his race; and behaviour becomes "conscious experience"—knowing, feeling or willing—under special conditions, that is, when conditions are such that what is of interest (the end as well as the means) has to be represented as a future good or evil (therefore of use and value) in relation to which the attitude of the individual must be framed, if need be through deliberation and choice. A sensation of "hot" is thus the consciousness that that which is hot will more or less burn if touched; the sensation is thus the index of the results to which a certain behaviour *viz.*, touching) will lead, and also of the uses to which those results can be put. It is use which assigns to each Centre its province of behaviour, and out of this province only a fraction is assigned to consciousness when the conditions of use are of a special kind. The conditions and limits, of a Centre's knowing, feeling and willing, are the conditions and limits of what is of use to that Centre or its group.

That there is a substantial element of truth in this statement of the case may be conceded by Indian Thought. Both the "world" and the experience of the world are fashioned for a Centre as the conditions of its own *Karma* and Enjoyment [1]—(the cumulative effect and resultant of those conditions)—require them to be fashioned. It is thus that the differing "Worlds" and experiences of one man and another, those of an ordinary man and of a Seer, those of stocks and stones and those of plants and animals, and so forth, are constituted: the differing organs and instruments of the different Centres are also due to the same factors, *viz.*, *Karma* and Enjoyment (presupposing

[1] Bhoga.

special need and use).[1] Consciousness is thus limited and specialised in a particular Centre—which, therefore, has, ordinarily, no consciousness beyond certain limits, and has, even in the zones of its conscious life, varying degrees and tones of consciousness ranging from subconsciousness and semi-consciousness to "wide awake" consciousness.

But these limits and degrees of Consciousness are "pragmatic" only. Individual Centres, according to their varying needs and uses, have these limits and degrees practically settled for them; but these do not cut up and circumscribe Consciousness itself. Because (1) the Universe being one undivided stress-system, (a system of mutual actions and reactions) the experience which takes the universe in, cannot really be a fragmentary and parcelled-out experience, though for the practical purposes of finite Centres it appears to be so; (2) that the so-called subconscious and unconscious are really inside Consciousness (not that normally accepted as such by a finite Centre), may be said to be shown by the fact that a Centre can more and more fully reclaim them as Consciousness or conscious experience by avowing what he has so far ignored, recognising, noting what he has "chaotically" felt; and from the fact that the whole universe (*i.e.*, the "fact") can be so reclaimed in, and as, Experience when that finite Centre is able at last to uplift completely the "veil" of ignorance and non-acceptance, and becomes, in consequence, one with the Immense Consciousness-Power. It follows from this that a Centre's ordinary experience is not the whole Experience because, though really having it and living it, he has been accustomed to ignore it as the whole and accept and avow it piecemeal; and he has been so accustomed because "the needs and uses" of

[1] Prayojana, Artha or Purushārtha.

his pragmatic existence as domicile in "the province of convention" have so required, and determined his experience to be pragmatic accordingly. Besides these two, there is also a third reason which requires that Existence and Consciousness coincide with each other: (3) the essential marks of Consciousness-in-itself are Joy and Freedom (or Free-Will-to-be-and-become). There is no form of existence—even "material" existence—which is not an expression of, and in its turn does not express (however veiled the expression may be in relation to certain "cosmic situations"), Joy and Free Power. Now if both Existence and Consciousness possess the same essential marks, it is reasonable to hold that one is the other, or both are manifestations of a Common Root. But since a Root more fundamental than Consciousness cannot be imagined (everything being representable as a mode of Consciousness, but Consciousness not being representable as a mode of anything else), it must hold that Consciousness = Being = Reality.

The above position is strengthened by the fact that the aspirant is able, it is claimed, by pursuing the appropriate method of realisation, to go round the whole circuit of involution and evolution—starting from ordinary pragmatic World-experience, passing through progressively higher and fuller "universes," coming at last to Pure and Perfect Experience which sums up all Existence, and then descending again to the ordinary pragmatic order of world-experience in the reverse order. In this an experimental proof is afforded as to the manner in which the common finite order of existence and consciousness thereof for a finite Centre, can be made to tend to, and ultimately become, Perfect and Pure Being-Experience, and, how again that Perfect and Pure Being-Experience, progressively evolves, and in evolving limits Itself as, the finite, pragmatic order of existence and consciousness which an individual Centre calls his "universe". The experiment is similar to that of a geologist (for example) who shows how a great rock or a layer of the Earth's crust has been formed by experimenting with a small sample of it in his laboratory. The aspirant shews in his experiment that all the elements of his universe (Solid Matter, Liquid Matter and so forth) can be, without leaving a "residue," dissolved into Consciousness, and that all partial and pragmatic universes can be made to fall into a Perfect Universe which is Perfect Consciousness; and also, in the reverse order, they can be made to evolve from It. This, it is said, shows that there is nothing ultimately but Being-Consciousness, and the Power of Consciousness to be and become.

CHAPTER I

CONSCIOUSNESS AS POWER-HOLDER AND AS POWER

THE concept *Chit* is unique.

Indian Thought in its highest form regards it as the fundamental Reality. In the West, there have been thinkers who have reduced the World to Idea, to Will, to Intention or to Imagination, but it is the Indian Vedânta—and other cognate doctrines based upon it—which makes the World *Chit*, in its root as well as in its manifestation. Chit as Power (*Chit-Shakti*) appears as the World but in so appearing never ceases to be in itself *Chit*. This is the essence of non-dualist doctrine. *Chit* is Being or Fact (*Sat*) and *Chit* is Bliss (*Ānand*). Veda says that the World proceeds out of Bliss, is sustained by Bliss and is reabsorbed into Bliss. Being is Bliss which is *Chit*. The latter as such, that is as distinguished from its Power, never *becomes* other than *Chit*. How Reality can change as the changing world and yet remain what it is—how in fact change and no change can be predicated of the same Reality—is a problem of which the Mâyâvâda of Shangkara is one solution and Shaktivâda or the Doctrine of the World as Power is another.

Chit is, to use an English term, the Spiritual Principle in man in which his universe of experience lives, moves and has its being. Not only is it the static *basis* of such universe, but it is that which by and as its own power (*Shakti*) *becomes* or appears as that Universe. This Spiritual Principle, which in itself is immense[1] and immeasurable,[2] becomes by its own Power[3] differentiated into a multiplicity of correlated Centres, some of which are the human selves. This Power by which the Immense and Immeasurable becomes *as such Centres* limited and measured, by which the "Fact" becomes veiled and ignored as "Fact-sections," is *Māyā* (which operates as a measuring, limiting or determining and therefore negating Principle).[4] Subjectively considered it is the sense of difference[5] by which the object of experience is seen as other than and different from the Self. It is no Cosmic Material, *foreign* to and *independent* of the Spiritual Principle[6] in man which evolves as the Universe of Mind, Life and Matter, deriving its efficiency from the presence of the Spiritual Principle (whose action on "Matter" is comparable to catalytic action in chemistry). Non-dualism says, firstly, that the Universe is *wholly* a product of the Spiritual Principle as Power, which is not only the "catalytic" source or prompter of its *efficiency*, but which is its *ground* and its *material* as well; secondly, that It, in so becoming the varied universe, does not require the operation upon Itself of a Power *other than* Itself; and thirdly, that in such evolution it presents two aspects, namely, a static, quiescent aspect or the 'Male' Shiva in which it remains the self-same Principle, and a dynamic, stressing aspect as the Mother-Power in which it moves and changes as the world of Mind, Life and Matter.

This reduction of the universe into a Spiritual Principle and its Power one with itself (or *Chit* working as Power), calls to mind the attempt of the modern physicist to reduce

[1] Bhūman. [2] Brahman. [3] Shakti.

[4] Mīyate anayā iti Māyā. [5] Bhedabuddhi. [6] As in Sāngkhya-Yoga.

the mass of Matter to electromagnetic mass alone which is referred to by way of illustration.

Is the mass of a material particle, charged with an electrical charge, partly mechanical and partly electrical? Or, can its mass, in the last resort, be reduced to the electrical mass alone? Is mass in its nature of one kind or two kinds—*non-dual* or *dual*? Now, the answer of modern Science has been clearly pointing to the non-dual alternative. The Electron Theory of Matter makes the mass of Matter of one kind; its mass is constituted by the masses of the positive and negative charges, protons and electrons (whatever be their precise number and distribution) which constitute an atom of matter. But even after such reduction of material mass to electrical mass, duality persists in another form. How is electrical mass related to Energy? Are they two and independent of each other? An electron (or unit charge of negative electricity) is in motion in a varied manner; its kinetic and potential energies in a given system are thus different. Now, does it possess the same mass whatever be its velocity and energy? Will its mass remain unaffected when, for example, its velocity approaches that of light? Physicists have shown that velocity—particularly when it is high—changes the mass of the moving thing: this is what is called mass-acceleration. Mass and Motion (or Energy for the matter of that) are not independent of each other: Mass becomes a *function* of Motion, that is, it varies (may be beyond certain limits only) as the latter varies. This indeed points to the unity of Mass and Energy which, however, it still remains for Science to definitely establish.

Electricity is a substance, which many have thought, to be Ether which is *quasi*-material. What, therefore, Science is now called upon to investigate is the exact relation which subsists between this Substance and Energy (or Motion).

It is practically confronted with the question: Are Power and Holder of Power[1] one or two? Translated into the language of Science, and restricted to the physical plane, this means: Is Ether (if we must separately retain it) and the Stress by which it is strained into various forms, which are probably the Prime Atoms, one or are they two? In other words, can we say this that the same substance, which considered in its static aspect is Ether, is *also* Energy when considered in its stressing or dynamic aspect? Or, to use the expressive language of the Shākta Tantra, can we say that the Ether-aspect is the *Shiva*-aspect (restricted to the physical plane), and that Energy at work subjecting Ether to various forms of stress-and-strain is the *Power* or *Shakti* aspect (restricted also to the physical plane) of the one fundamental Reality? The next problem is, how *Power* and *Power-holder* are related not only on the physical plane, but beyond on the planes of Life, Mind and on that of Powèr as the Radical Potential of which Life, Mind and Matter are the evolutes. In other words, Ether and its Energy must be brought into *rapport* with Life and Vital Power, these again with Mind and Will Power, and so on, until all pragmatic limitations of the data are dispensed with, and Substance and Energy are seen in their alogical identity (which man's logical thinking splits into aspects) in the complete Fact[2] itself which is *Chit*.

For a clearer understanding of the meaning of *Chit*, we should distinguish the different standpoints from which It can be regarded. In the first place, we must distinguish between the standpoint of the Whole[2] and that of the Part[3]

[1] Shakti and Shaktimān. [2] Pūrna.

[3] Kalā is a common concept in the Scripture dealing with Shakti and is graded as Pūrnakalāmūrti, Kalāmūrti, Angshamūrti, Angshāngsamūrti. There are no Kalās in Unmanī in Shivatattva. The Kalās appear with Samanī shakti in Shaktitattva.

between the complete view of Reality and the partial view of it. There is the former when Experience is avowed and accepted without the least veiling or ignorance of what is given—when there is absolutely no limitation of the data. This is Perfect Experience.[1] It is an experience of All-presentation or No-veiling. Man's centralised or individualised life is commonly a life of greater or less veiling or ignorance of the Given. By trying to remove the veil, or by trying to own and accept what has been disowned and ignored, he can more or less closely approximate to Perfect Experience which is the *Limit* (in the sense of consummation or perfection) of progressively higher and higher forms of experience; but which remains unattainable so long as his life, and therefore, his standpoint, remains centralised (*i.e.*, referring to a Centre such as the Ego) and individualised. Central reference or individualisation means a stressing and straining in a particular manner of Being and of Experience; by such stressing and straining Being and Experience is apparently limited, and circumscribed, so that this circumstance precludes the possibility of a complete avowal and acceptance of Being-Experience as it is in its entireness.

Man's view-point is therefore ordinarily partial, imperfect. He may indeed extend his frontiers, and thus more and more closely *approximate* to the All,[2] but so long as central reference, conscious or sub-conscious, remains, he cannot reach out to the realisation of the Perfect Being-Experience itself. His essay is therefore an essay of approximation, of nearer and nearer approach. Ordinarily he stops more or less short of the Goal or Limit itself which gathers, subsumes and perfects all. He stops because he refers to a Centre; because he is an Individual; and has therefore to know, feel and act practically with

[1] Chhāndogya, III, 14, 1.

[2] Pūrna.

reference to other Centres or Individuals in a correlated system or Kosmos or *Rita* as Veda calls it. Such knowing, feeling and acting in a correlated system is practical or pragmatic living, and it not only implies but requires limitation of the data, or ignorance of the given, or veiling of the concrete, which is called Ignorance.[1] For instance, life such as man ordinarily lives it would be impossible if at every moment he were to attend *impartially* to all that he felt, accept and emphasise *uniformly* all that he knew, and frame his actions *indifferently* with respect to whatever he felt and knew. As a matter of fact, he selects, ignores and emphasises in what he feels and knows; he owns and accepts a section only as being of interest or practically useful to him, and ignores and disowns the rest though given. Actions too are framed with respect to *selected* sights, sounds, etc., in the "objective" world, and selected ideas, feelings, desires, and so forth, in the "subjective". And such veiling and acceptance, such rejection and selection, is made (not always voluntarily by men) in a universe of Being-Experience which is undefined, seamless and alogical in itself, and which, in itself, cannot be labelled exclusively as either objective or subjective.[2] It is by such practical veiling and acceptance that we *seem* to see only a particular star or cluster of stars when looking up to the sky in a clear night; it is thus that we *seem* to hear a particular sound only in a "situation" in which not only many other sounds but countless sights, smells, touches, organic sensations, etc., constitute our actual *Given* of experience; it is also thus that we *seem* to have a particular idea, memory or desire in the mind when the *actual*

---

[1] That is relative to Vidyā or knowledge. Avidyā=na vidyate. This "ignorance" is a knowing of a limited kind.

[2] Isha. Up., 5.

universe of the moment is an undefined and undefinable whole of countless "objective" and "subjective" elements (*i.e.*, perceptions and ideas), most of which happen, for the time being, to be not of interest, and are therefore silently ignored. In a given universe of experience, attention is, for pragmatic reasons, focussed at a particular point which happens to be of interest for the time being; around this point of clearest attention or emphasis, spread tracts of comparative inattention till they merge into the outlying realm of the unfelt or unknown.[1] The process is analogous to the operation of turning the search-light of a vessel plying in a dark night upon different portions of the surrounding situation. The search-light is here Attention or Regard,[2] and the mechanism of its working is that of the tendencies or partialities[3] connected with a given Centre or Individual.[4] And it need be hardly pointed out that, like the vessel also, a Centre[4] cannot move to any definite purpose, if it be not provided with such special mechanism. It is useful and also indispensable in a certain sense.

We have therefore necessarily to select and refuse, accept and ignore in the midst of what we actually have. In all this a Principle of Limitation, selection or contraction[5] is operative. Now, in so far as its operation can apparently be traced to, and therefore connected with, the energising of a given Centre, it is called Ignorance;[6] and in so far as this veiling, measuring, limiting operation is the expression of a Cosmic Tendency or Will-to-become, and in

---

[1] See P. N. Mukhopādhyāya's "Approaches to Truth" for fuller discussion.

[2] Selective Attention or Regard, "Pakshapāta".

[3] Sangskāras. [4] Jīva.

[5] Sāngkocha; a common term in the Trika school of Māyā operating to produce the individual key.

[6] Avidyā.

so far therefore as it not only transcends but underlies (as generating activity) the life of the individual Centres, it is called Māyā, a power of finitization.[1] And whether we consider it cosmically or individually, it is patent that this Principle of finitization (which is the Power of Reality itself) is a limiting or contracting Principle—the Radical contracting force[2] by which the All,[3] without actually ceasing to be such, becomes Part,[4] by which Experience of Everything[3] without actually ceasing to be such, becomes Experience of something[5]: in brief, by which the "Fact" becomes "Fact-section".

The first distinction therefore, is that between Experience as whole,[3] and Experience as section or part.[4] The former remains for man a goal or "limit" only so long as there are central reference and selective regard in his experience. He can, however, more or less closely approximate to it. Nearer approach can be made to the All in proportion as the operation of the two conditions—*viz.*, reference to a Centre and selective attention—can be diminished. The All is realised when the operation of each ceases. To realise is to live and accept what has lived without being accepted. In realisation man does not veil or ignore what he has or rather what he is. His experience, therefore, does not *really* cease to be the All, when, on account of his having to refer to a Centre and bestowing his attention selectively, he has experience of parts or segments only; nor, on the other hand, does a previously non-existent All tend to be established and consummated, when, by making attention a-centric and impartial as completely as possible, man tends to come as near as possible to its realisation.[1]

---

[1] It is that by which things are measured (mīyate) that is formed.
[2] Kanchuka. [3] Pūrna. [4] Kalā. [5] Kinchit.
[6] It is Svarūpa-Vishrāntih or Svarūpa-Pratishthānam.

CHAPTER II

CONSCIOUSNESS AS THE WHOLE

THE preceding chapters have introduced the distinction between Consciousness[1] as whole or entire[2] and as section or part.[3] The former is Perfect Experience. Since all ordinary predicables or categories apply to only aspects or segments of experience, which are man's pragmatic facts, the Perfect Experience is beyond the reach of the predicables or categories.[4] That is to say, its nature cannot be adequately described by any of our concepts. Its description is therefore possible only by the mode of negation.[5] Those concepts are—to employ the classification of Kant—the forms of Time and Space, and the Categories of Quantity, Quality, Relation and Modality. By means of these forms and Categories, experience becomes thinkable, that is, logical. If these Forms of Thought (including the Categories) be withheld, the "Matter" or stuff of experience becomes formless, and therefore cannot be thought about and spoken of. By being cast into these moulds, the "Matter" becomes impressed with forms and thereby becomes thinkable and speakable.[6] That Experience becomes thinkable or logical by being circumscribed

---

[1] Chit. [2] Pûrna. [3] Kalâ.

[4] "Yatovâcho nivarttante aprâpya manasâ saha," Tait.-Up., II, 9.

[5] Nishedha; Neti Neti.

[6] Padârtha and Vâchya. The Forms and Categories are called—Nâma and Rûpa by which the Avyâkrita (undifferentiated) becomes Vyâkrita (differentiated).

in review is a fact that can be readily verified by intuition. The entire universe of sensations, feelings, ideas, memories, and so forth, which constitute total[1] Experience at any moment, can never be thought about *as a whole*; the whole must be limited and measured before it can be thought about and described. Even what is taken as "experience at any moment" is a cross section of the Experience as the whole or Fact.[2] In itself the Fact is time-less. Similarly, it is neither cause nor effect. What is known as cause or effect is a portion measured out of the Fact. These and other categories are applicable not to the whole as a whole[3] but to the whole delimited as part.[4] Perfect Experience is thus alogical. But though unthinkable and indescribable,[5] it is not on that account unknown and unknowable. It is Experience itself, Consciousness itself: no "thing-in-itself" beyond Experience. It is the Supreme Intuition.[6] It is unthinkable as is the Kantian "thing-in-itself," but its essence is Consciousness itself;[7] it is inscrutable[8] as Consciousness-Power.[9]

Experience becomes thinkable or logical by being circumscribed or limited. Now, since Experience, Consciousness or Feeling is ever what it is, its limiting can only mean this that it is ignored or veiled as a whole, and accepted or attended to in a part. In other words, the two facts, *viz.*, that we have actually at this moment a universe of experience comprising many sounds, sights, smells, touches, organic feelings, ideas, etc., and that we have at the same moment the perception of a particular sound or sight only, can be reconciled with each other only

[1] Akhanda which means sections. [2] Pūrna and Akhanda.
[3] Pūrna as Pūrna. [4] Kalā. [5] Avāngmanasa-gochara.
[6] Nija-bodha-rūpa. [7] Chit and Shakti Chidrūpinī. [8] Anirvāchya.
[9] See P. N. Mukhopadhyāya's "Approaches to Truth" for further discussion.

if we believe that the "universe," though actually given at this moment, has not been avowed and accepted as such, and that the particular sound or sight of which alone we seem to have perception at this moment is the pragmatic section of the universe especially selected and noticed by us. The pragmatic point or section has not indeed displaced or effaced the universe; even when attention is very nearly concentrated at a point or section, it does not cease to be slightly diffused, like twilight, over the outlying tracts or indeed over the whole "universe" that is actually given. The point or section always remains imbedded in that universe; always set on a larger background of experience. [The psychologist William James would call it (that background of actual feeling) the "fringe" of experience.] It is always there. So that the universe and the pragmatic point or section are *both* given as *actual* feeling. They can be both given in actual feeling only if the former, though given, is more or less ignored (*i.e.*, not attended to), and the latter given as it is as part of the larger experience, is, by reason of its special interest, especially attended to. Thus while we are especially attending to a point or section only, we have, and cannot but have, the "Universe" also. That it is not then attended to does not mean or constitute its ceasing to be an actual feeling: it does not become *no* experience. It then becomes or is an experience of a different tone or intensity—blurred, indefinite, confused. The pragmatic or interesting portion becomes lighted up, definite and discriminated. When, however, the experience of the moment the "universe" involving the points of interest is passed in review or thought about, it is commonly represented as though it were confined to or exhausted by the points of interest only. This is pragmatic thought giving the pragmatic facts, but which should be carefully distinguished from the Intuition of Fact. Circumscription or limitation of experience commonly means its veiling or ignoring as a whole and its avowal or acceptance in the "points of interest".

Veiling or contracting may, therefore, be defined as the circumstance which limits Reality considered as one aspect —as Power[1]—without making it other than what it is in its other aspect as Power-holder[2]: by which the whole[3] appears as part[4] and yet remains the whole. When, and in so far as, this circumstance operates in relation to the experience of an individual Centre, and its operation is immanent in it, it is called Ignorance.[5] When it operates cosmically, and its operation is transcendent to a given Centre, it is called Māyā. Evidently a Centre as so constituted, becomes a Centre of individualised stresses (potential and kinetic) in Reality which is Perfect Experience, because Experience by its own Power[6] so finitises and individualises itself. Veiling may be of two forms: (1) that which is done by the stresses (potential and kinetic)—that is, impressions tendencies and volitions[7] in the case of an individual Centre; and (2) that which is done by the Stress or Power of Reality itself underlying and evolving as the world of finite forms. In both cases the general definition of veiling applies. That is to say, Experience, and therefore Reality, never ceases to be the whole[3] because it has been veiled or contracted in an Individual Centre, or because it veils itself in evolving and appearing as the world of varied forms. When, for example, we appear to see a star only or hear a sound only, we actually have, and cannot but have, an undefined and indefinable "universe" of experience which is ignored except as regards the star or sound: so also in

[1] Shakti the Divine Mother. [2] Shiva Shaktimān. [3] Pūrna.
[4] Kalā. [5] Avidyā. [6] Shakti. [7] Sangskāras.

the case of "subjective" experiences, *e.g.*, a feeling in the mind, a memory, an idea. The "universe" never ceases to be such by being veiled in these cases, and emphasised in the points of interest. If we provisionally call that universe too the whole, then the whole remains as such while it appears as part.[1] In the cosmic or universal case also, where veiling has been called *Māyā*, the Immense and Immeasurable remains so even when it is to the individual eye finitised and measured. This finitisation, this evolution of *Brahman* as world, of *Shiva* as Power determined in a particular way,[2] is not, however, "illusive".

We may note also that between the cosmic case and the individual case, there is a threefold distinction as regards the circumstance of veiling. In the first place, in the individual Centre veiling or ignoring is partly voluntary and partly involuntry. When, for example, a person looking up at night wishes to see a particular star, he voluntarily veils (but cannot altogether efface) his universe of experience at that moment, and by that veiling his universe is *apparently* reduced to the perception of a single star or cluster of stars. In many cases, however, his universe becomes thus reduced not by an actual volition in his mind, but by the play of potential stresses in him which are his tendencies.[3] This is involuntary veiling. Such veiling may be either accidental or essential. It is accidental veiling when the total experience is ignored and a part accepted because of the working of a subliminal desire or subconscious interest in the mind which, for the time being, prevails most and vents itself in certain partialities. Thus even while we are not consciously attending to and selecting our experiences, we have

---

[1] Kalā.

[2] The thirty-six Tattvas as taught by the Advaita Shaivas and Shāktas.

[3] Sangskāras.

our experiences apparently dealt out to us in partials: certain sounds out of a great many actually given, for example, are apprehended by us; these are apprehended by us because certain predispositions, working subliminally and possessing the greatest causal efficiency for the time being, make us partial to them. But there is also a deeper kind of involuntary veiling which pertains to the essence of a Centre *as such*. We have referred before to the fact that an individual Centre's universe of experience cannot by Perfect Experience (which is ultimate Reality) in so far as that universe is referred to and organized round that Centre. Reference to, and organization round a Centre is itself a limitation of Perfect Experience. In fact, Perfect Experience limits or finitizes itself in appearing as such centre of reference and organization. This is the working of *Māyā* by which the Immeasurable is measured, the Indefinable is defined, the Infinite is finitized. With respect to different Centres again, (*e.g.*, amœba and man) stresses, potential and kinetic, are differently organized, so that what is ordinarily one Centre's universe is not that of another. Essential veiling means the limitation of Perfect Experience by reason of a Centre being a specialized centre of reference and organization.

It should be noted, however, that the difference between voluntary and involuntary veiling, and that between accidental and essential veiling, is a difference of degree and not one of kind. Ordinarily these differences seem to be fundamental like those between the voluntary and involuntary muscles, voluntary and involuntary nerve centres in the body. But by using appropriate means the jurisdiction of volitional control can be gradually extended over those centres which ordinarily lie outside it. The ganglia along the spinal axis, for example, which, according to some, are probably connected with race habits and instincts, can by proper discipline[1] be made amenable to voluntary control like the motor centres in the cerebral hemispheres. Such wakening of the spinal ganglia, is, it has been claimed, a collateral effect of the piercing of the "Six Centres" by *Kundalinī Yoga*. It may be incidentally observed too that such extension of the range of voluntary control over motor centres of the body which are ordinarily involuntary, has its parallel in the transposition and extension of sensory functions under hypnotism and *yoga*. *E.g.*, a hypnotic subject may "see" by the sense of touch. In the Psychic literature of the West many examples of such transposition and extension of special sensory functions are to be met with.[2] By training and effort[1] it may thus be possible for a given Centre to extend and rearrange its universe of experience (1) by extending the range of its voluntary control, (2) by extending the range of its sensory functions, and (3) by lighting up what is dark and subliminal in consciousness. By this process his universe can be made to approach to Perfect Experience. And ultimately Perfect Experience itself can be realized when a Centre is able to transcend itself as a specialized centre of reference and organization.[3] Then, what has been called essential veiling is done away with, and *Māyā* which measures and binds is transcended. A given Centre has *ordinarily* its universe of experience determined primarily by the Limiting Principle[4] by which it has been constituted a specialized centre, and secondarily by the circumstances of its own choice and

---

[1] Sādhanā.

[2] The Rishi Gotama, in ancient India, it is said, saw the face of his disciple Vyāsa by transferring his sense of sight to his feet, and so Indian tradition has given him the name *Akshapāda* (*i.e.*, one who has eyes in his feet).

[3] This is "Laya Yoga" of which Unmanī (lit. transcending Mind) is a conspicuous type.

[4] Māya.

control. Even ordinarily, his universe is thus partly at least an "intentional".

Now, let us turn to the cosmic case. It will be shewn later that the appearance of a primordial,[1] generic cosmic Centre is a condition precedent to the appearance of a multiplicity of special individual centres. Perfect Experience (or full Reality) must first "divide" itself as a Self and its Object or Universe, in order that such division may be reproduced in a multiplicity of particular centres.[1] Perfect Experience, is it is true, alogical; but *within* this Experience the polarity of Subject and Object must appear in order that the veiling and limiting process producing the world of finite forms may start. In the *Upanishads* we accordingly read how the Supreme Self was alone in the beginning, and then, how He began to see Himself (*i.e.*, made an object of Himself). In the *Kāmakalāvilasa*,[2] *Shiva*, whose nature is illuminating Consciousness or *Prakāsha* is depicted as seeing himself reflected in the "Pure Mirror" which is his Power as *Vimarsha*[3] on which the latter evolves as universe.[4] The *Vimarsha*[5] or Self-reflection of the Supreme Reality, by which act It knows Itself as a Perfect Universe, is the Perfect of Supreme Self.[6] Contrasted with this is the relative self[7], whose object of experienee is partial[8] compared with that of the Supreme Self whose object is All.[9]

---

[1] Jīvas or Purushas.

[2] Kāmakalāvilāsa, 1, 2.

[3] See note 6, page 57.

[4] It should be uoted that the order of evolution indicated, though stated as temporal, is really logical: it is not a question of *first* this and *then* that.

[5] See Kāmakalāvilāsa; and the Commentary of Natanānanda (Arthur Avalon's Ed.) where authorities are cited. See Katha-Up., "Na tatra sūryyo bhāti," etc.

[6] Pūrnāhantā or Parāhantā.

[7] Aparāhantā.

[8] Kinchit.

[9] Kritsna.

Now, the Supreme Reality makes use of Its own Power (*viz.*, *Māyā*)—(1) to appear as Supreme Self knowing Itself as a Perfect Universe, and (2) to evolve out of Itself a world of correlated finite centres. Unlike the finite centre, in which the operation of veiling is partly voluntary and partly involuntary, the Supreme Centre[1] exercises Its veiling power freely—that is to say, It is the Lord of Māyā[2] whose creatures the finite centres are. In the *Upanishads*, the Lord has accordingly been called wielder of Māyā.[3] To distinguish it from the *Māyā* of the Supreme, the "veil" in a finite Centre[4] has been called *Avidyā* (Ignorance). In Vedānta, the former is constituted by the predominant and lucid principle of unveiling and presentation whilst the latter is dark, opaque veiling. This is the first distinction between the cosmic case and individual case.

The second distinction is that whilst in the experience of the Lord knowledge of the particulars[5] co-exists with knowledge of the universals,[6] in the experience of the finite Centre,[7] knowledge of particulars is commonly possible by the veiling of knowledge of the whole, and *vice versa*. Thus while we are attentively regarding a particular star, we do so at the cost of, that is by veiling, the universe of experience we actually have at that moment; conversely, if we wish to abandon ourselves to the "universe" or the entire "given," we must disengage ourselves from the particular star which especially binds our interest now. Partial, especially focussed intuition and impartial and non-focal intuition (in so far as such intuition may be possible to a *finite Centre*) do not co-exist in man with an equal degree of psychic intensity, which means that the one must

---

[1] Pūrnāhantā or Parāhantā.
[2] Māyādhīsha.
[3] Māyāvin.
[4] Aparāhantā.
[5] Vishesha.
[6] Sāmānya.
[7] Jīva.

be veiled (without being actually effaced) in order that the other may rise to clearness and definiteness. In the Lord's Experience, on the other hand, the Fact, the Whole,[1] need not retire into the shade in order that the Fact-Sections[2] may come into the light, and *vice versa*. This is because *Māyā* which veils is His *Māyā*, and *Māyā* does not veil for Him who is the controller of it.[3] The Lord[4] is both knower of universals[5] and of the particulars,[6] and both these forms of knowing are eternal[7] in Him.[8] Therefore they co-exist.

The third distinction is that while *Māyā* (the veiling and limiting Principle which is but Supreme Reality regarded *as* Power to evolve as the world of finite forms) is immanent in the Experience of the Lord, it is transcendent in relation to the experience of a particular Centre. The consequences of this are important:—(*a*) whilst a world of finite forms is "objectified" in the experience of the Lord, it is not ejected and localised as something alien and existing outside as with man; in other words, Space is not a form of that experience in the sense in which it is a form with man; accordingly, there is no foreign "matter" seeming to exist by its own right outside of that experience.[9] (*b*) Accordingly, there is no need for *gradually* knowing that foreign outside matter and extending control over it in that experience; the Lord is Possessor of Perfect knowledge and power.[10] In the finite Centre

---

[1] Pūrna. [2] Kalā.

[3] There is, however, a distinction (as we shall see) between *Chit* as Pūrna and this "Pūrna" being objectified by the Supreme Self.

[4] Ishvara and as Divine Mother Īshvarī.

[5] Sarvvajna. [6] Sarvvavit. [7] Nitya.

[8] Even Nyāya Vaisheshika makes Jnāna nity in Īshvara.

[9] The Lord knows the world as Himself and as man sees it as non-self.

[10] Sarvvajna and sarva-shaktimān.

on the other hand, the veil has operated in such a way that an alien objective world lies outside of it in Space, which it essays to know and control gradually and partially.[1] (*c*) Time also is a measure which is immanent in the experience of the Lord; that is to say, the Lord, His experience and His Creation are not subject to temporal determination; on the contrary, these transcend Time; and what is Timeless in the Lord becomes temporal in relation to the subordinate Centres. The Lord's experience includes ideas of Time and Space, but, unlike man's is not subject to them.

The Shāstric symbols (which are also claimed as real experiences of the seers) which depict the Lord and His Power—the two being in reality one—as unclad, or nude,[2] imply this (1) that Supreme Experience which is Supreme Reality is an experience of no veil; (2) that though it of course *involves* the veil, it is not applicable to the Whole,[3] and that therefore no veil can be drawn over it; and (3) that consequently the categories and forms of thought such as Time, Space, Causality and so forth by which our Pragmatic Facts are dressed up, though all born out of, and immanent in, the Complete[3] Experience, are not forms by which the whole[3] itself can be dressed up or vehicled. In the above exposition, 'Lord' has been taken in the sense of the Superme Personality[4] which knows Itself as the Complete "I"[5]: it is Perfect Experience making an object of itself. This object is Power as *Vimarsha*. Between Perfect Experience and this Supreme I[6] there is a distinction which will be dealt with again in our study of Perfect

[1] Brihadāranyaka, III, 7, shows the Lord as Antaryyāmin (Controller) in respect of everything.

[2] Digambara and Digambarī or Mahāshakti or space-clad because being Brahman She is her own Māyā. See Hymn to Kālī.

[3] Pūrna. [4] Parāhantā. [5] Pūrnāham. [6] Being Brahman.

Experience and how the Tattvas are born out of it. Meanwhile, be it observed, that the distinction does not affect the position here stated, namely, that the Lord controls the Veil, and that Perfect Experience, involving Time, Space, Causality and so on, may be described as Experience of *no* veil. It is experience from which nothing has been ejected, held back; in which nothing has been ignored.

CHAPTER III

VEILING OF CONSCIOUSNESS

THOUGH the Supreme Reality is only realised in Yoga, the intellect gives, it is claimed, warrant in normal experience for the truth of the scriptural teaching. Let us then examine and reflect upon such experience. Recurring to the example already given let us suppose we have experience of a sound now. Commonly we think and say that our experience is, for the time being, of that sound only. This thought, though it does not represent to us the whole truth is practically useful. But evidently our whole experience at this moment is not confined to that sound. Several other sounds besides sights, smells, touches, organic sensations, feelings, ideas, desires and so forth, are in the universe of experience, though unattended, unnoticed, and therefore veiled and confused. Disengaging our interest from the sound which happens to lie on the apex of the curve of the presentation, and extending the range of attention, it is possible to explore this given universe. If we do that we shall discover two circumstances connected with that universe. In the first place, it is indefinable, so that no positive bounds can be set to it; we shall never be able to say that it goes thus far and no further, that it includes so much and no more. Beyond what we have "explored" by the search-light of attention, outlying vistas of semi-attended or unattended, and therefore more or less veiled and confused, tracts of experience will always lie.

In the second place, the veiled and confused zones are not exactly sub-conscious or subliminal; many of them are above "the threshold line; they constitute actual feelings; they, together with the sound which happens for the time being to be the point of interest, constitute our actual total experience (or "Fact") of the moment. But though they are above the threshold line, their curvature is low, the summit or apex of the curvature being represented by the sound now heard. When these two circumstances connected with the Fact have been discovered, the Veil drawn over the Fact has already been to some extent removed. Why not completely removed? We shall presently see.

Inspection of the Fact will further reveal to us two things. First, the whole "universe," involving as it does change, is sustained, "lives, moves and has its being" in a boundless and changeless "Ether of Consciousness".[1] In other words, the Fact *is* this boundless, changeless, quiescent background of Consciousness against which a Stress, infinitely various in its motions and forms, is at play. The Fact is thus both static and dynamic.[2] The dynamic, stressing, evolving aspect does not displace the static and unchanging aspect. They co-exist; they blend together into an inexpressible, alogical identity. Man is ever Consciousness *as* Power, though he commonly does not realize that he is so. He is commonly so much taken up with the "Fact-sections," the Pragmatic "Facts". When the veil of ignorance by which man ignores because of special

[1] Chidākāsha. This is a familiar concept of Upanishad. It is not meant that the physical ether is consciousness. For it is a product of Chit but that consciousness (as Chit) is like the ether an all pervading continuum. In a similar way the Shākta Tantras call the infinitely vast tract of consciousness the "Ocean of Nectar" set in which is the Bindu as the "Isle of Gems" (Manidvīpa) wherein is the Supreme Self as the highest concept in the logical order of the Alogical Real.

[2] "Gunātīta" as well as "Gunāshraya" and "Gunamaya".

interests in particular elements of Fact[1] has been so far uplifted as to give him a glimpse of the Ether of Consciousness and Stress playing in it,[2] then it is that he finds, in his own experience, a clue to the fundamental riddle of creative evolution, *viz.*, how Reality[3] evolves as the world-order and yet remains eternally what it is;[4] how, in other words, in one aspect appearing as all change it does not in the other aspect change; how, thus, its creative energising involves for logical thinking a contradiction—change and no change side by side. When man does not ignore himself, he knows that he is Consciousness which as the illumining Power[5] to *be* remains as placid, unchanging, sustaining and illuminating "Ether" of Consciousness, and as the becoming and illumined aspect[6] changes and evolves as a world of varied names and forms[7]; that the latter aspect, though opposite in character to the former, does not prevail by suspending or suppressing it. Man has warrant for this unthinkable, alogical blending of contraries in his own normal experience. The veil of pragmatic thought, when uplifted, will, it is claimed, show this to him.

The second point is this. The Stress or Power has a triple disposition in man. In the symbolic language of

---

[1] Or Pakshapāta.

[2] Of Kālī standing and moving on the prostrate inert body of Shiva, to use a very familiar Shāstric representation of the truth.

[3] Brahman, Shiva and Shakti. [4] Chit [5] Prakāsha-shakti.

[6] Vimarsha shakti. The word Vimarsha comes from the root Mrish to handle or pound. Vimarsha is that which is handled. It represents the objective side of existence and the power which produces it. It thus expresses a similar idea to that expressed by the terms Prakriti and Pradhāna or that which as its product is placed in front or an object.

[7] Nāma-rūpa, that is the psycho-physical 'sheaths' or bodies of Spirit. Tāntric Texts, Vol. X Ed., A. Avalon.

the Scripture, the Supreme *Bindu* (lit. Point)[1] which is fundamental, massive Potency to evolve ready for actual evolution, becomes a triangle[2] when it attains the condition of Primary manifestation.[3] Introspection will shew the "triangle" (the "Polar Triangle" as it may be called[4]) in the normal universe of experience. One fundamental disposition of Experience shews the polarity of Centre (*Aham* or "I"), its co-ordinate (*Idam* or "This") and their active correlation.[5]

Another fundamental of experience is this: There is the aspect of Pure Consciousness[6] in which man's universe appears, and by which it is revealed or manifested: and there is the aspect of Stress which evolves as that universe. The former is the aspect of Being-Consciousness;[7] the latter[8] is that of Stress-Becoming. By the former the universe is and is felt; by the latter it evolves and is determined. The former or revealing aspect is *Prakāsha*; and the latter or determining, "informing" aspect is *Vimarsha*. In the experience of a sound, for example, our analysis shews three elements: the sound *is*; it is *known*; it is *determined* or "informed" as sound and as a particular sound. These elements are of course aspects of one undivided *concrete* experience, and should not be taken as separate principles or entities. The aspects which analytic thought yields compose one indivisible unity of being.

---

[1] In the Shākta symbolism, Bindu means 'a drop of seed'.

[2] Trikona or Shringāta-rūpa.

[3] Uchchūnāvasthā, lit. swelled state.

[4] P. N. Mukhopādhyāya—Approaches to Truth.

[5] Vyavahāra. Matā Māna Meya is the gist (Sangkalitārtha) of Shakti.

[6] Chidākāsha. [7] Para-shiva. Parā Shakti. [8] Shiva-Shakti.

Hence Being and Becoming[1], the placid Spiritual Ether and the Point of Creative Stress,[2] Power Holder and Power,[3] *Brahman* and *Māyā* are not two, but one: or rather they are aspects, sundered apart by our analytic thought, of an alogical, ultra-numerical, Fact. Now, since the immensity of Fact or Experience or Being becomes circumscribed, and therefore veiled, in being determined (*e.g.*, when the total experience of a moment is represented as being that of a particular sensation or thought), it follows that the two aspects,[4] though connected with each other, are yet opposed to each other: the former being the revealing aspect of Consciousness, and the latter the determining, and therefore veiling, aspect of Consciousness. But determining or "informing," though it involves veiling, is not only that. When, for example, our experience is determined as that of a particular sound, the given, ineffaceable immensity of experience has undoubtedly been veiled or ignored, for the Universe in itself is still undefined and undetermined; and not only has that universe been veiled, but the emphasis of attention has moved from elsewhere to the place of the particular sound which, accordingly, now occupies the apex of the curve of presentation. The aspect of determining, or the Stress or Power by which Consciousness is self-determined involves, therefore, Veiling, Movement and Presentation.[5]

The two aspects of Revealing and Veiling[6] not only oppose each other but, as ordinary experience shows and

---

[1] Prakāsha and Vimarsha. [2] Chidākāsha and the Bindu as Stress.

[3] Shiva and Shakti. [4] Prakāsha and Vimarsha.

[5] Tamas, Rajas and Sattva gunas respectively of Sāngkhyan and Vedāntic analysis. If Veiling be called Āvarana Shakti, Movement and Presentation may jointly be called Vikshepa Shakti.

[6] Prakāsha and Vimarsha.

illustrates, they tend towards each other. That is to say, what has been revealed tends naturally and gradually to be veiled, and what has been veiled tends naturally and gradually to be revealed; what is undefined and unformed tends naturally and gradually to be defined and determined as forms, and *vice versa*. This mutual play of Revealing and Veiling[1]—which in the Scriptures is often symbolized as the mutual desire[2] of the "Divine Couple" Shiva and Shakti[3] is rhythmic, not only in the particular centres such as man, but in the life of the Cosmos, on account of which there is rhythmic cosmic evolution and involution, just as in man there is alternate waking[4] and sleeping.[5] This fundamental tendency shows itself on the physical plane as expansion and contraction of mass, on the vital plane as anabolism and katabolism and expiration and inspiration, and on the mental plane as knowing and ignoring, owning and disowning.[6] It is fundamental because it underlies the entire scheme of cosmic life, and because we fail to deduce this rhythm as a result or consequence from another law of operation more fundamental than, and therefore antecedent to, itself. It is a primordial law of the Fact to be rhythmically veiled and revealed, defined and undefined.[7] From homogeneity to heterogeneity evolution proceeds; but homogeneity is a condition of implicity[8] which condition gradually changes into one of explicity,[9] and this, back into implicity.[8]

---

[1] Prakāsha and Vimarsha. [2] Kāma.

[3] Hence named Kāmeshvara Kāmeshvarī or the fundamental "Libido". This "erotic" imagery, so objectionable to the prudery from which the Indian as most other ancient peoples were happily free, is not peculiar as some suppose to "the Tantras". So Br.-Up.: "He indeed was just as man and woman in embrace."

[4] Jāgrat. [5] Sushupti. [6] Perception is an act of "owning".

[7] See, as to "Elasticity" of Bindu later.

[8] Avyākrita. [9] Vyākrita.

It follows that the Veil (that which reduces, contracts, defines, determines the universe of Experience) tends—or in view of the law of rhythm it may be said, swings, or oscillates—between two limits, *viz.*, that of zero and that of infinity. In other words, the Veil tends to completely disappear, and it also tends to infinitely appear. In the former case, when it has completely disappeared, we have experience as the whole[1] or Perfect Experience. In the latter case, when it (*i.e.*, the Veil) has infinitely appeared, we have that condition of experience which is called dissolution[2] or Cosmic Sleep.

Infinity, however, may be either of volume or of mass, either of extensity or of intensity. When Power becomes infinitely intensive or concentrated its condition is called *Bindu* or "Point" (of contraction).[3] Such intensification or concentration presupposes a condition of Power in movement which as "heard" by the Absolute Ear is called Nāda or "Primordial Sound".[4] Energy must constitute a "field," and that field must be subject to an actual straining movement, before it can be supposed to be concentrated into a Point. This is true not merely of so-called physical energies, such as sound, heat or light. Heat or light, for example, can each be focussed, by means of a concave lens, from a more or less diffused condition. In each case, the field must be contracted, the diffused energy must be collected together. And this is true of Experience also—it is a law of Fact-operation which is the

---

[1] Pūrna. [2] Pralaya

[3] Sangkocha, that is, here potency ready to evolve as the contracted product or universe.

[4] The Shārada Tilaka says that from the Lord issued Power, from Power that state of it which is Nāda, and from Nāda Bindu. This latter becomes threefold as the universe of knower, knowing and known. See "Garland of Letters".

basis and model of all actual world-operations on the planes of mind, life and matter. Experience must be given as a continuum or universe, and that universe must be stressed and strained in a given manner, in order that attention may focus itself approximately in a point. If the placid, quiescent condition of the continuum be called *Shiva*, and Movement or Stress be called *Shakti*, then we see that the Continuum in Stress is the active union of the Power-Holder *Shiva* and Power or *Shakti*, and it is perceived why in the Shākta Tantras such active union (depicted, as often is the case, in "erotic" symbolism) is called *Nāda*, and also why it is said (carrying out the same symbolism) that *Bindu* (here Seed) issues from such union.

As an impregnated ovum or germ-cell is the concentrated form of the energies of a male and a female, so *Bindu* is the concentrated form of the substance and energy—if we may speak of them separately—of the entire perfect universe of Experience. It is the Whole[1] whose "mass" has become concentrated into a point. The Point or *Bindu* is therefore a universe, and the Perfect Universe.[1] It is the Universe in a *potential* from—the Seed of the Universe. The scheme of the organism is given in the seed; the plan of the planetary systems is possibly given in the atoms, and this is because all evolution proceeds on the plan of an universe being given in, and evolving out of, *Bindu*.[2]

In man's experience, the Point of Power[3] is given and is constantly active as "I"-ness. His whole experience has crystallized round the nucleus—"I". This is not to

[1] Pūrna.

[2] Bindu is called Paramākāsha or "Perfect Ether". Cf. also Chhāndogya-Up., which discusses the "Little Abode" which is also the Perfect Abode, and where there is Supreme Time, Parakāla, which in the former is broken up into the moments of Empirical Time (Kāla). So it is said "Time leads me in time."

[3] Ahantā.

say that "I"-ness, above "the threshold line," and the Point[1] should in all cases be identified with each other; the latter is there even when and where the former has not actually appeared, but whenever the former has appeared, it serves as the manifestation and representative of the Point[1] in the growth of the experience of a given Centre. Besides, the "Self" as the representative of the Point[1] works "sub-consciously" too. Now, It is this "Point" which in man, as well as in other forms of existence, "swells"[2] as the Polar Triangle of the measurer, the measured and the measure or measuring,[3] or Knower, Knowing, Known, and also, as it may be said from another standpoint, as that of "Base," "Index" and "Co-efficient" of the Fact.[4] It further assumes the forms of other Polar Triangles such as Power as Knowing,[5] Power as Feeling-attitude and Interest,[6] and Power as Willing and Volition.[7]

The second Triangle requires explanation. Whenever there is a given experience, analysis shows that it has a "Base" or substratum of immediate, intuitive feeling, an "Index" or superstructure of ideas and memories suggested by the "Base," and a "Co-efficient" or a background or store of possibilities or tendencies[8] which makes the fact change and grow like a crystal in appropriate solution. What is called Base and Index are commonly spoken of in Psychology as "presentative" and "representative" elements, as intuitive and ideational factors. Every perception is thus described as a presentative-representative complex. We hear a name (say *Shangkara*) uttered. The base of our experience is not only the immediate, direct

---

[1] Ahantā. [2] Uchchhūnāvasthā. [3] Mātā, Meya and Māna.

[4] In "Approaches to Truth," the doctrine is elaborated.

[5] Jnāna-shakti. [6] Ichchhā-shakti.

[7] Kriyā-shakti. [8] Sangskāra.

cognition of the sound, but it is, as introspection will show, a wide and undefined mass of many other sounds, sights, smells, touches, organic sensations, intuition of being and self and so forth, though all this great mass of feeling is, for the time being, masked under the veil of inattention and ignorance. The sound *Shangkara* is the place of emphasis and concentration, but it is obviously not the whole of what we immediately feel or what is directly presented to us now. This whole body of actually given feeling is the Base. The sound *Shangkara* calls up certain memories and suggests certain ideas; which memories and ideas associated with the name *Shangkara*, constitute the "representative element," and it is by them that the sound becomes intelligible, and conveys a meaning to us; what is a mere sensation becomes a perception to us. This halo or superstructure in, and by, which sensations are supplemented and understood, is the Index. Then again, it is patent to inspection that this complex of impressions and ideas, presentative and representative elements, is not a statical, unmoving, unchanging fact. It is an incessantly changing and growing experience. It changes both at the Base and at the Index: neither the mass of sensations nor the halo of suggested ideas ordinarily remains the same for two consecutive moments. Now, the tissue of potentials,[1] commonly lying below the threshold line of pragmatic consciousness, which makes a given experience change and grow like a crystal in a solution of the requisite kind and condition, is the "co-efficient" of the fact. The co-efficient partly determines what the fact shall be at the next moment.

We shall not study here the mutual reactions of the Base, Index and Co-efficient, but note only this that the

[1] Or tendencies—Sangskāra, Vāsanā. These have as their supporting and material cause (Shakti) as past direct experience.

first refers to the present tense of Time, the second generally to the past, and the last generally to the future. The "triangle" is in this sense three-dimensional in Time.[1]

The "triangle" involves, and is constituted by, veiling. This veiling process can be traced upwards and downwards starting from Perfect Consciousness. Perfect Consciousness veils itself when a Centre or Point of reference and operation appears in it. Consciousness is "partitioned" when it refers itself to and operates through a Centre. It seems to be no longer alogical, absolute and impartial when it so refers and operates. Ether no longer remains homogeneous, even and undivided when a strain-centre appears in it and constitutes a prime atom. By the appearance of such centre the mass as well as the energy of Ether becomes relative—assuming for one moment that they were homogeneous and uniform previously to the appearance of the strain-centres. Similarly, protoplasm becomes relative, both as regards mass and energy, when it assumes the nuclear form and becomes a cell. Lastly, experience becomes relative and partial by reason of the appearance of the ego or "I" in it. To be relative is to become partitioned or divided in a way. The strain-centre in Ether is distinct from, and, in a sense, separate from the rest of ether: it is a kind of hedging round. So in the case of the living cell, and in that of self-referring (either consciously or sub-consciously) experience. Now, veiling or contraction is the name that is given to this principle of hedging round or differentiation.[2] It is that which

[1] Kalikopanishat, 5, speaks of the "Trikonam" or Triangle of Kālikā which represents Reality especially as Time (Kālā), and the Devourer of Time ("Kālasya kālanāt kālī," etc.).

[2] This is variously spoken of in the Shruti as Brahman hiding Itself in a cave, dividing Itself.

gives us difference,[1] or duality[2] or separateness.[3] It does so by suppressing or concealing the sameness, unity and impartiality.[4] For veiling we must have therefore two circumstances. First, there must be difference, separateness and so on. But only this is not enough. Therefore, secondly, the whole in which the differences exist or appear must be suppressed or concealed in a manner. The whole must retire into a cave. The intrinsic strain-centre in Ether suppresses or conceals the Mother-Ether itself in this sense that it conserves itself, which means that it resists the encroachment of surrounding matter upon itself; resists the tendency to dissolution in the sea of ether out of which it has differentiated itself; and thereby maintains its own individuality as a prime atom of specific mass, constitution and energy. By resisting it maintains its separateness; and resistance is thus avoidance, rejection. The same reasoning applies to the nucleated cell of protoplasm. The nucleus is the physical seat and organ of a Principle of specific operation[5] and control, and such operation and control is possible not merely by acting upon the given mass of protoplasm and the energy contained in it, but also, to a large extent, by resisting the action of the portion of the protoplasm not made into a nucleus.[6]

Lastly, in experience the Ego acts as a Principle of specific operation and control, by reason of which Perfect Experience, like physical ether, is "strained" about a given

---

[1] Bheda. [2] Dvaita. [3] Vailakshanya.

[4] According to the luminous definition of Yogarāja or Yogamuni, "It is the function of Shakti to negate" (Nishedha-vyāpāra-rūpa-shaktīh) Karikā 4 Comm. on Abhinava Guptas' Paramārthasāra. This recalls the maxim "omnis determinatio est negatio".

[5] This is what is meant by Māyā creating Bheda or Dvaita.

[6] The disintegrating action is often called in Up. as "Mrityu" which, as Brih.-Up. says, assails the "Devas" of the Body and tends to produce "tiredness" in them.

centre; becomes hedged round or circumscribed, and thereby becomes imperfect, finite individual experience—the experience of the limited embodied self.[1] By being thus differentiated, such experience becomes the accepted and avowed segment of the Perfect Universe or Experience which has been pragmatically veiled, ignored or disowned. Like the nucleus of a cell of living matter, the Ego represents a system of countless tendencies,[2] a system of partialities, of selections and rejections. At every moment of its experience, it selects and rejects. Pragmatically, its experience is not the Perfect Experience, firstly because it is a centre of special differentiation, and therefore of circumscription, in the latter; and secondly because it selects in, and therefore cuts up, even that undefinable universe of experience which is its own "Fact". Thus a man may seem to hear a particular sound only in the midst of a given universe of experience comprising many sounds, sights, smells, touches, and so forth; and this given universe is the Perfect Experience strained and differentiated about a given Centre. Man's acknowledged feelings and so forth are therefore doubly removed from the Whole.

A Centre, whether in "dead" Matter, or in "living" Matter, or in Experience represents the metaphysical point or *Bindu*: which means that it is a concentrated, potentialized universe (an infinite sphere whose radii have been infinitely reduced), and consequently that it is a seed out of which a diffused, distended, actual universe is to evolve again.[3]

The *Bindu* is the Perfect Universe in a condition of maximum veiling but infinite potency. If we represent the Perfect Universe or experience by an infinite sphere

---

[1] Jīva. [2] Sangskāra.

[3] Sarva-Sāropanishat compares the "Seed" to that of a Banyan Tree in which the tree lies "hidden".

whose radius stands for infinite presentation or manifestation, then this sphere can be made to represent the *Bindu* when its radius has been infinitely reduced—that is to say, when its manifestation has been completely veiled. Since the sphere is not merely a mathematical sphere, but is dynamic—is a field of operative Power, its infinite contraction means infinite concentration or compactness of Power; so that the Para Bindu[1] or "Supreme Point" may be conceived as infinitely massive Power or Potency,[2] which is also, Power ready to evolve the Universe because, as further explained later, all evolution must start from Energy massed into nuclei or centres. It is as if an infinite coil of wire or spring were compressed infinitely till, in the limit, it became a Point. The more it is compressed, the less become its dimensions and the greater the amount of condensed energy or potency. In the limit, imagined when it has become a Point, its dimensions become infinitely small, but its potency infinitely great.

That such decrease of dimensions and increase of potency can go together, can be shown *à posteriori* from observed phenomena. Chemical action affecting the combination of atoms is, generally speaking, more powerful than physical or mechanical action affecting molar and molecular masses. In fact, greater bulk of operative power in the physical universe is probably derived from chemical action. But even chemical energy, great as it is, is nothing compared with the energy which is stored up in, and sometimes given out, as in radio-activity, by the atom. The atom is small but its store of energy is vast. But neither the atom nor the electron is infinitely small. Hence the energy of the atom or electron is not infinitely great. Infinitely

[1] Also called Īshvara-tattva.

[2] Niratishaya-ghanībhūta-Shakti.

vast energy is reached when the metaphysical "Point" or *Bindu*[1] is reached.

It is so because Mass *is* really Energy. Extension of Mass means diffusion of Energy. When the Mass is small, the quantity of Energy per unit area is greater than what it would be per same unit area when the same Mass occupied a larger volume. Mass, in accordance with the highly suggestive pictorial thinking of Faraday, may stand for so many and such and such forms of "lines of force". When Mass occupies a certain volume, we have so many lines of force packed together in a given area; when the volume contracts, the same number of lines of force becomes more closely packed together, so that, area for area, we now have force of a greater intensity. The Atom is matter in which lines of force are very closely conglomerated; in the Electron they must be still more closely packed, till we arrive at the dynamic "Point" in which they are infinitely closely packed, which means that in it force is infinitely intense. The dynamic Point is thus the "limit" in the mathematical sense of the "close packing" of lines of force *ad infinitum.*[2]

Now, for one moment let us consider evolution as it should be understood in this system.[3] It is a condition of cosmic dis-equilibrium. The stresses of centres do not neutralize one another so long as creative movement goes on. Placed in such a field of disequilibrium or unequal

---

[1] It is thus called Ghanībhūta or condensed massed Power.

[2] This is charama or niratishaya ghanibhāva of Shakti.

[3] Srishti, which is here used in its sense as evolution (Parināma) not of creation whether "out of nothing" or out of pre-existent material. Cosmic Evolution is an unfolding or making explicit of what is implicit in Shakti. The cause remains what it was and yet appears differently in the effect. The difference between this Parināma of Shaktivāda and the Vivartta of Māyāvāda lies in the fact that the former regards the effect as real, and the latter as neither real nor unreal.

tensions, a Dynamic Point or *Bindu* must tend to expand or swell.[1] That is to say, its infinitely closely packed lines of force (to continue the analogy of Electrical Science) will tend to distend or spread. Which again means that its infinite potency must commence to distribute itself about it as a "field". Such swelling of the Point is illustrated on the different planes of creation. In Matter it is represented by universal radio-activity. Every material particle allows its fount of energy to flow out in streams of radiation: and each material centre becomes surrounded by a field of force.[2] What Science now calls Atom is itself such a field—a little universe of revolving protons and electrons. Even these latter, being of finite magnitude, must be of the nature of "fields". In the world of Life, the cell of protoplasm is a field round about a nucleus. In a nutritive solution the cell "swells" and then splits up, divides, subdivides. In this way the cell multiplies itself, and then by integration and co-ordination creates organisms.[3] The material atom also multiplies itself in this sense that, in radio-activity, it gives out radiations each of which is a centre of force ejected from the body of the parent atom. By ejecting such new centres, it creates its field of influence, and slowly recreates itself. In Mind, too, the Self, which represents the "Point," swells and thereby evolves itself—in knowledge, feeling and action. Apart from such "swelling" or "field," the Self is a point at which countless tendencies[4] are, so to say, infinitely closely packed together. To use another physical analogy, it is the point

---

[1] Uchchūnāvasthā. [2] See Shvetāshvatara-Up., VI, 10.

[3] That even the formed body or organism is a radiating field of "magnetic" energy is proved by the laboratory researches of Western Scientists. Cf. the well-known passage of Shruti which means that "Hangsa" or Prāna radiates out (Shvetāshvatara-Up., III, 18).

[4] Sangskāra.

at which the battery of infinitely condensed mentative energy can be discharged *as well as* that at which it can be charged again. By continuous discharge, it ejects lines of stress, (*i.e.*, action and reaction) in all directions: and through and upon these lines of stress, its world of limited Experience evolves, starting from infancy. By these stresses again the battery or condenser is recharged—new tendencies are impressed. In its discharge upon the physical universe, the mentative force flows out at the point of the Self, and is converted into physical force by the mechanism of the brain centres which, accordingly, may be regarded as "converters". However that be, the Self is like a tap which, pressed in and out, discharges and recharges the infinite condenser or reservoir of Power or *Shakti* which every limited self essentially is. And not only is that self[1] so; organic matter is so; the atom of inorganic matter is so; the living cell of protoplasm is so; in fact, everything is so in which the *Bindu* or Dynamic Point of Power operates and tends to attain to the state of readiness for evolving action.[2] It should be noted further that this tendency, fundamental as it is, is rhythmic; that is to say, there is alternate expansion[3] and contraction[4] of the *Bindu*, in creation and dissolution, in life and death, in waking and slumber. And such rhythm ought on principle to be traceable in the "life-curve" of even the so-called "dead" atom of matter.

It has been already observed that in expansion the Dynamic Point tends to assume the form of the Dynamic Triangle[5]—that is to say, a triangle whose lines and points are not mathematical lines and points only, but are lines and points of force—a circumstance which can be aptly

[1] Jīvātma. [2] Uchchhūnāvastha. [3] Vikāsha. [4] Sangkocha.
[5] Trikona.

described by calling the triangle a "Polar Triangle".[1] A Triangle in comparison with the Point, is a condition of unveiling, manifestation. It becomes a Point again when the boundary lines or sides are made to shrink infinitely. The three poles are drawn infinitely close together, that is, are ultimately made to coincide. The Point or *Bindu* is, in one sense, the condition of maximum veiling or non-manifestation. It is infinitely condensed Power, but so long as it remains what it is, the lines of operation of Power are, so to say, packed up, that is, unmanifest. But if by manifestation we mean the condition of being given as Power, the *Bindu* is, as the Perfect Universe, the state of maximum manifestation. It is Complete Being-ness.[2] In it nothing is held back, nothing is incomplete, partial. Since again all operation, all movement, of whatever kind in the world, presupposes and starts from the *Bindu* it really means infinite potency to move and evolve.

In the Upanishads *Brahman* has often been described as smaller than the smallest,[3] and larger than the largest.[4] Now, if by *Brahman* we mean Perfect Experience or Universe, then we see how aptly the description applies to *Brahman*, particularly if we are careful to take the *Bindu* for what it really is.

---

[1] *E.g.*, the Kāmakalā of three Bindus, the first (Mahābindu or Parashiva or "Sun") holding within itself its aspects when polarised as Shiva Bindu ("Fire") and Shakti Bindu or "Moon". See "Garland of Letters". The triangle is the symbol of unity with diversity as the experiencer, experiencing and the experienced universe of tri-dimensional matter. The Triangle resting on its base is the Shiva or Power-holder, aspect, the reversed triangle is the Shakti aspect and the Hexagon (Shatkona) is the union of the two.

[2] Pūrna-Sattā.

[3] Anoranīyān.

[4] Māhatomahīyān.

CHAPTER IV

PURE EXPERIENCE

THE term 'pure' as appended to experience may mean three things. First, it may mean the unbounded Ether of Consciousness[1] in which an infinitely varied world of experience is in the stress of becoming. Whatever is felt and known, hoped and wished, in fact all the varied experiences of the limited self, appear and disappear, rise and fall, like waves in an infinite sea of Consciousness. Like clouds and myriads of heavenly bodies in Ether again, moving and revolving, man's experiences move and change, "live, move and have their being" in a perfectly placid Ether of Consciousness. Man's spiritual existence is never at any moment simply the aggregate of the modes of experience that he may have at that moment. For pragmatic reasons, he commonly ignores many of the modes themselves: he is commonly partial to a few and regards these as all that he possesses at that moment. But these are not all that is ignored; what is generally ignored, though it cannot be even for a single moment effaced or shut out, is the placid background or atmosphere of Consciousness in which all appearances take place. This placid Spiritual-Ether is patent to intuition,[2] though being the Primary Continuum,

---

[1] Chidākāsha or Ākāshātmā.

[2] Realizable in what Maitri-Up. calls "manah-kshaya" (melting away of Mind) and the Shākta Tantras and other Tantras calls "Unmanī bhāva," or Mindlessness.

the fundamental Basis and Light of all lights,[1] or Light of existence itself, it is not capable of being expressed except in terms of analogies which are themselves its inferior forms. Thus it is called Ether, Space, Illumination, and so forth. The Shāstra itself occasionally uses these and other analogies. Now, as man's spiritual being is never simply the sum-total of the modes of experience (as the sea is not simply the sum of its waves, or ether of the physical masses), so, conversely, his spiritual being is not reduced to nothing by eliminating or effacing the modes of experience. Modes may vanish but experience *as such* must remain: waves may die down, but the sea itself will remain placid.[2] This indeed is the quiescent, placid aspect of man's being—the *Shiva* aspect. Against it we have the stressing, dynamical, moving and changing aspect—the *Shakti* aspect. This experience as such, this universal, unlimited, ineffaceable (though commonly ignored) Ether or Mother-stuff of Experience, perfectly placid and homogeneous, impartial and undirected, is Pure[3] Experience.

This Pure and Primary Ether of Consciousness is *immanent* in the ordinary life of experience: it is given and cannot but be given, but it is generally not suspected; it is ignored. General and impartial Consciousness is never suppressed or superseded by particular, and partial "consciousness". It is always patent to intuition. But it is transcendent also. First, in the sense that it is never exhausted, taken up by particular consciousness, like Ether by the physical masses in, and of, it.

---

[1] As Br.-Up., calls it.

[2] Thus in Mahāpralaya which is cosmic slumber all determinations are effaced, all particulars are withdrawn; but consciousness *as such* does not cease to be.

[3] Shuddha.

It goes beyond. Immense or indefinable as the varied world of experience is, it is larger than that immensity.[1] Secondly, it is transcendent in the sense of being the fourth,[2] that is higher than, and going beyond, the three ordinary states of waking, dreaming and dreamless slumber. In this fourth[3] form, apart from the changing modes of the lower three (in which also it is undoubtedly immanent), it can be realized in that form of super-consciousness known to *Yoga*[3] in which Consciousness is realized as such, in its non-differentiated, impartial, placid form *only*—apart from all veiling differences[4] or modes or determinations. Even ordinary intuition establishes that it is immanent in the three states of waking, dreaming and slumbering. It therefore always persists, and unchangingly persists; because even in the three states, when Consciousness appears and evolves as the three states, it still remains as the sustaining and illuminating, placid and impartial Ether of Consciousness;[5] because in this aspect it does not change while appearing to change as the world of forms.[6] Accordingly, the *Māyāvāda* of Shangkara and of Gaudapâda, his grand-preceptor, which defines 'reality' as absolutely unchanging persistence, regards the Ether of Consciousness[7] alone as the transcendental real,[8] whilst the world which appears

[1] Mahato mahīyān. Shvetāshvatara-Up., III, 20.

[2] Māndūkya-Up. in particular, describes the four "pādas" of Ātman, and correlates them to the four mātrās of Om. The four states are: (1) "Vahih-prajna" (Mind acting through the senses of external perception and action); (2) "Antah-prajna" (when Mind feeds on its own ideas and sangskāras); (3) "Ghana-prajna" (consciousness is massive, undifferentiated as in dreamless Slumber); and (4) "Shānta" the Supreme State.

[3] Turīya. Nirvikalpa Samādhi.

[4] Vishesha.

[5] Chidākāsha or Shiva.

[6] Reality as such in contrast with reality as it appears is "Akshara" and "kshara".

[7] Chidākāsha.

[8] Pāramārthika sat.

and changes in it is pragmatically real,[1] though relative to the transcendent real,[2] "unreal"[3] in the term of non-persistence. This, however, is a matter of definition only.

Pure Consciousness, in the sense of the Primary Ether,[4] is patent to intuition which involves the turning of the light of attention in upon the Self and its experience. Intuition like outwordly directed attention, may be either pragmatic and centralized (*i.e.*, referring to and condensed about a centre), or non-pragmatic and a-centric.[5] The latter is an essay to review and accept the Fact as such, without allowing attention to be restricted to, and therefore concentrated on, particular sections or features therein such as particular sensations or feelings. The latter is not therefore swayed by special interests.[6] It looks upon and orders experience in its concrete entireness. Now, to this a-centric, non-pragmatic intuition, the Ether of Consciousness, with a universe of varied experience living, moving and having its being in it, is patent. Then again, this Spiritual and Ultimate Ether can be established by the method of Conceptual Limit and that of Perceptional Limit.[7] In using the first we ask ourselves this question: What ultimately, *i.e.*, in the limit, remains when we imagine or think away all modes, all particular determinations from the Fact or Universe of Experience? The latter method is approached and incompletely applied in many normal (*e.g.*, just going to wake, or just falling asleep) and abnormal (*e.g.*, certain kinds of so-called "unconsciousness," anæsthesia and so forth) experiences in which particular determinations tend

---

[1] Vyāvahārika sat. This is not recognised by Drishti-Srishtivāda form of Māyā-vāda.

[2] Pāramārthika sat. [3] Asat. [4] Chidākāsha.

[5] "Sabīja" and "Nirbīja"—with or without "Seed". [6] Rāga.

[7] See "Approaches to Truth", last section, for its elaboration.

more or less closely to the vanishing point without vanishing actually and absolutely. This method is said to be perfectly applied—so that the particular determinations of world-experience vanish and the Ether of Consciousness[1] alone remains—in the supreme *yoga* experience.[2] In the process of this *Yoga*, the common "Polar Triangle" of experience contracts into *Bindu*, and this latter dissolves, as an intrinsic strain-centre may be imagined to dissolve in ether, in the strain-less and stress-less Ether of Consciousness.

In the second place, Pure Experience can be taken to mean Experience which is not limited and conditioned and opposed by that which appears to be not Experience. Although really all is experience, yet ordinary experience seems to be limited, conditioned and opposed by what is commonly believed to be not experience, *e.g.*, by matter. There is thus the alien, objective, extra-mental enveloping order for the limited self. It is a system of correlated centres which are not believed to be co-essential with the experiencing self. Its experience is thus the result of the stresses of this external system of centres and those of other centres which are the limited knowing self. Thus duality is involved in the common position in life. The selves are reals entrenching themselves into the spatial, temporal and causal background of a Reality larger than themselves. Each has his own sphere or "field". With respect to the larger Reality, man's sphere, (an indefinable universe though it may be to intuition) is part or section.[3] But suppose we look at the Reality itself disengaging our attention from the sections. Sections are not indeed lost in that case; they lie imbedded in the immense Whole.[4]

---

[1] Chidâkâsha.

[2] Nirvikalpa Samâdhi.

[3] Angsha, Kalâ.

[4] Pûrna as Chitsvarûpa.

And what is this immense Whole? Experience and nothing but experience. There is no longer an alien, objective order conditioning and opposing Experience. Duality is gone. Reality as the Whole[1] is Pure Experience, not indeed in the first sense explained before, but in this that experience is not opposed by anything, (*e.g.*, matter) which is, or believed as, non-experience.[2] Suppose also, on the other hand, we begin with an individual sphere of experience, and gradually extend its boundary. The "alien" system of mind, life and matter centres which, in their mutual action and reaction on the given centre, constitute the objective order, is recognised as co-essential with the given centre itself, that is, as Consciousness[3] and its Power;[3] Reality in the infinite richness of its expression is recognised as *Chit*, or Consciousness, and in its infinite variety of functioning as the play[4] of *Chit-Shakti* or Consciousness as Power.

Perception is (though we commonly do not suspect it) an act of *owning*; that is, establishing an essential identity between Self and Not-Self, Spirit and Matter.[5] The essential Basis or Common Factor of all existence, whether objective or subjective, is this Consciousness. Every act of perception brings out this common factor, without, however, the action ordinarily suspecting it. Everything is in, and of, *Chit*; the Subject-Centre as well as the system of Object-Centres. In such "knowledge"[6] therefore, experience is the Whole[7] again; and since then there

[1] Pūrna as Chitsvarūpa.

[2] This is the experience of "Sarvāsmi" or "Brahmāsmi"—I am all: nothing is other than, alien to, Ātman. "Pure Experience" in the first sense would be—"chinmātro'ham," "Niranjano'ham," "Buddhajnānamasmi"—*i.e.*, I am pure, "undifferenced" Chit.

[3] Chit.

[4] Līlā of Shakti.

[5] Pramāna-Chaitanya, Pramatri-chaitanya, and Prameya-chaitanya.

[6] Jnāna.

[7] Pūrna.

remains nothing other than, and conditioning and opposing, experience, we may call such experience Pure Experience, *i.e.*, Experience and nothing else.

In the third place, 'Pure' may mean 'of one kind or quality'. Perfection of purity in this sense is of course reached in the Ether of Consciousness which is undifferentiated (therefore having no qualitative variations) experience.[1] But apart from this, and in degrees inferior to this, man may have uniform experience which are, therefore, pure in this sense. In his ordinary experience there are, for example, the three poles of Base, Index and Co-efficient explained above. Base stands for immediate, direct perceptions or intuitions;[2] Index for actually recalled and suggested elements, gathering around intuitions and constituting their "halo" of meaning. Co-efficient stands for tendencies[3] by, and in, which the given experience grows and changes like a crystal in the requisite solution. Now, suppose we imagine an Experience which is all Base with no Index and no Co-efficient; that is, an experience which is wholly, in all its elements, actual, direct, immediate.[4] Nothing is, or requires to be, recalled or suggested; nothing which is merely possible (*i.e.*, tendency) is, or requires to be, actualized. Then this is Pure experience in the sense of being of one kind or order. It should be noted in this connection that in dreamless slumber,[5] the Co-efficient is at its maximum, Index is almost nil, and Basis at its minimum, being only a vague, undifferentiated but, as the Shâstra tells us, pleasant[6] feeling of being. In dream[7]

---

[1] See last Chapter but one for further explanation of Shuddha (Pure) and Ashuddha (Not-pure).

[2] Aparoksha jnâna. [3] Sangskâras. [4] Aparoksha.

[5] Sushupti. [6] "Happily I slept. I knew nothing."

[7] Svapna.

all the three poles exist, though the emphasis seems to lie on that of the Index. However that be, Pure Experience which makes the Base the whole of Experience, which is not limited by any unrealized tendencies or possibilities, and which has no admixture of any element that is only a suggestion of another, not directly given, is experience which, in a sense, is whole [1] or Perfect.

Similarly, experience which is only statical or only dynamical will be pure in the sense of being of one kind. The Sangkhyan self [2] or Vedantic Ether of Consciousness [3] is purely statical: [4] it is perfect quiescence. Sāngkhyan *Prakriti*, though not recognised as Consciousness-Experience in Sāngkhya, is purely dynamical, because it always moves, whether homogeneously [5] or variedly.[6] *Shakti* in Shakti-vāda is essentially Consciousness-Power; and Consciousness, has both a statical, quiescent aspect and a dynamical, stressing aspect. But quiescent Consciousness [7] is also Power,[8] in this sense that Consciousness remains and continues as such (that is, unchanged) by its Power: it persists, it conserves itself. If to suffer a change implies power, not to suffer a change also implies it. In fact, persistence or self-conservation is one of the fundamental expressions of Power—the Power by which Reality or Substance is constituted and held together as such. Hence if we say that *Shiva* in one sense is pure rest, we must say that in another sense He is pure motion or action. A substance that merely stops but does not persist, does not continue, is

[1] Pūrna.

[2] Purusha, which is neither Kārana (cause) nor Kāryya (effect) and is chinmātra.

[3] Chidākāshā.

[4] It is the Shiva aspect of the Shākta's Shiva-Shakti.

[5] Sadrisha-parināma. [6] Visadrisha-parināma

[7] Shiva. [8] Shakti.

one that is dead and gone. To persist or continue, it must move or act; though, to ensure unchanged continuance, it must be absolutely uniform, invariable or pure action. Its action is analogous to uniform movement of Sāngkhyan Psycho-physical Principle.[1] Hence *Shiva* is actionless[2] as well as (as *Shakti*) acting,[3] not merely as, and in the aspect of, the changing world, but even as Ether of Consciousness.[4] These two aspects (actionless and acting) of *Shiva* in the Ether of Consciousness[4] do not however contradict each other: they do not constitute duality. They are merely two ways (from man's point of view) of expressing one and the same fact. *Shiva*-Experience is therefore really non-dual experience,[5] one essentially indivisible experience, and is, therefore, according to the definition stated, Pure Experience.

Power is both Power to persist and to change. It is the latter which is commonly called Power,[6] though, as we have seen, the former is equally so. Pure action is commonly regarded as no action, pure movement as rest. It is so regarded because commonly and practically man is interested in change or variation. But this is, for reasons above explained, a pragmatic and partial view. In the complete view, rest and pure action can both be predicated of *Shiva* as Ether of Consciousness,[4] because they mean the same thing; they express one non-dual[5] Fact.

On the other hand, Power[6] is that aspect of Consciousness in which it stresses and changes as the world-order. As such changing action is commonly called action or movement, Power[6] is regarded as the moving, acting dynamical aspect of Consciousness.[7] If Consciousness[7]

---

[1] Prakriti. [2] Nishkriya. [3] Sakriya.

[4] Chidākāsha. [5] Advaita. [6] Shakti. [7] Chit.

which is the essence of Power,[1] be veiled, that is unrecognised, then Power[1] is the creative Impulse that continuously changes as the world—there being no rest, no endurance, no permanence. Such Power[1] becomes acceptable to such philosophies as that of Heraclitus of old and of Bergson to-day. But it is essentially a Power of Consciousness;[2] there is no warrant for going beyond and behind Consciousness[2] in searching for the common root of the world and experience. And though Power[1] is dynamic, is Movement, it cannot but be set against, and sustained by, a quiescent background of Consciousness,[2] the Ether of Consciousness,[3] the Supreme *Shiva*. In fact, an all-change, all-movement view of Reality cannot be assumed without destroying the warrant of experience, the only warrant and sanction of unimpeachable authority that man possesses. Not only does *Shakti* presuppose *Shiva*; *Shakti* is *Shiva*. She is that not merely in the sense that She is *Chit* as Power to move, act and change; but also in the sense that She is *Chit* as Power to persist; in other words, *Shakti*, though dynamical, also possesses the essential character of the Ether of Consciousness,[3] of Substance and Reality. As such Ether[3] is statical in one sense (*i.e.*, in the sense of unchanging) and dynamical in another (*i.e.*, in the sense of persisting or continuing), so *Shakti* is dynamical in one sense (*i.e.*, in the sense of moving and changing), and statical in another (*i.e.*, in the sense of persisting as such). *Shakti* is always *Shaktī*; She is eternal,[4] in creation and dissolution, in action as well as in rest, in latency as well as in potency; She becomes never other than *Shakti*, and is never

---

[1] Shakti. [2] Chit.

[3] Chidākāsha. The Mother is Chidrūpinī. [4] Nitya.

dissociated from *Shiva* or *Chit.*[1] Even Perfect Power cannot do away with itself—cease to be other than Power. Now, if the experience of such Ether,[2] quiescent and persistent, was pure experience according to the definition given, so must be that of *Shakti*, moving and persisting as such. The latter like the former seems to involve a contradiction in itself—movement and persistence. But, as in the former, the contradictories blend into one non-dual[3] fact in the complete view, having arisen only from the circumstance of man's partial and pragmatic survey. To know (realize) *Shakti* is therefore pure Experience.[4]

---

[1] Na shivah Shakti-rahito, na shaktir vyatirekinī (Shiva Drishtih III, 23). See also "Wave of Bliss," vi.

[2] Chidākāsha. The Mother is Chidrūpinī. [3] Advaita.

[4] Shakti-jnāna is Shiva-jnāna and Brahma-jnāna. The Abode of Shakti is the abode of Shiva or Vishnu. See v. 44, Shatchakra Nirūpana.

CHAPTER V

PERFECT EXPERIENCE

PERFECT Experience can be best described by the negative method.[1] The Ether of Consciousness[2] as undifferentiated pure Consciousness, is also describable by the negative method. One is, however, not exactly the other. In the first place, Perfect Experience is an Experience of *no* veiling.[3] Veiling treats and disturbs experience fundamentally by setting up Dynamic Points or Centres of strain and stress, whereby Experience becomes referred to, determined and limited by the action and reaction of, correlated Centres. Centralized experience is essentially veiled and cramped experience. Then, secondarily and incidentally, veiling proceeds to create aspects and poles in experience. Thus there arise such distinctions as that between actual experience and possible experience, presentations and tendencies,[4] conscious and sub-conscious experience; that between clear, accepted experience and obscure, ignored experience; actual experience and pragmatic experience; that between the "Fact" and "Fact-Section"; experience and beyond; that between statical aspect and dynamical; changing and unchanging; and so on. Briefly it *limits* experience firstly by setting up separate "universes" in it; secondly by cutting up each universe into aspects and

---

[1] Nishedha, vyatireka, neti. [2] Chidākāsha.

[3] See the explanation of Shuddha-tattvas in the last chapter but one.

[4] Sangskāras.

planes such as statical-dynamical, actual-possible, latent-patent; thirdly, by making man partial to sections, pragmatically unmindful of the whole. Now, in Perfect Experience the veil must go in all these three forms. In other words, Perfect Experience cannot be limited to particular "universes," to particular aspects and planes, and to particular sections or features. Conversely, an Experience which is that of a particular Centre operative as such; which is statical only or dynamical only; which is actual in part and possible in part; which is accepted in sections and ignored in the whole;—is not Perfect Experience.

In the second place, Perfect Experience, which is also the Supreme Fact, is alogical.[1] It cannot be reached and expressed by the logical categories. For instance, the Supreme Fact is not a numerical Fact: one and many are categories which do not apply to it. So as regards the categories of Time, Space, Causality. Fact is not now and then, here and there, cause and effect. But, then. two things are to be noted as regards the alogicality of Perfect Experience. First, though transcending all categories, it involves them all. That is, categories of quantity, quality, relation and modality are all immanent in it; arise out of the Power of Consciousness;[3] relate to particular determinations wrought by that Power; and therefore to all "Fact-sections" contained, and even to their sum-total.[3] Thus Consciousness,[2] both in the sense of Ether of Consciousness[4] and that of Perfect Experience, is unreachable by thought and discourse.[5] This is the true

---

[1] Parā Samvit which is Tattvātīta or Beyond the Tattvas or Power defined in a particular way. See *post*, last chapter but one.

[2] Chit. [3] See "Approaches to Truth" for further discussion.

[4] Chidākāsha. [5] Avāngmanasagochara.

characterization[1] of Consciousness as Chit.[2] Secondly, we may have nevertheless an approximate characterization,[3] based upon man's experience and thought: that though the categories of judgment do not apply to the fulness and perfectness of experience (which is therefore alogical), yet some concepts come nearer to it than others, and therefore, some concepts may be thought as giving an approximate representation of it. It is thus allowable to speak of it as one, immense and infinite, whole and perfect.[4] Nevertheless, in seeking to completely possess and express the alogical by means of logical concepts, we ultimately discover ourselves as dealing in contradictions. To think of the unthinkable, to speak of the unspeakable, involves, *ipso facto*, contradiction. And since man cannot help sometimes thinking and speaking of his Experience, in its perfectness as well as in its segments, his thought does sometimes necessarily involve contradiction. We should expect it rather than be surprised.

For example, we find, in thinking about Consciousness and the World, that *Chit* does not and also does change: that it stresses and changes as the world, and yet it remains unchanged as Pure *Chit*. In trying to cure this logical defect, we commonly do two things. We say either with *Māyāvāda* Vedānta that from the absolute standpoint changing is unreal, that *Chit* does not really change at all; or with *Shākta* and some other forms of Vedānta that changing and unchanging are both

[1] Svarūpa-lakshana.

[2] Mahānirvāna Tantra, III, 7, gives the "Svarūpa" and III, 9, gives "Tatastha-lakshana" of Brahman.

[3] Tatastha-lakshana.

[4] It is this, together with Sat, Chit, Ānanda, which is commonly given as the Svarūpa-lakshana which is a definition that always applies to Brahman; and which never becomes contradicted (Vādhita).

real, and that they relate to two aspects of Consciousness.[1] But in either solution the contradiction remains unsolved. The former soon finds that contradiction turned out by one gate inevitably returns by another. *Māyā* or the "hypnotic suggestion"[2] by which unchanging Consciousness[1] appears as the changing world is said to be neither real nor unreal,[3] nor partly real and partly unreal, and hence inscrutable.[4] Contradiction thus reappears in the statement of *Māyā*, and inscrutableness or alogicality is ultimately recognised as the only answer. The crux of the whole problem is this: Though of course the changing world is not real in the sense of 'being persistent in the three tenses of time,'[5] yet it is there in a way; and it can never be said that it does not exist.[6] And this changing existence (call it unreal if to change is to be unreal) of the world-experience side by side with unchanging existence of Pure Experience[7] is a Gordian knot which (some may say) we do not either untie by any theory of cosmic hypnosis, or cut by any logical or dialectic weapon. It is best to frankly recognise that Reality (though Consciousness[1] itself) in its wholeness is alogical, and that, therefore, any attempt, direct or indirect, to clothe it in logical concepts must involve us in contradiction.

---

[1] Chit.

[2] "Indrajāla."

[3] Sadasad-vilakshanā. Tattvā-tattvābhyām anirvachanīyā, as Shangkara's Commentary has it. See also Sarvasāropanishat for definition of Māyā.

[4] Anirvāchyā.

[5] Kālatrayāvādhitatvam.

[6] Non-existent like the aerial flower, hare's horn, child of a barren woman, etc. The world possesses admittedly not only Prātibhāsika but Vyāvahārika sattā. Compare however the position of the Ekajīva-vādin who recognises only Pārmārthika and Prātibhāsika forms.

[7] In Jāgrat, Svapna and Sushupti as immanent, in Turīya or Samādhi as transcendent.

Neither is the contradiction solved by splitting up Experience into aspects. Aspects help us to imagine pictorially different functionings of one substance; but, as for understanding, they tell us no more than this that the functionings, and therefore, the corresponding powers are different, and that they are experienced as such. Consciousness[1] by its quiescent,[2] mind-transcendent[3] Power[4] remains the Pure Ether of Consciousness[5] or *Shiva*; and by its active, stressing[6] immanent-in-mind[7] or involved Power[4] changes as world-experience. This is, from the point of view of understanding, no more than saying that Consciousness[1] exercises two different (and one may say, opposed) functions, and that we do not know how and why. In spiritual intuition, not swayed by any pragmatic interests whatever, Consciousness[1] is beyond the antithesis of quiescent and moving[8]; beyond the antithesis of active and passive, agent and patient;[9] beyond the antithesis of negation and affirmation;[10] and even beyond "thatness" or the antithesis of this and that, immanent and transcendent.[11] 'Beyond'[12] here means this: Consciousness[1] while presenting to thought the antitheses, polarities or dualities of active-passive and so forth, is not, in its completeness, summed up and expressed by those correlatives. It is Absolute.[13] The correlations are, however, not to be dismissed as mere illusion or an unreal imposition ("unreal" even in *Māyāvāda* means something different); since it is

---

[1] Chit. [2] Shānta. [3] Unmanī. [4] Shakti.
[5] Chidākāsha. [6] Sakriya. [7] Samanī. [8] Shāntātīta.
[9] Kriyātīta. [10] Vākyātīta. [11] Tattvātīta. [12] Atīta.

[13] In that form of Sādhanā which is called Kundalinī yoga, the Ajnā-chakra (the two-petalled lotus at the forehead) represents the last stage of duality or correlativity (which is symbolized by the fact that it has two "petals"), beyond which is the "place" of Parama-shiva, in which Shiva and Shakti unite, which is nishkala (aspectless) as well as paramakalā (the Supreme Aspect).

Consciousness[1] itself which, primarily as the Supreme Centre or "I,"[2] and, secondarily, as Finite Centres or the individual Egos,[3] thinks itself in, and as, such correlations.

For example, again, let us ask this: is Consciousness—without or with aspects?[4] In *Kundalinī yoga*[5] we have the "place" beyond the sixth[6] Centre, where there is the thousand-petalled lotus representing perfect dynamic[7] Reality, Universe or Experience as well as the perfect static Void[8] which represents pure Reality or Experience.[9] This is to say that contradictions meet here in non-dual[10] experience. So that it is "beyond"[11] all categories of dual experience[12] *as well as* the "Supreme"[13] of all categories—the "Limit" of all definitions. Thus it is Supreme Reality in its aspect as the source of all which is partial:[14] supreme Time,[15] supreme Ether, supreme Sound, supreme Speech, infinitely concentrated Power, and supreme *Shiva* and *Shakti*.[16] Even ordinary experience, reviewed apart from pragmatic interests, indicates such a solution of contradictories in a way; but for a perfect proving appeal must be made, however, to Supreme Experience—that is, Experience of the *yogī* beyond the sixth Centre.[6] "Supreme"[17] in

---

[1] Chit. [2] Parāhantā. [3] Aparāhantā.

[4] Nishkala or Sakala [5] See "Serpent Power".

[6] Or Ājnā. [7] Sakala.

[8] Parama Vyoma, or Parama Shūnya: the Nishkala aspect.

[9] Nishkala, Nirguna, *i.e.*, Chidāsha.

[10] Advaita. [11] Atīta.

[12] Such as rest (Shānta), action (Sakriya) and so forth.

[13] Paramakalā. [14] Kalā.

[15] That is transcendent time not split up into sections as is empirical time through the action of sun and moon. Supreme Time is God from the time aspect, sectionless and ever enduring.

[16] Paravyoma, Paranāda, Paravāk, Parabindu, Parashiva, Parashakti.

[17] Parama.

the above characterizations means an experience which subsumes all dual and imperfect experiences; which, with reference to Centres, becomes dualized and polarized as subjective-objective, active-passive, statical-dynamical experiences.[1] When, for example, it has been said the Experience has both statical and stressing aspects,[2] it remains to be recognised that there is an Aspect of Experience of which these both are dual, polarized manifestations, and which therefore is not in itself completely expressed either by the one or by the other. This fuller Aspect is the Supreme Aspect.[3] So also as regards subjective-objective and other polarities.

Let our next question be this: is Consciousness as *Chit* statical or dynamical? Whether Western psychologists may or may not agree, it has generally been patent to Indian thought that Consciousness presents two aspects—the unmoving, undifferentiated aspects of "Consciousness-Ether," and the moving, diversified aspect of particularized experiences. Now, Consciousness as Perfect Experience (*i.e.*, in its Supreme Aspect) involves and subsumes both; is alogical and cannot be defined or characterized by either. Any attempt to treat logically (*i.e.*, by categories) the Alogical and Perfect Experience will lead sooner or later to a tangle of thinking. Suppose one were to say first that Perfect Experience is moving, evolving *ad infinitum*. But how can Experience be perfect which is in the making, which is unevolved? How can knowledge be perfect the bounds of which are ever widening and widening? Shall we say, then, that Perfect Experience is not an "Ideal" merely, realizable in an infinitely distant time, but that it is an actual Fact that it *is* completely realized, evolved and

[1] See last Chapter but one for evolution of Tattvas; also "Garland of Letters" and "Shakti and Shākta" on the 36 Tattvas.

[2] Kalā.

[3] Paramā Kalā.

statical? The Perfect[1] has no need to move, and it does not move. It has nothing to add to it; no deficiencies to supply; no ends to realize. Why should it move, or change? But this view also involves difficulties. The whole[1] does not move; but the parts imbedded in it, the experiences of the Centres living in it, do move. Now, how can the whole be imagined to remain unchanged, unmoved, while the parts in it are changing and moving? To say with *Māyā-vāda* that the parts and their changes are unreal is no solution for those who cannot but accept their reality. To say again that the changes of the parts neutralize one another and do not therefore disturb the equilibrium of the whole is no solution either, for the analogy of physical equilibrium cannot be extended fully to Experience which to be full[1] must sum up the experiences of the parts, must subsume the *changing* experience of the parts. Hence we find ourselves between the horns of a destructive dilemma in attempting to "rationalize" the whole.[1]

The dilemma is this: to say that Perfect experience changes and evolves is to deny that it is Perfect; and to say that experience is unchanging and statical is to deny that it is the whole of Experience as it actually is. But as a whole it must be either moving or unmoving. There is no logical escape from the dilemma.[2] In spiritual intuition, the whole[1] is alogical, and, to the analytic understanding, it presents the two aspects of statical and dynamical. It is known as the whole[1] in spite of all immanent movements: additions and subtractions do not affect it, as expressed by the mystical saying—"even if the whole[1] be subtracted from the whole,[1] the whole[1] remains."[3]

[1] Pūrna.

[2] This is the meaning of the famous "Tarkāpratishthānāt" in Vedānta. Vedānta Sūtra, II, 1. 11.

[3] See Brihadāranyaka, V, I, 1: Īsha-Up. (opening Mantra).

The question whether Perfect Experience is subjective or not, will be found, if pressed home, to lead to a similar dilemma. By subjective experience is meant an experience that is referred to and "owned" by a Centre or Self. If, therefore, we hold that Perfect experience is subjective, we must imagine a Perfect Centre or Self as the owner of it. In other words, we must define Perfect Experience as the experience of the Lord.[1] Approximately, that is, to the highest reach of our understanding and expression, it is so, of course. Perfect experience, in so far as it can be owned at all, can be owned only by the Supreme Self.[2] That is to say, after alogical non-dual[3] Perfect Experience has been polarized into the aspects mentioned,[4] there arises the relation of owner and owned, subject and object, and Perfect Experience thus polarized, becomes the experience of the Supreme Subject or Lord. It is obvious from this that the Perfect Experience which is polarized into aspects and the "Perfect" Experience which as one aspect is owned by another aspect, are not logically of the same order. The former is extralogical. The Lord[5] owns and makes an object of Perfect Experience. To express it in other terms, the Lord,[1] is the highest logical construction[6] (not fiction) that man can put upon alogical Perfect Experience. This, however, is not to say that the Lord is "our" construction merely. For the existence of the Supreme Centre and for the Supreme Experience owned by it, man, according to Vedānta, possesses as sure a guarantee as he possesses for

---

[1] Paramātmā or Īshvara. For the technical sense of Īshvara-tattva see last chapter but one.

[2] Parāhuntā. [3] Advaita.

[4] Prakāsha and Vimarsha (see ante).

[5] Ishvara.

[6] In the Evolution of 36 Tattvas, Īshvara-tattva represents the third "stage". See post.

his own self and his own experiences. It is more than a mere speculative idea. The Lord is the *Brahman* and the mind which conceives Him is the work of His Power.

Before we pass on, it should be observed that "Perfect" and "Supreme" as epithets applied to the Lord's Experience mean perfect or supreme in the logical order or hierarchy in which we, together with countless other centres, are placed. The Lord is the "Limit" or Ideal of logical or rational experience. He is thus the Supreme Cause; the Supreme Agent; the Supreme Knower; the Supreme Being as regards Infinite Time[1] and Space[2] and so on. He is thus the "Limit" of perfection of the logical categories (Causality, Time, Space, etc.). He is thus the perfection of "rational" existence. But as man's own experience, and therefore existence, is not wholly rational or logical, as, in other words, his experience presents two aspects to him (that of the alogical Fact, and that of "Fact-sections" logically treated), so also in Vedânta does the Lord's Supreme Experience. His Experience has a logical or rational aspect, and an alogical or ultra-rational aspect, and, as in man's case, it is the latter which is larger than, subsumes and sustains the former. Man's experience is alogical while it is being logically known, treated or constructed by him. While in his experience a self knows an object, the experience is not wholly either the one or the other. Nor is it merely the sum of the two. So also in the Lord's case, the Lord's Supreme Experience presents to Himself and to man's thought the poles of a Supreme Self and a Supreme Object; but it has, and presents to the Lord, another and a "more" supreme aspect,[3] *viz.*, a Whole[4] and alogical Experience or Fact in which, and of which,

---

[1] Nitya.

[2] Sarva-vyâpî.

[3] Paramâ Kalâ.

[4] Pûrna.

Supreme Self, Supreme Object and the rest are but modes, which is not therefore wholly one of these modes. This indeed does not belittle but really establishes the greatness of the Lord. It says that He has an aspect of being and experience larger than and transcending what He presents to man's thought and belief (*viz.*, the rational or thinkable aspect). As the famous *Purusha Sūkta* in Rigveda and Atharva-veda has it: "He is thousand-headed, thousand-eyed and thousand-footed; He, while completely pervading all this, exceeds all this by the measure of ten fingers (so to say)."

Next, we deal with the moral and æsthetic question: Is Perfect Experience (or Being) good or evil, beautiful or ugly? Does "Perfectness" as applied to experience mean or connote ethical and æsthetic perfection? Undoubtedly it does connote it; but it is more than ("exceeds by ten fingers" so to say) ethical and æsthetic perfection. Good and Beautiful are undoubtedly aspects of it, but we cannot say that Perfect Being is Good and Beautiful *only*. Is It then Evil and Ugly *also*? Yes, according to the Hindu view, for these are also aspects of It. It means this: Good and Evil, Beautiful and Ugly are categories which are applicable to Experience (=Being) when it has divided and manifested itself as aspects or polarities; it is good or evil, beautiful or ugly *in so far as* aspects or poles exist in it and divide it. But apart from, or without reference to, aspects or poles, it is unreachable by either pair of categories. Even while it is taken into poles or aspects, it is agreeable to these pairs of categories in so far as it is taken into aspects or poles; but even then, in its wholeness, "it exceeds all this by ten fingers". The categories belong to the logical, rational or thinkable order; they are therefore applicable when, and in so far as, that order has appeared. And since Perfect Being is of the alogical, ultra-rational and unthinkable order even when the logical, rational and thinkable has evolved in it, the categories are not applicable to it as the whole.[1]

Well; but are they applicable to It as Experience of the Supreme Self, as Lord's Experience or Being? Is not the Lord's Being perfectly good and perfectly beautiful? Undoubtedly it is. But since according generally to the Hindu conception, the Lord's being is the "Limit" or "Supreme Position" of the logical, rational or thinkable order, we cannot restrict His Being and manifestation to one set of poles only such as good and beautiful, leaving out the correlative poles such as evil and ugly. These latter are also in Him and in His manifestation. Hindu thought has again and again, and boldly, attributed all possible polarities or pairs of opposite categories to the Lord's manifestation. Thus He is at once beautiful[2] and fearful,[3] righteousness[4] and unrighteousness,[5] light[6] and darkness,[7] knowledge[8] and error,[9] and so on. The Mother *Kālī* who holds Her blood-streaming sword and the severed head of the demonic *Asura*, both dispels all fear and gives all blessings. As the supreme synthesis[10] of the logical (*i.e.*, presenting polarities, correlations, aspects) order of experience, the Lord's experience cannot evidently in this view be narrowed down to one set of poles, correlations or aspects only; and not only His experience but His being. A purely ethical God and the existence of Evil (moral and physical) in the world have never been successfully made to fit in with a monistic scheme of the world-order: they have involved an ill-concealed dualism or pluralism. Without however, discussing this aspect of the question, it

[1] Pūrna. [2] Shovana. [3] Bhīshana.
[4] Dharma. [5] Adharma. [6] Jyotih. [7] Tamah. [8] Jnāna.
[9] Bhrama. And so Mārkandeya Chandī salutes the Devī as in the form of Error. [10] Parākāshthā.

may be observed that by setting up a God in whom poles and contradictions live side by side, the basis of human morality and religion is not necessarily undermined. Good and Evil both exist in Him, both flow out of Him as streams that variously mingle in the world; but man has, and knows that he has, his law that is the law *his* essential being,[1] given to operate in the line of righteousness; he has his satisfaction and happiness in operating along that line; his progress and ascent in the pursuit of it; and ultimately his liberation, when he again goes beyond the realm of law.[1] To be thus essentially constituted in spite of his apparently being a mixture of good and evil,[2] is part of the Divine outburst, is organic to the cosmic plan. This is, to say in one word, his law of being. Hence the same Power which stands surety for the cosmic plan also stands surety for man's law.[3] There is thus divine guarantee for human evolution.

Summing up we find that Perfect Experience is not in Time and in Space and yet it manifests itself as beginningless and endless cosmic flux and cosmic configuration; it is not Cause, and yet it is ultimate Basis of causation; it is not a Centre, and yet countless subjects and objects are in varied stress on its bosom; it is not Cosmos, and yet myriads of worlds appear and disappear in it like bubbles on water; it is unthinkable and yet all thought and speech proceed from it; it is the Whole and yet all aspects are Its aspects.[4]

---

[1] Dharma. [2] Dharma and Adharma.

[3] Dharma. Dharma and evolution are dealt with in a later section.

[4] *Cf.* the statements that Brahman is with "four feet," "sixteen limbs or parts", and so forth.

CHAPTER VI

CONSCIOUSNESS AND REALITY

THE fact which in Vedānta is absolutely beyond doubt is not exactly, as Descartes thought, "I think" but the indefinable universe of experience of which 'I think' is a logical—and by no means an inseparable, adequate and complete—treatment and description, that is, limitation. It is a logical representation of what is presented as alogical. Remembering the definition of Fact given before, we may say therefore, that Fact or Experience is, Reality. This Reality is defined as *absolutely doubtless*[1] *Being Experience.* By "Being-Experience" is meant an experience which does not discriminate between 'thought' and 'thing,' and which feels those two aspects or 'poles' as identical. It is the alogical Whole[2] which may, and often does, involve these and many other aspects or poles, but is not partitioned into, and expressible in terms of, aspects or poles. Intuition of the total universe of experience which we have "at any moment" (without our commonly recognising, however, that we have it, because we are pragmatic and partial) will it is said readily prove that such experience is both being and experience, and absolutely doubtless and undeniable

[1] Maitri-Up., VI. 32 (ka)—speaks of Ātman as "the Real of the Real". (Satyam satyasya.)

[2] Pūrna. Chhānd.-Up. calls it "Bhūman"—the Great, or Immense which is also the meaning of Brahman which comes from a root denoting "bigness".

7

being and experience. This indefinable[1] Whole of experience *is* and it is *Consciousness*—that is it is Being[2] and Consciousness[3] undistinguishably given.[4] This Whole of experience is neither metaphysical nor physical, neither transcendental nor empirical,[5] and yet it is all. It is the Given which may or may not, at any given moment, involve, these and other correlate aspects; and which, under logical operation, yields these and such other aspects.

To be absolute or perfect Reality, Experience must be perfect in the sense of the Whole.[6] That is to say, it must be taken as Supreme Aspect[7] which involves and yet transcends all particular varied aspects[8] and pure or undifferentiated.[9] To narrow Experience down to either of the subordinate aspects is to cut down the perfectness of Reality—is to make Reality *relatively* real. This is the root of the matter.

Thus, suppose, we define with *Māyāvāda* Vedānta Reality[10] as Consciousness[3] in its pure aspect,[9] because this aspect persists in and through all states of experience, and is never effaced or cancelled,[11] and because the other aspect is one of incessant change or flux. We have seen that Pure Consciousness[3] or "Ether of Consciousness"[12] is

---

[1] Brihadāranyaka, IV. 2. 4. says—" Sa esha neti netyātmā grihyo na grihyate "—He can be only negatively referred to; he is unreachable by thought and speech, and so. cannot by them be reached.

[2] Sat. [3] Chit.

[4] Chhānd.-Up., VI, 8, 9, 10 . . . 16—" Idang sarvang tat satyang sa ātmā tattvamasi shvetaketo," etc.—which establishes an identity, *viz.*, World=(Idam)=Reality(Satyam)=Consciousness(Ātman)=Self (Tvam).

[5] Chhānd.-Up., VII, 25, 1.—" Sa evādhastāt sa uparishthāt "—the Brahman Consciousness is here "below" as well as there "above".

[6] Pūrna. [7] Paramā Kalā. [8] Sakala. [9] Nishkala

[10] Sattā. [11] Vādhita

[12] Chidākāsha.

an inalienable feature of experience in all its states and forms. If therefore Reality is unchanging persistence or ineffaceable being, then Pure Consciousness[1] is Reality. But, then, how can we be sure that this *alone* is Reality in the sense of ineffaceable being? It is true that Consciousness in the other aspect is stressing and changing; that the consciousness of this moment is not that of the next; and that possibly in ecstasy[2] or in the "fourth"[3] state the stressing and changing aspect may altogether vanish and the pure and quiescent aspect alone may remain. The world of name and form has by some been likened to an hypnotic suggestion,[4] a dream, an illusion, so that with the passing of this suggestion or dream, pure, changeless and aspectless *Chit* alone abides. Let it be granted for the sake of argument that this may be so. But if *Chit* thus always abides, so also does *Chit* as Power—that is, Power to be and appear in and as different aspects.[5] If *Chit* changelessly persists in all the states by its own Power (and we have seen that to be or to persist is of the essence of Power), it also changes or stresses by its own Power; and in fact, to change and persist while changing (it may be as *Māyāvāda* says, apparently), and in ecstasy[6] and liberation[7] to cease to change at all, are all equally undeniable manifestations of *Chit* as Power. Hence this Power—*i.e.*, to be and appear as different aspects and forms—is an inalienable feature of Consciousness,[1] is in fact Consciousness[1] itself; and if the latter is real in the sense of being ineffaceably given, the former is also so. Consciousness[1] as Power projects the world-order remaining itself pure Consciousness[1] all the while; Consciousness[1] also as Power withdraws

---

[1] Chit. [2] Samādhi. [3] Turīya, Shānta.
[4] Indrajāla. [5] Sakala. [6] Nishkala. [7] Sakriya

the world into itself which thus it bursts upon itself, as it were a bubble on the surface of water, as *Māyā-vāda* often puts it. It follows therefore that Power *as such*—that is as distinguished from different forms or directions of it—is, even from the Māyāvādin's standpoint, real.

But what, it may be asked, do we gain by discriminating Consciousness[1] from its Power? Do we know anything beyond the fact that Consciousness is and changes; that it changelessly persists while changing and that it may cease to change? Why do we then interpose a Power between *Chit* and this fact? The reply is—we do not interpose anything between them. Our Power is simply the expression of the whole fact. We simply say that Consciousness[1] by itself persists, changes and persists again; that there is nothing else than Consciousness[1] which so persists and changes. *Māyā* of *Māyā-vāda*, on the other hand, has a residual element of unconsciousness[2] and unthinkable alienness[3] left in it, after the attempt has been made to dissolve in non-duality the Sāmkhyan *Prakriti* which is absolutely unconscious and alien to *Chit*.

Again, though an individual Centre may realize Pure *Chit* and the world of distinction and change[4] may cease to exist for him, yet, generally, it is admitted that the world-order as a flow is beginningless and endless, though it has a rhythmic life of evolution[5] and involution.[6] During the latter[6] the world is withdrawn into *Brahman* and remains there as potency; during creation it is projected into manifestation again. Now, if by Power we

---

[1] Chit. [2] Achit Jadatva.

[3] Māyā is neither Brahman nor independent of it. It is taken not real nor unreal nor partly one and partly the other. To the Shākta Māyā is the Mother-Power—Mahāmāyā—Who in Herself (Svarūpa) is Consciousness and Who by Her Māyā appears to be unconscious.

[4] Nāma and rūpa. [5] Vikāsha. [6] Laya.

mean nothing else than the fact that cosmic being-experience of itself rhythmically passes into the conditions of seed and fruit, slumber and waking, than we cannot be mistaken in saying that the Power of Consciousness[1] to thus rhythmically change eternally persists, and is, therefore, as much real as Consciousness itself.

Or else, shall we say that the Immense by its own Power veils and finitizes itself and thus becomes the world of varied name or form,[2] of correlated Centres; that the Immense and Immeasurable by its own Power is also gradually unveiling and realizing itself; that the complete unveiling and realizing of itself by itself will mean liberation; and that, therefore, the cosmos can attain to liberation only as a whole, there being no actual liberation for individual selves?[3] This is to make *Brahman* the only real self,[4] binding itself and then liberating itself by its own Power. The multiplicity of selves[3] means only so many reflexes or "virtual images" of the one real individual self[5]; so that there is no question of individual antecedence and subsequence in the matter of bondage and liberation. There has been bondage for "all" since *Brahman* has limited itself and there will be liberation for "all" when *Brahman* fully reasserts or reaffirms itself. *Shuka*, *Nārada*, *Vāmadeva*, *Vyāsa*, *Vashishtha* and others are all reflexes with mutual variations, of the one *Brahman*, masking itself by Its own "play"[6] as an individual self,[3] and though possibly, in point of spiritual purification, the persons named have advanced farther than other reflexes, they have not yet attained to perfect liberation, because that of which

---

[1] Chit-shakti.

[2] Nāma and rūpa, that is ideas and ideas objectified.

[3] Jīvas.

[4] Jīva; the doctrine of Eka-Jīva-vāda.

[5] Jīva.

[6] Līlā.

they are reflexes,[1] is still there as *Brahman* masking itself, as the individual self.[2] The principle is this—there is no liberation for individual selves while the individual [3] type is there; there is no vanishing of the reflexions [3] while the original [4] is there and veiling (which like variously shaped and curved mirrors variously reflects) is there.

Continuing the metaphor we may say that what we have called "reflexes" are double-reflections: we have the first or original reflexion when *Brahman* on the mirror of its own *Māyā*,[5] reflects itself and sees itself as "I am this all".[6] This is the Supreme "Personality,"[7] the first Reflex, the individual Self.[2] Then by variously constituted veiling, the Type is elaborated into infinite variations which are the "double" or secondary reflexes.[8] However this may be, the question which is now pertinent is this: The Immense undoubtedly changelessly persists[9] as Pure[10] *Chit*, even while It thus binds itself and then tends to liberate itself. By veiling and reflection,[11] its essential nature as Consciousness[12] is never for one moment abrogated or effaced. But what about the Power by which it thus binds (*i.e.*, limits) and liberates itself? By 'Power' is meant the *fact* that it does of itself thus limit and reaffirm itself.

Now, having put the question, let us ask: Is this self-denying (or limiting) and self-affirming operation in Time? Is it that *Brahman* limited itself actually in the past and is tending to reaffirm itself in the future? Or shall we say that the temporal determination or scheme is

---

[1] *i.e.*, of the Vimba, the prototype or original. [2] Jīva.

[3] Pratibimbas. [4] Vimba.

[5] Vimarsha as Kāmakalā-vilāsa has it, using the very same metaphor of the mirror—"vimarsha-rūpa-vimalādarsha."

[6] Pūrnāham. [7] Parāhantā. [8] Aparāhantās.

[9] Kautasthya. [10] Shuddha. [11] Vimarsha. [12] Chit.

itself a product of the limiting and defining operation,[1] is immanently applicable to all processes and phenomena incidently and subordinate to the fundamental limiting operation; but is *not* applicable either to the fundamental limiting operation as a whole, or to *Brahman* which appears to subject itself to this operation? In other words, the Immense and Immeasurable may not as such have a "life history" of bondage, striving and liberation; and the denying and affirming may not belong to past and future tenses of real Time. Time may be a scheme for the "Reflexes"—the First Reflex as well as the "double reflexions": a Reflex (in the sense of limited Chit, not of unconsciousness[2] appearing as[3] consciousness,[4]) may thus have and think its experience in accordance with the temporal scheme. From its standpoint, therefore, that scheme is real. But the Immense and its fundamental operation of self-limiting may both be alogical, and beyond the temporal scheme.[5] Argument has been offered to show that it *is* so; and if it be so, the Power which thus alogically and extra-temporally denies and affirms itself is a Power that *is*. And once we lay aside the temporal notation (*i.e.*, the tenses) "changeless persistence in the three tenses of Time," which is commonly the *Māyā-vāda* definition of Reality, can only mean being as such. Since the Power of the Immense to Limit itself is as such (we are no longer thinking and speaking in the tenses), and undeniably is, it is Reality. In fact, this is only to say that the

---

[1] Kāla (Time) is one of the Kanchukas.

[2] Achit.

[3] Chidābhāsa.

[4] Chit.

[5] Yoga-drishti, and, what in the West are now called "Psychometry," "X-ray vision" and so forth, place before us certain phenomena (*e.g.*, reading of the past and the future which is held to be established) seem to force the conclusion on us that, in reality, past, present and future meet in a point; that they co-exist as a seamless, indivisible tissue of facts which our pragmatic thought and habit (sangskāra) takes to pieces. In fact, they meet in the "Bindu".

Immense is as Pure Consciousness,[1] and is as Power to limit itself as Consciousness. There is warrant for this in pragmatic experience.

But suppose we think as a Reflex must think—that is, logically, and, in accordance with the temporal notation. *Brahman* has made an individual Self[2] of himself, and is tending to liberate himself. When will liberation come? In finite time or infinite? If the latter, then the limiting Power infinitely continues; and since no absolute beginning either can be thought of in relation to the operation of this Power, it eternally continues; and as Power (*i.e.*, apart from modes and directions) it ever is what it is. The definition of Reality is, therefore, satisfied by this Self-limiting Power of *Brahman*. But, on the other hand, to remove this prospect[3] of perpetual "bondage," if we say that self-limiting, though perhaps beginningless, has an end, so that the limit may go one day, then also, it should be clearly observed, the eternality of Power as Power is not affected; because, if to limit itself connotes Power, to do away with the limit and to rest in, and as, Perfect Experience also connotes Power. In fact, binding and then unbinding constitute one single fact, though our thought may split it up into two; and if it is agreed to describe the first half of the fact as "Power," there is no reason why we should refuse to describe the second half as "Power" also. And if the whole fact is or presupposes Power, Power as such eternally *is*. It is therefore Real.

But what if we interpret the term "changelessly" rigidly in the sense of the *Māyā-vāda* definition of Reality? Change, like difference[4] may be of three kinds:[5] One

[1] Chit.

[2] Jīva.

[3] Dismal to some though it may be the reverse of dismal to those who see self (ānanda) only in the continuation of the Līlā or World-play.

[4] Bheda.

[5] Svagata, Sajātīya, and Vijātīya.

thing while remaining essentially the same may change so as to present differences of detail. Thus Power, remaining essentially the same Power, may change from a condition of latency to one of patency. Or else, while Power as a whole remains unaltered, its components may severally vary.[1] Or, Power may change from one form and direction into another form and direction; but it remains the same kind of Power. Lastly, Power may change into one of a different kind.[2] Now, in all the cases we have mentioned, Power of *Chit* may be supposed to continue eternally as Power; but since in all the cases change from latency to patency, and change of form and direction are involved, we are justified in saying that what eternally persists is Power of the same kind (if we do not hold change of form and direction as constituting difference of kind); but we can hardly say that the self-same Power in the same condition persists for all time. If it were so, there would be no creation at all; or there being creation, there would be no dissolution; briefly, no change, apparent or real, in the Given. Power, therefore, while remaining as such, changes its condition. And if it does, it is not changelessly persistent, and not, therefore, real.

The objection can be met in two ways. First, we must consider Power as a whole and not in cross-sections. What remains the same Power unchanged is the whole. That is to say, what remains the same Power unchanged in creation, maintenance and dissolution is simply, and nothing less than, Power as creating *and* maintaining *and* dissolving. Suppose we split up this Power into three components or aspects corresponding to these three aspects of the world-process. Then of course we cannot say that

---

[1] This is Svagata—intrinsic or immanent change.

[2] These two are Sajātīya and Vijātīya respectively.

Power as creative activity is the same as Power as sustaining activity, and this again the same as dissolving activity. The Devīs *Brahmānī*, *Vaishnavī* and *Raudrī* are thus different, because they do different kinds of work. But as Primordial Power[1] which now creates, now sustains and now dissolves, it is, and must be, one. Difference is in the sections: non-duality[2] is in the whole.[3] But still we may be told that it involves intrinsic or immanent[4] difference. The aspects or components of Power change. And if they do, absolutely changeless persistence (excluding even immanent variations of form or condition) cannot be predicated of Power considered even as whole;[5] and if not, Power is not real.

Hence, secondly, let us consider this; Is Pure *Chit* absolutely changeless in the sense that its condition remains the same for ever, though it may be now veiled and now unveiled? *Chit* is manifestation itself;[6] and yet in ordinary experience—in the three states of waking, dreaming and slumbering—its perfect illumination veils itself in a way, without ceasing to be or being effaced, as intuition, it is said, will directly show. The object of religious striving and its practical method[7] is to raise the undeniable veil. Now, surely, between veiled or ignored "Ether of Consciousness"[8] and unveiled and recognised "Ether,"[8] we must admit a difference of condition. It is undoubtedly a difference that does not affect the Ether as it is in itself.[9] Ueveiling here merely means acceptance and recognition of what has been given in consciousness, but

---

[1] Ādyāshakti. [2] Advaita.

[3] Pūrna. Brihad.-Up., II, 4, 13; IV, 5, 15.

[4] "Antarlīna" and "Antargata".

[5] Pūrna.

[6] Svaprakāsha. Prakāsha-mātra-tanuh as Kāma-kalā-Vilāsa, 1, has it.

[7] Sādhanā. [8] Chidākāsha. [9] Svarūpa.

practically ignored. Still from veiling to unveiling or *vice versa* is a change of condition. To say that veiling and unveiling are both immaterial, unsubstantial,[1] is not to deny the change. For, in experience, even a fancied change is an actual change of condition. A rope does not indeed become a snake when illusion makes it appear so; but experience of a rope and experience of an illusory snake are not the same experience. Hence though Pure *Chit* remains Pure *Chit* even while it is veiling or unveiling itself, we must admit a difference (whether superimposed or immanent) between the veiled condition and the unveiled. And if we must, what becomes of "absolutely changeless persistence" as assuring the reality of Pure *Chit* alone? We have seen that as regards the Power-aspect of Consciousness, we must admit immanent differences of condition to explain the different conditions of of the world-process; we now see that as regards the illuminating-aspect[2] of Consciousness also, we must admit difference of condition to explain the differences in the four states of waking, dreaming, slumbering and ecstasy[3] and also that between bondage[4] owing to ignorance[5] and liberation[6] on account of "knowledge".[7] "Absolutely changeless" in the definition of Reality is, therefore, in the absolute sense, applicable neither to Power-aspect nor to Illumination aspect.[3] Or else, if we be satisfied with only an approximation, then the definition applies to both. Both are real, and both are one.

We have to be satisfied with an approximation because we have proposed a logical definition (and also pragmatic, for the matter of that) for that which is essentially alogical.[8]

---

[1] Avastu. [2] Prakāsha. [3] Samādhi (turīya).
[4] Bandha. [5] Avidyā. [6] Mukti.
[7] Jnāna. [8] Pramāna.

The Real is the Whole, the Complete and Perfect Given. This Given as given cannot be doubted, questioned, challenged and contradicted. We may indeed pragmatically enquire as to whether a particular section of the "Fact" is, or is not a fact; is or is not evidence.[1] But as Whole[2] the Fact is above the distinction of fact or fancy; beyond the antithesis of true or false. The wildest fancy as part of the Given Universe of Experience *is* experience and has therefore as such absolutely assured being. That it is experience and as such is there, can never be questioned. The 'illusory snake' of Vedānta undoubtedly exists as a mode of consciousness. The illusoriness arises when we pragmatically enquire about the correspondence of this particular mode of consciousness to certain other modes, *viz.*, a group of sensations which Analytic Psychology takes as the representative of a snake. Hence as intuition will readily establish, we touch the absolute ground only in the alogical Given; in any circumscribed portion or aspect of it, we have only the realm of approximation. And a realm of approximation is a realm of doubt, of contradiction.[3]

The so-called transcendental[4] definition of *Māyā-vāda* is really therefore a pragmatic, definition[5]—a definition of approximation seeking Reality still in the realm of limitation and doubt. The definition suffers from two defects.[6] We have seen how the fact of Pure *Chit* being ever absolutely changeless is, rationally speaking, open to doubt. If it were so, there could be no veiling and unveiling of it, no ascription[7] of the "magic" of a world upon it as *Māyāvāda* requires. It is of course undeniable that the Ether of Illumination continues uneffaced even while it is being veiled or unveiled, even when the 'magic' is on or off. This is

[1] Pramāna.

[2] Pûrna.

[3] Apratishthā and virodha.

[4] Pāramārthika.

[5] Vyāvahārika.

[6] Avyāpti and ativyāpti.

[7] Adhyāsa.

unchanged persistence of an unmistakable nature. But still, as already pointed out, the circumstance of veiling and unveiling, the incidence of the 'magic' and its removal, does constitute a kind of difference. On the other hand, the definition as an approximation is applicable not to the illuminating aspect[1] of Consciousness only, but also to the Power-aspect. It is true that the persistence of the former[1] is more patent than that of Power; that is because the former is manifestation and being itself, and the latter, to man at least, is manifested by the work it does, so that no power is suspected by him when no work is being apparently done. Thus, while to him, Illumination[1] is revelation itself, Power seems to require a revealer.[2] That is why unchanging persistence has been affirmed of the *Chit*-aspect, but denied to the Power-aspect. But this is, absolutely speaking, an unwarranted denial.

Vedānta recognises various orders of Reality. We have referred to the transcendental[2] order already, and explained why the definition must be regarded as a definition of approximation and the order as not the supreme and absolute one which is the alogical Given or Fact called the Whole.[3] The transcendental[2] reality limits us to a "partial" or aspect only of the whole, *viz.*, the Illuminating[1] or Pure aspect. *Māyā-vāda* does so with purpose; realization of the Transcendental[4] aspect of Experience is its objective. The definition is therefore pragmatic.[5] The absolute, supreme Reality can neither be an aspect of the Fact, nor a pragmatic one. It must be above not only thought and speech but use.[5] And this is satisfied by the Complete Fact alone. Reflection will show that the Fact

[1] Prakāsha. [2] Prakāshaka, Abhivyanjaka. [3] Pūrna.

[4] Nishkala, niranjana, shānta sachchidānanda.

[5] Vyavahāra. The word artha (purpose or sense) in Pāramārthika implies that.

as an unlimited, entire Whole is alogical, and cannot be put to uses.[1] Thoughts can relate to, and motives can be formulated upon, sections only. Only sections can be judged as true or false, valuable and desirable or otherwise. The Supreme Absolute Reality should therefore be called not Transcendental Being[2] but Being which is the Whole,[3] as it is the Supreme[4] That of which Illumination and illumined[5] are both aspects.

Below this Supreme order we have the so-called transcendental[2] order of which the definition (approximately) is—"changeless persistence". We have shown that under this order we must according to the view here dealt with place not only Pure Consciousness,[6] but also its Power aspect,[7] though from man's practical standpoint, the former as Being and Illumination[8] is more patent than Power which is commonly associated with Becoming and manifested by the work it does. But the association of Power with Becoming only is a mistake: Power is Being-Power *as well as* Becoming-Power. And Power finding its revealer in work is also due to man's pragmatic veiling which makes him hide his power in latent capacity and then discover and recognise it in actual work and achievement. Consciousness[6] or Chit as Power to be and to become is therefore transcendental Being.[2] Whatever becomes,[9] does not belong to this order. Whilst Consciousness[6] as "Ether"[10] and as Power to Be and Become

[1] Vyavahāra. [2] Pāramārthika Sattā.

[3] Parama Sattā. It is Pūrna. Chhāndogya, VII, 23, 24—calls it "Bhūman," or Immense and It is beyond all specification.

[4] Paramākalā. [5] Prakāsha and Vimarsha.

[6] Chit. [7] Chit Shakti. [8] Prakāsha.

[9] The evolved Tattvas or Principles, the world of Nāma and Rūpa, or the Psycho-physical.

[10] Chidākāsha.

"changelessly persists," the world of name and form changes, and it is its nature to change.

Next comes in *Māyāvāda* Pragmatic,[1] relative, limited Reality. It is pragmatic because such reality is constituted by, and essential to, the uses of the practical living of Centres; it is relative because, as compared with Consciousness[2] and its Power, it changes and may be dissolved in the latter which, therefore, persists even after it (*i.e.*, the changing order) is no longer there; it is limited because, in the first place, it is necessarily limited to sections only of the Fact, and because, in the second place, its persistence is limited in time. Thus the world of ordinary experience and its things and processes belong to the pragmatic, relative, limited order of Reality.

This is not to say that the world is an "illusion". Compare the alogical universe of "Fact"—even in the veiled and centralized form in which man has it at any moment—with what he *takes* as the world of his practical thinking, feeling and acting. It will be found that the latter is a limited realm accepted out of the much larger and indefinable Given which is, except in the part accepted, ignored; that which in the actual Given all is real as being-experience, in the accepted realm the distinctions of real-unreal, subjective-objective, inner-outer, desirable-undesirable, etc., are set up according as certain sections or features in the realm do or do not satisfy certain practical tests, or do or do not serve certain practical ends. Thus certain features or elements being "thoughts" only and not "things"; certain elements being fancies only and not facts, and so on;—arise out of the special disposition of Consciousness' Power in the accepted realm; but those distinctions either do not arise in the entire Given itself, or arising, do not affect either the alogicality of the whole Fact, or the reality, in the sense of

[1] Vyāvahārika Sattā. [2] Chit.

undeniable being-experience, of the elements thereof. A "fancy" as an element of the Given is as much real as any "fact" in it; it is regarded as a fancy because, compared with a fact, it does not satisfy certain practical tests, or what commonly amounts to the same thing, does not possess certain characteristics (vividness, permanence, requisite tone of belief, etc.) which indicate that it will satisfy certain practical tests. The accepted realm is thus an "intentional world," in the defining and constituting of which potential stresses[1] play, however, a greater part than actual stresses which, broadly speaking, are man's "intentions".

The world of experience is not "illusion,"[2] though it is based upon and leads to use.[3] We have said that it is limited Reality in the sense of being limited in time. But here we must draw a distinction. Conventional experience[4] may be eternal or non-eternal.[5] All Scriptures[6] starting from the *Vedas* assert that the world-flow is beginningless and endless; and that the general cosmic scheme or plan (the Types, for example) persists from one cycle of creation or *Kalpa* to another through the intervening "Night" of cosmic slumber.[7] They pass from a state of evolution to one of involution, and this is an unending rhythm. Through this rhythm of evolution and involution they persist; and though such persistence is in a sense changing persistence (*i.e.*, the persistence of alternate appearance and disappearance), and though possibly, the appearance in one cycle

---

[1] Sangskāras.

[2] Brihadāranyaka, I, 6, 3, calls Nāma and Rūpa "Satyam": also Brih.-Up., IV, 3, 20, which describes the supreme experience as "Sarvvo'smi"—All is "I am". Also Chhāndogya, VII, 25, 2. "Ātmaivādam sarvamiti," also, Brih.-Up., IV, 5, 7.—"Idam sarvam yadayamātmā."

[3] Vyavahāra. As regards when Vyavahāra is possible and when not, see Maitri-Up., VI, 7, (Ch.) and (Chh.); and also Chhāndogya, VII, 24, 1.

[4] Vyavahāra. [5] Nitya or anitya. [6] Shāstras. [7] Laya.

may vary somewhat in detail from that in another, still, in a general sense the cosmic plan or scheme is persistent, and as such, is real.[1] The Generals[2] of the *Nyāya-Vaisheshika* Philosophy are eternal[3] (as also some other entities); and, from one standpoint, their being[4] is real.[5] Particular things such as a jar have non-eternal reality,[6] unless we subscribe to the theory that the world-order as it is in one cycle repeats itself exactly in another. Nyāya-vaisheshika believes in the antecedent non-existence[7] of a particular thing, and this[7] is beginning,[8] though it may be it has an end,[9] as when that thing actually ceases to exist. That thing, again, when destroyed has an unending destruction.[10] About the non-persistence[11] of particular things, the First Standard raises no difficulties.

The difficulty arises when we come to the Second and Third Standards which agree in equating Cause and Effect, and conceive destruction[12] as only dissolution of the effect in the Cause. Consistently and rigidly applied, this principle will not admit the absolute beginning or the absolute ending of anything, general or particular: nothing comes to actually exist which did not already potentially exist in its cause; and nothing ceases actually to exist but has again a potential existence in its cause.[13] Not only the twenty-four "Principles"[14] of *Sāngkhya* but all their particular modes ought, therefore, according to this principle, to be eternally persistent either patently as effects or latently

---

[1] This is Nitya-vyāvahārika sattā. [2] Jati. [3] Nitya.

[4] Sattā. [5] Nitya vyāvahārika.

[6] Anitya vyāvahārika sattā.

[7] Prāgabhāva. [8] Anādi. [9] Sānta.

[10] Dvangsa. [11] Anityatā. [12] Vināsha.

[13] Nāsato vidyate bhāvo nābhāvo vidyate satah.

[14] Prakriti, Prakti-vikriti and Vikriti.

as causes. We shall not pause here to discuss this question which does not admit of an easy solution.[1]

Cause may be common[2] and uncommon.[3] The Will of God, "Space" and Time[4] and so forth are, according to Nyāya-Vaisheshika, the common cause of every phenomenon that takes place. Each phenomenon has also its own special assemblage of conditions which, according to this system, are threefold.[5] Vedānta reduces them to two kinds.[6] Prepared clay is the first in the case of an earthen jar; the putting together of the parts, the wheel and the stick[7] as well as the agent belong to the other group or kind. Now, when an effect is produced, we can consider it in its three elements: (1) its matter or stuff (which may be in some cases mind)[8]; (2) its energy, kinetic and potential; and (3) the particular collocation[9] of the matter and energy which constitutes the special form[10] of that effect. In equating Effect to Cause we have, therefore, to equate all these three elements.[11] Of course in seeking to equate we have to consider both Cause and Effect completely and not partially. For instance, it may be necessary to consider the entire antecedent condition of the universe as the cause of the entire subsequent condition of the universe. But even doing so, will it be possible to prove in every case of causation not only that the matter and the energy of the effect were already in the cause, so that there has really been neither addition to them nor subtraction from them (a possibility to which the Physical Theory of Conservation

[1] See, however, "Power as Causality and Continuity".
[2] Sādhārana. [3] Asādhārana [4] Dik, Kāla.
[5] Samavāyi, Asamavāyi and Nimitta.
[6] Samavāyi or Upādāna and Nimitta.
[7] The volition of the pot-maker. [8] Antahkarana. [9] Sangyoga.
[10] Rūpa. [11] See "Power as Causality".

of Matter and Momentum lends countenance), but also that the *special* collocation of matter and energy which makes the special form[1] of the effect was there in the cause, may be latently, and is not, therefore, anything new and previously non-existent?[2] Was, for instance, the particular form of the cloth woven existent in the fibres of the cotton, in the spinning and weaving machinery and in the volitions of the spinner and the weaver—distributively or collectively? When a sculptor is chiselling a figure from out of a block of marble, the figure may be supposed to exist as an idea in the mind of the sculptor, and it may be supposed to be "given" latently even in the block of marble. Again it may be thought that, what the chisel of the sculptor does is to knock off the portions which conceal, suppress or fold up the figure given in the block of marble. But this seems to be an apparently strained supposition leading to interminable intricacies. For instance, we must suppose that not only the particular figure in question but every possible figure is latent in the marble like all meanings[3] in a letter as postulated in the *Vyāsa-Bhāshya* on *Patānjali's Yoga-Sūtra.* The typal case of evolutionary causation is the seed becoming a plant, though even here variations have to be accounted for. And it is certainly not easy to conform all kinds of effects (*e.g.*, that of production of water by the mixing of Hydrogen and Oxygen; the weaving of cloth from fibres of cotton, etc.) to the seed-model. We do not, however, further discuss this.

Causation is an unsolved riddle; and it must remain so. The world being a manifestation of the Play or *Līlā*[4]

---

[1] Rūpa. [2] Prāgabhāva-vishishta. [3] Arthas.

[4] It is very necessary to distinguish this Trinity and other Divinities of the Māyika world from the Supreme Cause or Mahāmāyā. The supreme Mother-Power which is Consciousness (Chidrūpinī) itself as explained later.

of Primordial Consciousness-Power, and the nature of *Līlā* or " Play " being freedom, we can never, except to bring the world-order to any logical account, expect approximately and pragmatically. The Shāstra says that " Even *Brahmā*, *Vishnu* and *Rudra* have not understood the Līlā of the Mother-Power ". Time in our pragmatic analysis of causation, is a form necessary to the concepts of Cause (which is antecedent), and Effect (which is consequent). But, in reality, they co-exist, and are aspects (arranged by man in the perspective of " before and after ") of one single fact. The whole past + the whole present + the whole future = a " Point " or *Bindu*.

But is it a statical, unalterable, *Bindu*? In other words, Is the whole cosmic order (including the Not-yet or Future) absolutely given and determined or fixed? If so, it may be said that it cannot be the manifestation of spontaneity or *Līlā* but of Blind Necessity or " Fate "; and the individual Centres also have no freedom, *i.e.*, no *Karma* properly so called. It is here that there is a riddle. The Ancients believed, and many " psychic researchers " have now come to believe on fresh evidence, that foreknowledge (even as regards details) of the future is possible, which implies the pre-existence of the future in the present; the past also is not in any way lost in the present; which together lead to the conclusion that the Cosmic Order is eternally and unalterably fixed and condensed in a " point " (since the whole can be deciphered from the minutest detail, as for example, when a " medium " is alleged to be able to " read " the past and the future of persons unknown to her and of other persons connected with him, by " looking at " a flower or piece of paper touched by him). Now, if the Order be so unalterably fixed, what becomes of *Līlā* and *Karma*, both of which imply possible change, and an undetermined future? We can essay to answer this only by supposing that the Cosmic Order is susceptible to change by *Karma*, but that the change in itself, need not be in Time; that is, not a fixed but a changing universe is given in the timeless *Bindu* we have postulated. So that a "medium" *en rapport* with the *Bindu* can "read" an event freely wrought by a Centre, which man's pragmatic, "temporal" thinking must, however, place in the realm of Not-Yet or Future. Imagination doubtless fails to conceive how this may be, as for instance, it fails to conceive Dimensions higher than the third. Analogous is the idea of the *Vaishnava* who believes in an eternal Heaven[1] wherein there is eternal Play.[2]

Pragmatically speaking, the collocation of matter and energy in the effect is either previously existent in the cause (or assemblage of conditions) or non-existent. If the latter, then every moment thousands of phenomena are happening around us which, though persistent in their *types* and also in the quantities of matter and energy involved, are as special collocations new, previously non-existent and ephemeral. These phenomena belong to the transient conventional class.[3] If, on the other hand, the collocation be previously existent as latent in the cause, then, waiving all difficulties to the view, we may again distinguish between two classes of phenomena. There may be certain particulars (not *genera* or types) which as particulars may substantially and actually endure till the end of a *Kalpa* or age of a given cycle of cosmic life or till final liberation is attained; but there are countless others which do not thus actually endure, but are speedily dissolved in their causes, and in the Root Cause[4] during dissolution,[5] to be projected

[1] Nitya Goloka: Go does not here mean cow but sound and light.
[2] Nitya Līlā.
[3] Anitya Vyāvahārika.
[4] Prakriti.
[5] Pralaya.

into actually again during the succeeding *Kalpa*. Thus *Brahmā* and others as particular forms of *Chit-Shakti* have their fixed age to live through; and at the termination of this age a particular *Brahmā* or other ceases, to exist, though the type remains. The particular objects of experience have, however, no such prolonged actual life-duration.

Let us pass on to Apparent Reality in Māyāvāda.[1] It is the reality of an illusory perception while the illusion is not suspected as such. It is contradicted and corrected by pragmatic reality,[2] *e.g.*, the rope-snake of an illusion. The rope-snake possesses some marks of reality, but is soon discovered not to possess others which practically settle for us the question of reality of the snake. The tactuo-muscular sense is commonly set up as the judge of reality because practically in the matter of living and self-preserving it happens to be the most important. In dealing with this order of Reality we are introduced to the pragmatic distinction between Right Knowledge or Evidence[3] and false knowledge.[4] In the "Fact" knowledge is simply knowledge and as such undeniably is. The basis of all evidence (even of Perception[5]) and the ground of absolute certainty is Experience as Experience.

With the two other forms of Reality[6]—we shall not deal elaborately. The first is Being-Experience as intuited by each individual Centre for himself.[7] It is the universe of Fact as defined with reference to a given Centre—"You" or "I". It is what you or I totally feel or experience—apart from all pragmatic interests. At this moment I am, for example, pragmatically experiencing the sound of a

---

[1] Prātibhāsika sattā. [2] Vyāvahāra. [3] Pramā. [4] Bhrama.

[5] Pratyaksha. [6] Prātismika Sattā and Anirvachanīya Sattā.

[7] Pratisma.

distant whistle, but actually I have or am an universe of experience comprising many sounds, smells, touches, sights, ideas, etc., of which the particular sound happens to be the prominent element. This universe, though in itself indefinable, is pragmatically defined by myself; and the defining line is a flexible one—now closing, now receding. We may, however, represent it by a circle or a sphere. Then the universe of another Centre is another circle; that of another is a third circle; and so on. In one sense, these spheres all lie outside of one another. What one feels cannot, exactly and in the same relations, be felt by another. What you feel is somewhat like what I have felt. But in another sense these spheres cut one another, and two spheres, A and B for example, have a common element, C. Thus while A's headache is not in B, or B's idea is not in A, both hear the sound of the distant whistle, see the greenness of the lawn, smell the odour of fresh blossoms and flowers, and so on. In fact, it is the common element that is objectified, and it is there that the different Centres bargain with one another—it is their province of Convention.[1]

It is with reference to this province again that an approximately common standard of Reality is fixed upon by the interacting Centres; it is commonly that which proves the fittest in practice, what is most safely workable in such mutual Experience.[1] Thus: In A there is a wild fancy which is not in B and others. Now, as experience the fancy unquestionably is: its reality in that supreme sense is undoubted. But commonly A does not accept it as reality because it cannot be found in the common province of Conventional[1] being, because it is not "marketable". There can be ordinarily no practical transaction between A and B on the basis of that fancy. A, therefore,

[1] Vyâvaharâ.

defines his practical Reality not as whatever he experiences (which is Reality in the supreme sense), but what he feels in common with others and what, accordingly, can be made a basis of transaction with others. Thus, ordinarily, experiences have " value " for him which have a " currency ". Sometimes possible " currency " is enough. A sees the *Mānasa-sarovara* lake in Tibet, and though many others may not yet have actually seen it, he believes his to be a real experience because of its possessing marks of possible currency. The pain of an headache, though subjective and which remains so, yet possesses certain marks which, while not placing it in the first class of experience, makes it a real experience in another way. A actually feels the pain and he cannot wish it away : the feeling appears to have him in possession. A fancy, on the other hand, is also there in him as experience, but it seems to be dependent on his pleasure as regards whether it should be there or not there. We have, therefore, three orders : (1) experience as such which absolutely *is*, and it requires no marks to establish its title to reality ; (2) " subjective " experiences which possess certain marks such as vividness or " clear tone," relative permanence and independence of the Subject's wish ; and (3) " objective " experiences which are approximately common to a group of Centres and also possess certain marks of actual or possible currency.

Marks in the second and third orders are pragmatic marks : they are demanded because certain practical ends have to be served by us. The demand postulates a condition, raises a question and is formulated as an " if ". *If x* possesses such and such marks, it is real, otherwise not : this is how we judge in the second and third classes. Pragmatic reality is therefore conditional, hypothetical reality. The first order is unconditional, categorical. Experience as Experience is unconditionally, unquestionably real. We have called it therefore Fact.[1] It will be seen also that howsoever obstinately man may pin his faith to the pragmatic order of reality (and to a certain extent he cannot help doing it), the first order, that is Experience, as Experience, is still tacitly reserved by him as the ultimate criterion of judgment on questions of reality. A "common" experience is also my experience, or can possibly be my experience.[2] I may commonly waive my right in favour of the experiences of an expert some of which I do not now actually have; but the right *is* reserved nevertheless. I could possibly experience that which the expert says he is now experiencing: the reality of *his* experience is admitted subject to this condition. On the other hand, where I have an experience but others not, I certainly expect that, conditions being satisfied, others will also have it; but if the conditions be not satisfied and others do not share it, still I feel that I have a right to hold to my own experience as a reality. All this points to where the native soil of Reality is to be found. The *Veda* in the primary sense means Perfect Experience; in the secondary, partial sense —A body of classical experiences obtained by the *Rishis*, and always obtainable by those who are fit to share in them.[3] In matters supersensible,[4] the classics are evidence as direct evidence;[5] but still, so long as it has

---

[1] "Satyasya Satyam." See "Introduction to Vedânta Philosophy" (Sreegopal Basu Mallik Fellowship Lectures, 1927, Calcutta University) by P. N. Mukhopadhyaya: Lects. XI and XII.

[2] Ātmânubhava.

[3] Yogya Adhikârî. See "Garland of Letters" for Veda as Perfect Experience. See "Introduction to Vedânta Philosophy," by P.N.M.—Appendix.

[4] Atîndriya.

[5] Pratyaksha (like the solar light in the manifestation of rûpa as Shankarâchâryya puts it).

not been or cannot be verified by my own experience,[1] it remains or belongs to a conditional order—subject to an "if". The relation between experience[2] intuited by each individual centre and complete experience[3] will be further considered when we come to discuss *Chit* and Its Forms.

Inscrutable Being[4] in *Māyā-vāda* Vedānta is the name commonly given to *Māyā* which is the Principle of apparent or unreal change[5] such as that of a rope into snake in illusion. The snake of illusion has two parts: the apprehension of mere "thatness" or "thisness,"[6] and the suggestion of the characteristics of a snake projected and superimposed upon the basis[7] of the apprehension of "this".[8] The basis "this"[8] is real;[9] that is, in the illusion of rope-snake, the part which is real is the apprehension of this.[8] The superstructure laid upon it is an inscrutable transformation of ignorance[10] the function of which can be analysed into two components: veiling,[11] and movement and imposition.[12] Thus of the real rope before us, the mere "this"[8] part is rightly apprehended, but the special form (and qualities[13]) of the rope is veiled and that of the snake is imposed. This imposed structure of form[13] is the product of the ignorance-tendency[14] (operating, as Western Psychology would say, through association by similarity) and prompted to operate in a particular way by the subjective and objective conditions—dimness of light, defective vision, mental predisposition and so forth—then prevailing. Now,

---

[1] Anubhava. [2] Prātismika. [3] Pūrna
[4] Anirvachanīya Sattā. [5] Vivartta. [6] Idantā.
[7] Adhishthāna. [8] Idam.
[9] See Vedānta-Paribhāshā (Pratyaksha-parichcheda).
[10] Avidyā. [11] Āvarana. [12] Vikshepa. [13] Rūpa.
[14] Avidyā-Sangskāra.

this imposed structure or *Rūpa* which cannot be said either to be existent or to be non-existent or to be partly existent and partly non-existent, possesses inscrutable Being.[1]

A right perception, *e.g.*, that of a real rope is regarded as a transformation[2] of mind;[3] while a false perception as that of the "rope-snake" is regarded as a transformation of ignorance;[4] and the difference between Mind[3] and Ignorance[4] is not one of kind, but of degree—the former being a purer[5] and the latter a cruder[6] form of Māyā. In man this "double" framework of *Antahkarana* and *Avidyā* exists, and from them proceeds a double line of transformations—one line giving him "real" perceptions, the other illusions and so forth. We see that the projections of ignorance[4] on the plane of perceptional experience—which look like perceptions but are not really so—are supposed to possess inscrutable being.[7] Now, *Māyā-vāda* seeks to establish a ratio proportion: the world of ordinary experience[8] is to the ultimate experience as Pure *Chit* what an illusion is to ordinary "real" experience. Conventional or pragmatic being[9] is therefore really inscrutable being[10] which is the being[7] of apparent, seeming change.[11] Between the real rope and the "rope-snake" the difference is not one of kind, but mainly of duration. Both are liable to be contradicted and cancelled,[12] one only a moment later, the other perhaps ages after when Pure *Chit* is realized. Illusory being[13] is also inscrutable Being.[14]

---

[1] Anirvachanīya sattā which is also tuchchha or alīka sattā. The term "tuchchha" is given a special meaning sometimes.

[2] Vritti. [3] Antahkarana. [4] Avidyā [5] Sattva-prevailing.

[6] Tamas-prevailing. [7] Anirvachanīya sattā.

[8] Or the Vyāvahārika order. [9] Vyāvahārika sattā.

[10] Satta. [11] Vivartta.

[12] Vādhita. [13] Prātibhāsika sattā. [14] Anirvachanīya Sattā.

But this Māyā-vāda conception of the apparently real will not be found to be free from difficulties. Either all is *Brahman* or all is not *Brahman*. If the latter, then we have a second, independent Principle[1] and the reality of that Principle and its products is not inscrutable[2] in the sense above explained. If the former, then all is *Chit*, all is Being,[3] all is Joy,[4] since *Brahman* is so. It may be that *Brahman* by its own Power appears as other than *Chit* (*i.e.*, unconscious[5]), other than Being[3] (*i.e.*, non-being[6]) and other than Joy[4] (*i.e.*, pain[7]). But it may be asked: Is that Power other than *Brahman* or the same? It must on the monistic hypothesis be the same as *Brahman*. Is the appearance other than *Brahman* or the same? It must be the same again. It follows, therefore that at base the so-called unconscious[5] is *Chit*, the so-called unreal[6] is real,[3] the so-called pain[3] is joy.[7] To the limited, pragmatic review of finite Centres,[8] the antithesis of conscious-unconscious, real-unreal, pleasurable-painful appears and for it counts. But if we start with Being-Consciousness-Bliss,[9] and have never anything else to reckon with, then we cannot really make it end in becoming anything other than itself. A finite, interacting Centre cannot but think in antitheses, poles, dualities. From its standpoint, therefore, a definition of Reality making a distinction between Reality as uncontradicted[10] experience and Reality as contradicted[11] experience—that is, between transcendental being[12] and inscrutable being holds.[13] But this standpoint is essentially a dualistic standpoint. Whatever definition of Reality we may fashion from this standpoint will

---

[1] *E.g.*, a Sāngkhyan Prakriti.

[2] Anirvachanīya. [3] Sat. [4] Ānanda. [5] Jada. [6] Asat.

[7] Duhkha. [8] In mutual vyāvahāra. [9] Sat-Chit-Ānanda.

[10] Avādhita. [11] Vādhita.

[12] Pāramārthika Sattā. [13] Anirvachanīya Sattā.

involve dualism, open or veiled; and, we may point out by way of illustration, that the definition of *Māyā* as inscrutable being[1] does involve veiled dualism. All attempts to define the indefinable will bring us to such a pass. If we must stand by the Absolute One[2] itself, and not tolerate any dualism, open or veiled, then, we must take, that is be, Experience as the Whole.[3] We must not limit ourselves to any aspects or partials; must not set up definitions which partition the non-dual[2] into opposites such as Conscious[4] and Unconscious.[5] And doing this we find that the Whole[3] is inscrutable[6] in the sense of being alogical, indefinable; and also is transcendental being[7] in the sense of being indubitably given, of unquestionable "being". Thus in the Whole,[3] the senses of the two kinds of being,[8] which hold good only in the realm of limitation and convention,[9] are modified; and necessarily so. And since the whole[3] is the basis and synthesis of all "kinds" of being,[8] and yet as the whole[3] transcends all kinds, we have called it before (following *Āgama Shāstra*), Supreme, Absolute Reality.[10]

We must be warned therefore against extending the definitions or their senses which are pragmatically valid to that which is above all limitation and all pragmatic use.[9] Thus the transcendental[11] definition approximately applies to one aspect of *Brahman* (lit. the Immense or Whole[3]) as against another aspect. It is a definition that serves while we are the thinker and analyser of *Brahman*. It does *not* serve when the Centre is (in being as well as intuition) *Brahman*. When the Whole has to be consciously

---

[1] Anirvachanīya (Sadāsad-vilakshana) Sattā.
[2] Advaita. [3] Pūrna. [4] Chit. [5] Jada. Achit.
[6] Anirvachanīya Sattā. [7] Pāramārthika Sattā.
[8] Sattā. [9] Vyāvahāra.
[10] Parama Sattā. [11] Pāramārthika.

lived, and not aspects only have to be *thought* and talked about, we must either leave aside all definitions or else applying them, must not employ them in the senses which suggest, and are valid in the realm of, the limited, thinkable and "usable" order of experience only. Here, we must not, for example, define Reality as "changeless, uncontradicted persistence" only; for that at once sets up a correlate Pole, *viz.*, that which changes and is contradicted. Here, Reality is Experience as Experience, and since here Experience is all, all is real.[1] So, here, all is at base Consciousness as *Chit* (nothing in itself being unconscious[2]); and all is in essence Joy[3] (since, Pain is impeded, obstructed, limited being); and in the whole[4] there is no impediment, obstruction or limitation. As the *Chhāndogya* Upanishad profoundly observes[5]—Immensity[6] is Bliss[7] and littleness or restriction[8] is the negation of Bliss.[9] Experience as *Brahman* or immensity[6] (which the *Chhāndogya* goes on to define as Experience above the relation of knower—knowing—known[10] or pragmatic experience[11]) sees the universe, therefore, not as something in any degree alien to the *Brahman* but as being Divine Mother Herself who is Being-Consciousness-Bliss.[12] It is She who is called *Mahāmāyā* and by many another name.[13]

Not only the above pragmatic definition of Reality but other similar variations of it suffer under the same

---

[1] Sat. So the "Upanishad" says—all this is Brahman—Sarvamkhalvidam Brahma.
[2] Jada.
[3] Ānanda.
[4] Pūrna.
[5] See *Ante*.
[6] Bhūman.
[7] Sukham or Rasah.
[8] Alpa.
[9] Sukha.
[10] Pramātrī-Pramāna-Prameya. This relation is the gist (sangkalitārtha) of Shakti.
[11] Vyāvahāra.
[12] Sachchidānandamayī.
[13] Lalitā (the player or Creator) Mahātripurasundarī, Mahavaishnavī, Mahākālī and the rest, more than a thousand names being given in the Lalitā Sahasranāma.

essential disadvantage: they cannot be, in their senses, extended to the Whole.[1] Shall we say, for instance, that the Real is that which is universal,[2] and the unreal is particular?[3] The first is defined as what is not limited in space and time:[4] what is everywhere and always. This is also called without exception.[5] The second is limited in space and time—is here but not there, is now but not then. It is with exceptions or limitations.[6]

Now, as before, in having to apply this test to Experience or *Chit*, we must first analyse *Chit* into aspects, reduce the alogical Fact to a logical order amenable to the categories of Time, Space, and so forth. Supreme Being[7] must in this way, be adjusted to our thought or standpoint. After that adjustment, we find that the universe of experience is analysable into five aspects.[8]

Any object, Self or Not-Self, is, is known, is pleasant (in some relations or others), has a name, has a defining set of qualities.[9] These are the five "predicables". Of these the first three are common to all object-experiences.[10] The fourth and the fifth differ from object to object—the name of one and the form[9] of one are not those of another. The first three, which are Being[11], Consciousness[12] and Bliss[13] respectively, give us the "own form"[14] or nature of *Brahman*, and are, according to the definition, real; the rest stand for the world-order,[15] and are said to be "unreal".

That a dividing line can thus be drawn after the first three need not be questioned. Let us assume that a "thing" or object is, and must be, a form of *Chit* or Consciousness.

---

[1] Pūrna. [2] Sāmānya. [3] Vishesha.
[4] Parichchhinna by Desha and Kāla. [5] Avyavichārī.
[6] Vyavichārī. [7] Parama Sattā.
[8] Asti, Bhāti, Priyam, Nāma, Rūpam. [9] Rūpa.
[10] They are Sāmānya and Avyavichārī. [11] Sat. [12] Chit.
[13] Ānanda. [14] Svarūpa. [15] Jagat-prapancha.

We shall see as we proceed what basis there is for this. All objective or subjective objects, and the Self amongst them, are then experiences. Now, comparing all modes of forms of experiences we undoubtedly discover some common elements. For example, a tree is, an idea or desire is, an illusion is, void is, nothing is. The names and forms vary, but being or "is-ness" is everywhere and always given, and there is no escape from it even in the case of the void.[1] The void is known or felt as *is*. It is, in this pure sense, real[2] and not unreal.[3] Void is the negation of all determinations[4] but is not the negation of "is-ness" as such. That is the fundamental omission of the *Mādhyamika Bauddha*. In fact between is[5] and is not,[6] the common element is—is.[5] Often this invariable is[5] is there as "this".[7] Thus we feel this tree, this desire, this illusion, this void. Very often again our judgments of facts of experience are not given or stated explicitly as judgments. "Tree is" is an explicit judgment; this tree," suppressing the predicate, is an implicit judgment. Sometimes this[7] also is not explicit there: thus we feel and say—"tree," "desire," "illusion," and so on, simply. But whether this[7] or "is"[5] be explicitly stated or not, the experience of tree and so forth is undoubtedly felt as this[7] or is.[5] It is an inalienable element or rather basis[8] of experience. In some fully explicit judgments both this[7] and is[5] occur.[9]

Next consider *Bhāti* or revelation. Experience means illumination[10] or manifestation.[11] It is manifestation as Consciousness or *Chit*. Thus in the above examples, we have: a tree is felt or known; a desire is felt or known; void

---

[1] Shūnya. [2] Sat. [3] Asat. [4] Vishesha.
[5] Asti. [6] Nāsti. [7] Idam. [8] Adhishthāna.
[9] *E.g.*, in "ayam ghatah asti", (this jar is).
[10] Prakāsha. [11] Bhāna.

is felt or known. The feeling, cognition or consciousness has of course different forms[1] and names[2] in the different examples, but everywhere and always it is *feeling* or consciousness. Even the Void is feeling or consciousness of, or as, the Void. There is no escape from *Chit* as such, as there is no escape from Being[3] as such. The *Mādhyamika Bauddha* has again omitted to recognise this. In slumber or swoon in which nothing seems to be known (possibly because nothing but the sense of blissful sleeping is remembered afterwards) what is, or can be, meant by "nothing" is form[1] and name[2] (that is, particular determinations); it does not, and cannot, mean feeling or consciousness, pure and bare.[4] The common view which looks upon particularized consciousness as alone consciousness, and determined consciousness as no consciousness, is a pragmatic view which sees only what it has interest and need to see. The *Yogāchāra Bauddha* whose object, inner or outer, is a mode of experience only, that is, who recognises no "thing" apart from the feeling or thought; and whose experiences[5] are transitory,[6] leaving a real gap between one experience[5] and another, as they succeed one another in time, is also suffering from the Pragmatic Illusion. The so-called experiences[5] are really like the waves moving on on the surface of a continuous fluid; are like clouds passing in the sky. And this continuous "fluid" or "sky" is, as intuition will show at once, not void[7] in an absolutely nihilistic sense, but *Chit* as *Chit* or Chidākāsha or *Ākāshātma*. This Perfect Ether fills all "gaps," sustains and pervades all modes. The "gap" in

[1] Rūpa. [2] Nāma. [3] Sat.

[4] Māndūkya-Up. calls this state of Slumber—"Ghana-prajna" (massive, undifferentiated consciousness); see Brihadāranyaka, Chhāndogya, etc., for fuller description of this state.

[5] Vijnāna. [6] Kshanika. [7] Shūnya.

every case is born of the non-recognition of Pure Consciousness as Consciousness. The "Light" of *Chit* in, and by, which all modes of experience are revealed[1] cannot be extinguished, nor can it be imagined as ever being extinguished.

We have regarded *Chit* as being the essence of "Thing"; so that though there may be extra-mental objects or objects lying outside the pale, or independent of, the individual's ordinary consciousness (thus Matter being as real as Mind), yet we have thought that "things" cannot be outside or independent of (1) *Chit* as *Chit*, and (2) *Chit* as "Fact" or the Perfect Universe or Experience. This view disposes of the difficulty that, though illumination[2] is the common element of all objects experienced, it has nothing to do with countless others which are not experienced. For example, a jar experienced is known, is a mode of consciousness; but what about the jar not experienced, or even about the "real" jar which, though experienced, exists in its own right independently of experience? The real jar or the unknown jar is non-illumination[3]—the opposite of illumination.[4] If it be asked is it not so? From the pragmatic and centralized point of view of experience, Yes. From the real and whole[5] point of view, No. From the latter point of view a "thing"—Matter, Mind whichever it may be—is in, and of *Chit*, and as such is *both* "Is" and Illumination:[6] though its beingness,[7] and more particularly, its illumination[8] may be, and often is, doubly veiled or ignored by individual Centres, firstly because they are Centres of specialized function and reference, and secondly, or rather secondarily, because Centres are, owing to their pragmatic interests, apt to

[1] Bhāti. [2] Prakāsha.
[3] A-bhāti. [4] Bhāti. [5] Pūrna.
[6] Asti and Bhāti (because Chit is both asti and bhāti.)
[7] Astitā. [8] Bhātitā.

limit and narrow down their "Facts" or universes of experience to special aspects or sections only.[1]

Lastly, let us consider *Priyam*, that which is pleasant and gives happiness and which seems to present greater difficulties. The Self presents no difficulty. In fact, the Self is the model of objects as regards the three characteristics—*Asti, Bhāti, Priyam.* The Self *is*, it is *conscious* of itself and other objects. The Self is supremely *pleasant*[2] to itself. Even in wishing to die and be no more, the Self loves itself, and never ceases to be supremely pleasant to itself; it is only dissatisfied with a certain kind of existence, and chooses death because, rightly or wrongly, it thinks that it will be good, that is pleasant, for the Self to be rid of that kind of existence. A philosophic nihilist may desire to put an end to existence as such, to stop all experience.[3] This is because he thinks that it is on the whole better, that is more pleasant, for the Self not to continue than to continue, since continuance, in any form of existence, is sure to give it a surplus of pain over pleasure. Longer existence is greater pain on the whole; to be extinguished and be merged in nothingness is therefore thought to be the best thing. Best thing for whom?—The Self. All acts of self-sacrifice, self-abnegation, all altruistic impulses, again, have their root of inspiration and their basis of support or sanction and their test or standard of value in a sense of self-satisfaction. Bliss[4] is the substance and expression of the Will-to-be-and-become which, not only the living but all existence is.

---

[1] The unknown jar (ghata) or the so-called independent ghata—that is, independent of Chit—will be found to be a victim of such doubt, ignorance or rejection.

[2] Niratishaya-premāspada. Love (by the self for the self) in its uttermost limits is Joy (Ānanda). The Essence of the world is that.

[3] Vijnāna, which is Para Nivriti or Para Nirvāna.

[4] Ānanda.

The Self conserves itself, or expands and then retires or withdraws into itself; and this Will-to-be-and-become is really Joy,[1] and the activity which expresses it is "Play".[2] Not only the Supreme Self, but every centre down to the "material" particle, has its Joy[1] and its Play.[2] "All things are sustained by a measure of this Joy"[3] which[3] as the Whole[4] is immeasurable. Between the Self and, say, a material centre, the difference is not in essence or in kind, but in the form and degree of veiling. Each is Consciousness[5] and each is Joy,[1] but in the latter, these are veiled to such an extent (with reference to man at any rate), that they have the appearance of not being either. Even the human Self is more or less veiled. Hence, though we can be made to perceive that the Self is essentially pleasant,[6] still the great amount of pain and suffering which we have to bear in life, the "unconsciousness" of swoon and slumber, the dull, vapid, indifferent tone of many experiences, the making of sacrifice and the occasional courting of death among other things, would seem to indicate not indeed that existence is pain as out-and-out pessimists, ancient and modern, have contended, but that it is of a mixed nature, and often of an indifferent nature. But, in the case of the Self, it is comparatively easy to see through the appearance of pain and indifference. The difficulty, in some respects, is with other objects. But be it easy or difficult, the Scripture says that: The mother is wholly Joy[7] and Play[8], and all Her creatures, whatever their grade in evolution, must have a share in and be made of Joy[1] and Play.[9]

---

[1] Ānanda. [2] Līlā. [3] Brihadāranyaka, IV, 3, 32.

[4] Pūrna. [5] Chit. [6] Priya.

[7] Līlā. A doctrine which Āgama Shāstra elaborates and in practice acts upon.

[8] Dvaita. [9] Vyāvahāra.

It is the law of veiling first to conceal, then to invert (*i.e.*, change the sense and direction) of a thing. It is the Principle of Polarity[1] in creation. And all pragmatic experience[2] and action[3] is based upon duality.[1] If Being,[4] Consciousness,[5] Bliss,[6] while remaining so, do not also appear as other than so, then there will be no pragmatic experience,[2] no *karma.* Action or movement is to realize the possible, know the unknown, and attain the unattained joy[6] or get rid of dissatisfaction.[7] That which not yet exists, is not yet known, is not yet satisfaction, is therefore presupposed. If all be displayed and realized, then there can be no play for the Centres, for the play is essentially one of hide and seek. Hence Being,[4] Consciousness,[5] and Bliss[6] are variously veiled and unveiled in the universe of experience. As the Whole[8] and the Immense,[9] Joy[6] is pure and perfect. As soon as a limit is drawn, Joy[6] becomes circumscribed; and it is this bar, this impediment, this restraint which is the seed of all pain.[10] Joy[6] is thus the essence and index of perfect freedom of being and functioning.[11] Since centralized life and existence is necessarily limited, impeded being and functioning, we have pain as an incidence of life. The "throes" or "travail" of birth, and the first cries which the new-born babe utters, are symbolic of this. But though limitation imposes pain, it cannot efface the sustaining background of Joy.[6] If that were effaced, the Self, the organ and cells of the organism

---

[1] Dvaita. [2] Vyāvahāra. [3] Karma. [4] Sat.

[5] Chit. [6] Ānanda. [7] *i.e.*, impediment to Ānanda.

[8] Pūrna. [9] Bhūma.

[10] The "bar" is Kanchuka born of Māyā.

[11] Called "Sahajāvasthā".

could not live, for vitality[1] itself is Joy.[2] As at the back of all finite modes of experience the "Ether of Consciousness"[3] remains, so behind all the pain and joy and "indifference" of life, the basis of Joy[4] is given. As the little[5] life is pain, as the great[6] life is Joy[7] (a term which, like *Chit*, is untranslatable). Pain, therefore, may be defined as the feeling of restriction of Bliss.[4] What man calls pleasure and even happiness belong to Pain, with this difference, that while feeling them he attends rather to that which is restricted than to the restriction itself, to what is affirmed rather than to what is denied; he looks to what is within the circle of limitation and not to what is outside. In feeling pain as pain he feels the restriction, the denial, the negation rather than what is circumscribed, given and affirmed. In his bitterest and deepest sufferings, the positive but circumscribed background of joy[4] can be recognized, but then he may be interested in not what is given, but in what has been denied him. By changing the direction of his interest and regard, he can, and sometimes does, touch this ground of Joy[4] while he feels himself as being drowned in "a sea of troubles". Feeling of pain, involving as it does, feeling of restriction, can be made to change its quality as well as intensity. Greater regard on the restriction or drawing closer the restricting line, will serve to intensify the feeling; regard on the positive side may change its quality and make it one of pleasure; and finally, merging all restrictions in the Whole[7] itself, will make it Infinite Bliss.[8] Pain is the negation or restriction of something positive. The First and Second Standards

---

[1] Prāna. [2] Ānanda. See Taitirīya-Up., Bhrigu-vallī.

[3] Chidākāsha.

[4] Ānanda. The whole process of appearance as given in the scheme of the 36 Tattvas is through increasing contraction or Sangkocha.

[5] Alpa. [6] Bhūmā. [7] Pūrna. [8] Bhūmānanda.

defining Liberation[1] as the complete cessation of Pain[2] would seem to imply that Pain is something positive and *Ānanda* merely the negation of this. But Vedānta conceiving Liberation[1] as realization of Supreme Bliss[3] makes Bliss[4] positive; Pain is merely the negation of it due to restriction.[5]

As in cognition it is only the point of pragmatic interest in the total Given which is regarded as the fact cognised and the rest though given in consciousness, is ignored, so in the matter of "affection" (pleasure and pain). The ignored parts of the given universe have all the gradations from "self-consciousness" to "sub-consciousness" or "evanescent consciousness". Thus while I am fully conscious of the star Sirius now, I am hardly conscious of the neighbouring stars, of the sounds I may be hearing, of the touches, smells and so forth, I may be feeling, of the ideas and memories I may be entertaining in the mind. All this wealth of actual experience is silently buried in ignorance, because not then useful. It fades into semi-consciousness and sub-consciousness. In fact, the dividing line between conscious and sub-conscious or unconscious is due to the habit of selective attention and regard[6] having been so consolidated as to practically operate as an opaque partition or wall between what is attended to and what is not. It is owing to this practical tendency[7] that mental life becomes like a floating ice-berg the greater part of which lies in sub-consciousness. It is thus that experience like an

---

[1] Mukti

[2] Apāya or Atyanta Nivritti.

[3] Paramānandāvāpti.

[4] Ānanda.

[5] As Upādhi (Brahma-Sūtra, I, 1. 12, and the Shruti Texts quoted in the Bhāshya thereunder) or Sangkocha.

[6] Pakshapāta.

[7] Sangskāra.

ascending and descending curve, now rises above the "normal line," now goes below it. The "normal" is settled by the tacit consensus of intercentral practice. This practical tendency[1] often acts therefore as a wall to shut out the "not-wanted" in experience, or, from the point of view of the "not-wanted," as a sort of crust more or less completely concealing the fact that it is being experienced. By wanting the not-wanted we can to a degree remove this crust; and by *yoga* this partition between conscious and sub-conscious may be brought as near as desired to the vanishing point.[2]

The same with Bliss.[3] We are practically used to regard as pleasurable or painful such experiences only as lie between certain limits. As our eye commonly sees only between certain limits, our ear hears only between certain limits, so experiences affect us as pleasures or pains only between certain limits. Beyond those limits the "affective element or tone" is supposed not to exist. Experience is said to be toneless or indifferent outside those limits. Inherited tendency[4] has erected a wall and built a crust here as it has in cognition. Many experiences or objects experienced are thus thought of as being without "value". Consider, as a typical cause, a block of stone lying at the foot of a hill. What has it, we may ask, to do with Joy?[3] To answer this we must raise and decide three issues. (*a*) Is it in itself joy?[3] (*b*) Does it know or feel itself as being so? (*c*) Is it an object of joy[3] (*i.e.*, *priya* or dear) to others? —that is, is it pleasing or pleasant?

Taking the last issue first we put two queries: (1) Is it pleasing to ourselves? and (2) Is it pleasing to some

[1] Vyavahāra sangskāra.

[2] In Yoga this is called "seeing" the Sangskāras which are, in fact, subtle (Sūkshma) presentations or impressions.

[3] Ānanda.

[4] Sangskāra.

other than ourselves? We separate these two because we are commonly so much occupied with ourselves and our own likes and dislikes that we do not care to consider whether a thing, not being useful and pleasing to us, may or may not be useful and pleasing to others. Let us turn up the stone and we shall find that, possibly, many worms and insects live under its shelter, so that that stone is as useful and dear[1] to them as our own sheltering roof is useful and dear[1] to us. And, for anything we know, that stone may be dear[1] not merely to the worms that our eyes may discover there, but to myriads of other unnoticed creatures living on, about, and in the pores of the stone. And we can generalize and say that what is true of a block of stone is true of everything: there is not a thing but is dear[1] to some in some relation or other.[2] In this sense, to be "dear" is a common mark of things. Now, coming next to ourselves, the stone may be dear[1] to us if we have the interest of a geologist or of one who loves the landscape of which it is a part. But let us suppose that apart from such special interests and associations (and not, moreover, stumbling and getting ourselves hurt by it), we are looking at the block of stone at the foot of the yonder hill. Is it dear? This is an important question which, being answered, will lead to a decision as regards the first and second issues raised above.

Let it be considered merely as an object of perception. Now as an object of perception apart from all practical interests, it is a measure[3] of Joy.[4] The play of practical interests will make it either pleasurable or painful; but its nature as Joy[4] is given in perception as such. Since

---

[1] Priya.

[2] *i.e.*, to some in certain "cosmic situations" or Adrishta.

[3] Mātrā. [4] Ānanda. As Brih.-Up., IV, 3, 32, has it.

man is not commonly interested in this basis of joy,[1] but rather in the superstructure of pleasure or pain raised on this basis by the "organic" reverberation of "resonance" evoked by that perception, we veil and ignore it, and think as though it were in itself a "toneless" and indifferent perception. But this is a mistake. Suspending for a time all practical interests, and looking up to the blue vault of the sky, or looking at the wide stretch of a field or a mass of water or a forest, we can certainly experience a kind of serene, quiet satisfaction, which is the basis of Joy, normally given in every perception, but which is perhaps less veiled in the cases just cited than in others. We can touch and realize this basis more and more closely in proportion as we can rid ourselves of our ordinary practical interests in modes of perception tending to produce organic resonance, as pleasures and pains. Strikingly analogous is the case of sound. We hear a variety of sounds and are interested in them. This prevents our attending to a kind of continuous sound (a continuous *Om*) which is the basis of all sounds, and which some may hear by disengaging their attention from the varieties, and listening in a quiet place and in their calmer moments. In a crowded place, a moment is never quite quiet, for there are then at least "dispersed" sound vibrations in the atmosphere (like dispersed light-waves during twilight). But in the country-side and in a secluded place, one can listen and perhaps hear the uninterrupted *Om*. A similar experiment may be necessary for verifying the normal basis of Joy[2] given in every perception. "Civilization" however which removes us from life in Nature and according to Nature, removes us from this basis of Joy[2] which is Life, though it may create for us varieties of pleasures and pains. In the *Vedas*, as also in

---

[1] Ānanda. As Brih.-Up., IV, 3, 32, has it. [2] Ānanda.

other ancient Revelations, such everyday natural occurrences as the rising and setting of the sun, the coming of darkness, rain, thunder-storm and flashes of lightning, and so on, are experiences of intense Joy, and we now almost wonder how it could ever have been so. We have learnt to ignore the normal joy of natural perceptions. In however the *Rigveda* and in the *Upanishads*, the very wind, earth, water, sun, plants, etc., are perceived to shed drops of "honey";[1] are seen to live, move and have their being in a measureless Joy;[2] are loved as beautiful.[3] In such a view the philosophy of, and outlook on, life and existence is such that death is *not* death to him who sees; old age[4] is not such to him; pain is not pain to him, because he recognises that the Self or *Ātma* is *Sat-Chit-Ānanda* (Being-Consciousness-Bliss), and as such cannot die, age, and be touched by pain and sorrow.[5]

Evil and pain there are in the world, and what man ordinarily calls pleasure may be hardly better than pain. But evil and pain exist by veiling and limiting essential joy which life and existence is; so that even when pain is there, there is also the veiled background of joy pervading it and enveloping it on all sides. Evil and pain is not, and cannot be in Vedānta, the true word and the last word for man. Consistently with this outlook on life, the *Shāstra* forbids for example, the writing and enacting of tragic dramas: union and joy must be the last word even in a play instead of death and sorrow. From witnessing a tragedy we come, on the other hand, laden with sorrow, possessed by evil and sorrow as if these were *the* realities in existence compared with which our pleasures and joys

[1] Madhu Ksharanti. Cf. The well-known Madhu-vidyā described in detail in Chhāndogya and Brihadāranyaka-Ups.

[2] Ānanda. [3] Sundaram. [4] Jarā.

[5] See, in particular, Chhāndogya, VIII.

are felt to be "iridescent air bubbles now gay in the sunshine and then broken by the passing wind". A real tragedy thus tends to invert the true order, relation and proportion of joy and sorrow in life and existence: it seems to fill all existence with an unfathomable abyss of pathos on which the so-called joys of life burst like empty bubbles. The Hindu has not countenanced this tendency in his ancient drama, which, though it admits evil and pain as a subsidiary element, has refused to admit it as the fundamental, essential, primary and final theme.

That every object is a measure of Joy is implied in the Vedānta view of Perception. Perception is an act of owning—cognition is recognition—a recognition of the essential identity between the Self which knows and the object that is known. The Self has its own veils of limitation—successive layers, so to say, of the Veil of increasing grossness, from the sheath of Joy[1] to the gross physical body.[2] The "object" has its own "layers" of crust too, according to its past action or *Karma* determining its present condition.[3] Both have *Karma* and enjoyment of pleasure and pain,[3] and both have sheaths[4] appropriate to the needs of their special kinds of *Karma* and enjoyment.[3] The latter has its "Self" and Play[5] too, as later explained. Now, when the first perceives the second, there is recognition of the *essential* identity between the two by the first. The crusts of both are so to say pierced in the act of perceiving, the essence of the one coming directly in touch with that of the other, and both being recognised as "the same". This is *owning*. And what is the Self[6]

[1] Ānandamaya kosha.

[2] Annamaya kosha. See Taitirīya-Up. for treatment of the five Koshas.

[3] That is Adrishta or Bhoga.

[4] Kosha.

[5] Līlā.

[6] Pramātā.

beneath the sheaths?[1] What is the innermost being of the *Ātman* but Joy? Hence, there could be no act of owning, and therefore of perceiving, if the Self, in perceiving a block of stone, did not recognise it as essentially Joy also. Perceiving is thus Joy leaping up to joy; one battery of Power as *Chitshakti* sparking out to another. The ancient Vedic practice of producing fire by the friction of two pieces of wood[2] may be treated as symbolic of this.[3] Fire, latent in both, is evoked by friction. So *Chit* and *Ānanda* or Joy, latent in both the self and the stone—maybe, more latent in the one than in the other—is evoked by that action which we call sensing and attending. The Vedic parable of two clouds, charged with "celestial fire," between which lightning passes, is again suggestive of this. A really unconscious thing[4] could not be known—because it is on that hypothesis, not what the knower and knowledge[5] are, *i.e.*, *Chit*. The third "Pole" of the "Polar Triangle,"[6] *i.e.*, the Known, must be of the essence of the other two.

In many Vedic "parables" *Indra* is described as killing *Vritra* by *Vajra* (commonly translated as lightning). Clouds have gathered but it is not yet raining. Why? Because the minute raindrops forming the clouds are by some hidden influence prevented from gravitating together and forming drops big enough to fall. That hidden influence is *Vritra*. But behold, flashes of lightning begin to pass from cloud to cloud, whereby the resisting power of *Vritra* is overcome; and it now begins to rain. By *Vajra Vritra* has been

---

[1] The Ishīkā inside the munja as the Kathopanishad puts it: Katha-Up., II, 3, 17.

[2] Arani.

[3] See Aitareya Brāhmana detailing the process (III Ch.) Agni thus produced was called Mathitāgni.

[4] Jada. [5] Jnātā and Jnāna. [6] Triputī.

killed. From rain comes food, from food "beings".[1] This is the meaning on "the physical plane". But it may be made to yield a deeper meaning also. It symbolizes the commonest of facts. In the act of knowing, there is the knower and there is the object to be known. The knower does not yet know it. Why? Because each is encrusted in "ignorance". Because each has constituted itself an alien with respect to the other—because the latter has been disowned and flung away as unconscious.[2] This Power[3] we may symbolise by *Vritra; Indra* is then *Chit Shakti* functioning as Self and using the mind and the senses. *Vajra* is the attentive direction of the mind and senses by which the coverings of Self and the object are pierced, and one is brought into rapport with the other. Both *Mind* and *Matter* are Joy from which creation proceeds.

In so-called "idol" worship, for example again, the worshipper first purifies himself by the preliminary rite called *Bhūtashuddhi*.[4] He calls to mind that all Principles[5] and Divinities[6] are in him, have evolved from the Supreme Self,[7] and return again to It. All the Principles and their *Devatās*[8] evolve from and are resolved into the Supreme Self.[9] These two afferent and efferent activities are represented in the *Mantra-Shāstra* by *Hangsah* and *So'ham.*[10] After *Bhūtashuddhi* comes mental worship,[11] and then finally

---

[1] Vrishterannang tatah prajāh.

[2] Achit or jada.

[3] As Āvarana and Vikshepa.

[4] This rite is enjoined by the Shākta Tantras as the preliminary of all worship being the purification of the subject about to worship the image or symbol of worship. See "Serpent Power" and "Shakti and Shākta".

[5] Tattvas.

[6] Devatās.

[7] Ātmā Sachchidānandamaya.

[8] Or controlling Chit-Shaktis. Each Divinity is a special aspect of the one Causal Consciousness.

[9] Sat-Chit-Ānanda as Īshvara and Īshvarī.

[10] See "Garland of Letters"—"Hangsa".

[11] Mānasa-pūjā.

external worship or worship on the plane of matter.[1] These are the three stages of assimilation of the worshipper to the *Devatā* or Divinity of his worship. In the first, the former calls to mind that he and all else are in ultimate essence—*Sat-Chit-Ānanda.*—The Yogic expression of this is *So'ham* (I am He), Sā'ham ("She I am"). In *yoga* all veils are lifted.[2] In Sādhanā (as worship) the Subject and the Object of worship are both invested with the veil of the refined "stuff," that is, "Mind."[3] The worshipper, though he has previously assured himself of the essential identity between himself and the Form worshipped, yet places his Mind[4] in a worshipful attitude with a view to as nearly as possible assimilate it to that of the Divinity or *Devatā* which is, *ex hypothesi*, purer and more potent than his. Lastly, comes worship on the vital and physical planes.[5] In this, what has been realized by the worshipper within himself, that is on the higher planes, namely, essential identity as *Sat-Chit-Ānanda*, and assimilation of Mind as nearly as can be to that of the Devatā, is projected on to the vital and physical planes.[6] By such projection, lines of mentative energy (or substance-energy) are made to impinge upon the "matter" of the "Image" worshipped. These lines or streams of mentative and vital substance-energy[7] envelop the matter of the Image, create

---

[1] Vāhya-pūjā.

[2] As Maitri-Up., VI, 27 (Ga, Gha, etc.), says, we enter the "Abode of Brahman, by piercing the four sheaths".

[3] Antahkarana (Vijnānamaya and Manomaya Koshas).

[4] Antahkarana.

[5] Prānamaya and Annamaya Koshas. Vitality is dealt with in the Prānapratishthā rite.

[6] By Nyāsa, Prāna-Pratishthā, etc.

[7] For the "stuff" of mind (Antahkarana) and vital force (Prāna) flows out with or as energy (Shakti).

round about it an aura of "radiant"[1] energy which so acts upon the "material" crust of the idol that, whilst remaining apparently as matter to the senses, it becomes dematerialized for the worshipper in this sense that Consciousness, Mind and Vital Force[2] ordinarily latent or folded up in it (from the pragmatic standpoint), becomes evoked, awakened and patent. This is what *Prānapratishthā* or "Life giving" rite means, or is supposed to effect. After this, the Image[3] is no longer to the worshipper "matter" only. It becomes in perception as it already was in reality Consciousness, Mind and Life.[4] And these are not a mere reflex, as the image of the sun in the mirror is a reflex of the sun. The worshipper's Consciousness is not simply reflected in, and, imaged by, something which is unconscious and remains so. In other words, it is not unconsciousness[5] looking like Consciousness.[6] What the projective action of the worshipper does is to cast the "radiant" energy of his own inner being (vastly potentized by *Bhūtashuddhi* and mental worship)[7] over the matter of the Image thereby evoking, unfolding, "waking up," adjusting the "radiant" stuff and energy folded up in it. This is, so to say, piercing the crust of Matter, evoking Consciousness,[7] Life[8] and Mind[9] in it, and bringing the whole into rapport with the Consciousness and Mind of the worshipper. The "awakened"[10] *Devatā* is thus no mere "creature" of the worshipper, and thus "smaller" than him. The degree to which this can be effected is determined by the extent

---

[1] Taijasa. [2] Chit, Antahkarana and Prāna.

[3] The Pratimā or that which is placed "before" one as the object of worship, not "Idol".

[4] Chinmayī, Manomayī, Prānamayī. [5] Achit.

[6] Chidābhāsa. In Shakti doctrine there is no Chidābhāsa.

[7] Chit. [8] Prāna. [9] Manas. [10] Jāgrat.

to which the worshipper has been able to evoke and dynamize himself, spiritually and vitally. The worshipper then sees, after the life-invoking ceremony,[1] not something alien and unconscious[2] in relation to himself, but an embodiment of Power as *Chit*, Power as Mind[3] and Power as Life.[4] The preliminary *Bhūtashuddhi* rite has enabled him to recognize this essential identity (*So'ham*). To the Divinity he has in part assimilated himself in mental worship.[5] It now stands before his senses as an Embodiment of fuller Power of knowledge, will and action[6] (similar to but fuller than himself which he now worships for the four desirable forms of Good).[7]

This, briefly, is the theory of the practice, as properly understood: whether this theory, and this claim can be substantiated is not so much a matter for speculative argument, as one for experimental proof. But in any case, worship or *Pūjā* is at base a recognition of essential identity and an experimental assimilation, as near as can be, of the form of the worshipper to that of the *Devatā* on the planes of Mind[3] and Life[4] at least, since Matter, being the principle of inertia and solidity,[2] does not easily (though it does, however, upon the necessary conditions being fulfilled) change its form since it is *guru*—that is heavy or ponderous. And what is more important to our present enquiry—the theory of worship[9] is also substantially the theory of Perception. Perception, as Vedānta holds, is an act of assimilation between the Subject and the Object, effected by the Mind[8]—energy of the former going out

[1] Prānapratishthā. [2] Jada. [3] Manas.
[4] Prāna. [5] Mānasa-Pūja.
[6] Jnāna-shakti, Ichchhā-shakti and Kriyā-shakti.
[7] Dharma, artha, kāma and moksha.
[8] Antahkarana. [9] Pūja.

through the senses to where the object is, enveloping it and assuming its form, and revealing its essential nature as *Chit* and as Bliss.[1] And this is what is supposed to be effective in the Life-giving rite or *Prānapratishthā*. Thus *Prānapratishthā* is perception and perception is *Prānapratishthā*. In both it is seen that what is "here" (*i.e.*, in the worshipper) is also "there,"[2] (*i.e.*, in the image). In the course of worship with a lamp, a fivefold flame of light is waved.[3] This symbolizes the play and offering of the five vital forces[4] as well as of the five senses of perception (as also, the five elements of matter, envelopes and so forth).

The Self is, in its substratum, recognized as Bliss.[1] Perception is really the perception of essential identity between the Self and the object, whether in the review and statement of the perception, which are commonly swayed by practical interests, expression be given to such identity or not. In the review of the perception the object may possibly figure as a stranger, as a rival or even as an enemy. But the superimposition of these characters does not destroy the basis of essential identity felt implicitly in perception. It follows therefore that the object of experience, in its substratum, is, like the Self, implicitly felt as Joy or *Ānanda*. This conclusion follows deductively from the premises about the nature of the Self and that of Perception. And it has been shown before that, apart from practical interests and tendencies which variously limit experiences and oppose them to one another, experience of objects, as of Self, is actually and intuitively an experience of bliss,[1] upon the basis of which pleasures and pains may variously intermix and inter-play. Thus the first question we raised before,

[1] Ānanda.

[2] As the Vishvasāra Tantra says. [3] Ārati. Pancha Pradīpa.

[4] Tattvas—Kshiti, etc., the five Tanmātras—Rūpa, etc., the five sheaths, koshas—Annamaya, the five Kanchukas.

whether a block of stone is in itself joy[1] is answered. By "thing" we mean of course "thing as experienced".

The second issue raised before, *viz.*, whether a block of stone knows itself as Bliss[1] as the Self knows itself, is one which cannot be directly decided, because here the question is not what the thing may be to us, but what it is to itself. We are driven therefore to infer from signs or marks. We are to proceed either *à priori* or deductively or *à posteriori* or inductively.

In the former case, we begin with a general view of existence (being and becoming) such as is given in these premises: Being is *Chit* or Consciousness. It becomes or evolves as Power. In becoming It finitizes and centralizes Itself as the selves, whereby different Centres with finite "fields" of being appear. These are the Centres of Power as Matter, Power as Life, Power as Mind. But since Chit alone is working as Substance-Energy, these Centres of Matter, Life and Mind are essentially Centres of *Chit-Shakti*. And since the *Ātman* manifesting as the Self is not anything other than a Centre of *Chit-Shakti*, the *Ātman* is everywhere—in man, in the amœba, and in a particle of dust. The forms or "sheaths" of *Chit-Shakti* differ of course in the different cases. But in principle, *Ātman* is everywhere —in an atom of Hydrogen, for example. It is as Power, the Centre-making Principle, and it must be there, where there is a centre of being and operation. A material particle, an amœba, a plant, an animal, a man—all are *Ātman* which is Consciousness, though in the last named that Consciousness has become evolved to such an extent as to appear as what is called "Self-Consciousness".

Self may be experienced in three forms: sub-consciously as in the amœba and other low organisms, intuitively as

---

[1] Ānanda.

perhaps in some of the higher animals including man; and rationally or logically as perhaps in man alone (excluding for the moment higher Spiritual Beings) who thus formulates his self-consciousness in definite judgments such as "I know this jar," "I will do this action", and so forth. The operation of practical interests and tendencies in man commonly determines him to note and accept life and existence only within certain limits; and sometimes the limits have been imposed upon his organism and his instruments of cognition. Thus the eye, the ear, and so forth can know only within certain approximate limits. Attention also has its limits. These practical limits, so useful in ordinary experience,[1] are responsible for the experience of the "developing" man being graded into three or four orders. Thus, according to one scheme, there are experiences—gross,[2] subtle,[3] and supreme.[4] According to another we have—gross, subtle,[5] causal,[6] and supreme or transcendent.[7] The experience of the developing man develops into these orders or forms. That of the ordinary man is commonly restricted to the gross order or form. Thus it is gross experience to feel that there is "no" life in a block of stone; "no" consciousness and bliss in it or even in the plant which is taken as "living"; "no" self anywhere except in man. Some of the Cartesians went so far as to deny consciousness or feeling even to the higher animals. Thus man is made to stand quite apart from the rest of creation. The denial of consciousness and life to other world-forms is due to man's ignorance and to the fact that he has learnt to commonly recognise and accept the Self only within certain limits. We have given to Self pragmatic definitions which reduce it commonly to the plane of gross and ordinary experience.

---

[1] Vyavahāra. [2] Sthūla. [3] Sūkshma. [4] Para.
[5] Sthūla, sūkshma. [6] Kārana. [7] Turīya.

Even in ourselves we do not commonly know the Self as a whole but only in a part. Man's Self is really the Presiding Self of a number of selves that are in him. Every cell, every organ, every sense of the body has its own Self[1] which, as such, is the manifestation of the *Devatā* which is the cosmic mode of a particular form of Consciousness as Power or *Chit-Shakti.* The microcosm[2] repeats and involves what *Chit-Shaktis* are at play in the macrocosm: *Āditya* ("the Sun"), for example, is the *Devatā* of the eye.[3] Each *Devatā* in the body has his own sphere[4] of domestic control and economy. The Self of man's Common Self-consciousness,[5] is only the president of a particular collectivity[6] —the "united states," each domestically controlled by its own *Chit-Shakti.*[7] In fact, there is no creation where the polarity of *Chit* as Efficiency Power (*i.e.*, *Chit-Shakti*, technically so called) and *Chit* as Material Power (*i.e.*, *Māyā-Shakti*) is not involved and repeated. Everywhere there is "material" to be controlled and fashioned, and a "Controlling Principle".[8] In every cell, for instance, there is "Matter" undergoing incessant metabolism, and the "Agency" whereby this is done and supervised—which Biology vaguely describes as Vital Power—is a Form of

[1] Chit-Shakti and its associated Māyā-Shakti. So in Kundalinī Yoga described in the Tantras each bodily centre (chakra) has its presiding Divinity (adhishthātrī Devatā). Divinity (Devatā) is the cosmic aspect of individual function. See also the Nāthas described in Introduction to Tantra-rāja Tantra.

[2] Kshudra brahmānda.

[3] See Chhāndogya, Brihadāranyaka and some other Ups. Brihadāranyaka, V, 5, 2 ; Chhandogya, I, 6, 6, and I, 7, 5, identify the Devatā in the Sun and the Devatā in the Eye.

[4] Adhikāra. [5] Jīvātmā. [6] Sangghāta.

[7] *Cf.* the dispute between Prāna (the Chief Devatā) and the Devatās of the Eye, Ear, Speech, etc., described in some of the Upanishads.

[8] See "Power as Life"—Appendix.

Chit-Shakti, a *Devatā*. Now, according to this conception, man's "Self"[1] is only the Chief of the *Devatās*, their *Indra*.[2]

But even the government of this Self is not ordinarily complete. There are many "States" in our organism which, apparently and directly, lie outside its jurisdiction. The activities or affairs of those States, though affecting the general tone and character of experience, are commonly both sub-conscious and involuntary. Several systems of ganglia in the spinal column, for example, are of this type. They may be seats and organs of many race-instincts, individual habits, reflex and automatic actions, and so on. They have their own *Devatās* or Selves. These Selves, though generally co-operating with the "Self," are commonly outside its cognisance and control. If "selective or purposive action" be accepted as the test of *Chit-Shakti*, then, it may be shown by experiment that all nerve-centres are centres of *Chit-Shakti*: all select their action. Those who have experimented with animals in which the cerebral matter has been removed, affirm that such an animal can be made to go through almost the whole round of reflex and instinctively selective actions which constitute the normal life of the animals. The noticeable difference, as William James points out, seems to be increased inertia or loss of spontaneity in its actions. This can be explained by the hypothesis that the lower ganglia have their own Controlling Principle or Self, and though this Self may keep itself somewhat in the background and hide its activity in sub-consciousness while the "cerebral Self" is there, it may rise into prominence and do office for the cerebral Self where or when the latter is inactive or its control ineffectual. In the

---

[1] Jīvātmā.

[2] Bṛihadāraṇyaka IV, ii, 2 and 3, place Indra and his wife in the right and left eyes respectively, and explain.

experiments cited, the "lower" self becomes a substitute for the "higher".

In certain hypnotic subjects, again, there is effected what may be called exchange or substitution of functions between one sense and another, *e.g.*, the sense of sight and that of touch. And since, according to the *Shâstra*, the human birth is preceded by countless other forms of birth, and tendencies of different births are as tendencies stored up, there is in man not only the "cerebral self" and the selves of other ganglia, organs and senses, but the countless selves of the previous births (a few, perhaps, are human or super-human, whilst most are sub-human) brought over and folded up with their characteristic impressions and tendencies.[1] Of the innumerable "groups" of tendencies[1] those only fructify which are pertinent or relevant to the human birth, by the Law of Similars, the rest, though given, do not unfold and make themselves kinetic.[2] In man therefore there is a Plurality of Selves or Personalities. Sometimes two or more "Personalities" may dissociate from each other and each becomes, or tends to become, an independent conscious Personality. Cases are on record in which in hypnotic patients or in mediums or in somnambulists, or else in yogins, Personalities with widely contrasted characters appear and hold their sway.[3] In many forms of practical method[4] again, particularly in Initiation,[5] there is effected superimposition of a higher Self upon a less developed one whereby the latter's development is extraordinarily

[1] Sangskâras.

[2] See Pâtanjala Darshana, IVth Chapter discussing the whole question.

[3] Kâya-Vyûha.

[4] Sâdhanâ.

[5] Dîkshâ.

accelerated.[1] We need not adduce further examples. The point sought to be established is this that of the manifested self[2] as a whole in us we commonly know but little. Our interest is so little and so partial, and our ignorance so deep and so great.

But let us consider the familiar marks of the existence of Personality. A stone or even a dog is commonly to us not a "person"; it is only an "individual". But is this an absolute distinction? Let us try the marks. There are several marks by which we recognise Self in another human person. All these are at the root expressions of one fundamental mark: action springing out of Bliss,[3] that is, free or spontaneous action. Action arising out of bliss[3] is play.[4] Hence the Self is what is capable of, and in fact does, play.[4] The Supreme Self or Lord is full of play,[5] the world being His play.[6] The finite Self is a finite reproduction, is made "in the image,"[7] of the Lord. Play[4] is threefold: in creation, in sustenance, in dissolution. Wherever there is Self, we must have evidence there of "Play" in these three aspects. That is, Self must, out of essential bliss[3] create, maintain and destroy. But there is a difference between the Supreme Self and the finite Self created by the Veiling

---

[1] The inner significance of the repeated fight between Devas and Asuras, in which the latter often depose Indra from his lordship over the three worlds (*i.e.*, the three states of experience—waking, dreaming and slumber) and deprive the "gods" of their adhikāras or authorities, but are finally ousted by the grace of the Supreme Power, is in one sense, the fight between co-existent but opposite Personalities in the sādhaka as man.

[2] Vyavahārika.

[3] Ānanda. [4] Līlā. [5] Līlāmaya.

[6] Līlā. Brih.-Up., I, 3, 3.—"Sa vai naiva reme"—Alone He could not enjoy: Also, Maitri-Up., II, 6 (Kha). Brahma-Sūtra, II, 1, 33—"Lokavattu līlākaivalyam."

[7] Kulārnava Tantra, I—"Tadangsha jīva-sanggakāh . . . yathāgnan visphulingakāh."

Principle which veils and finitizes and conditions Consciousness,[1] Bliss[2] and Play.[3] The Supreme Self is the Lord of *Māyā* (the veiling and conditioning Principle) but the finite Self is subject to it. Hence in every finite Self both Bliss[2] and Play[3] are relatively and variously veiled and conditioned. The essence of the Self, which is Bliss and Play, can nowhere be completely suppressed and effaced, however. It may be more veiled and conditioned in A than in B, more in B than in C, and so on. We have accordingly a descending series of Bliss and Play manifestation, starting from the Supreme Self down to the densest or grossest matter.[4] As we descend, we have play[3] more and more veiled, more and more conditioned, till coming to Matter we are presented with the appearance of "insensate" being where behaviour, as physicists believe, is "absolutely" determined. Matter, thus, appears to us as the vanishing point of Bliss[2] and Play.[3]

But it is not really that. In matter an inexhausted residue of Bliss[2] and Play[3] is still left, though ordinarily man has no suspicion of it. Ordinarily he is not interested in looking for Play[3] beyond certain familiar terms of the series referred to. It is said in the *Shāstra* that after gross, solid matter has been created, *Shakti* or Cosmic Power becomes "coiled"[5] or rests. As such, She is given at the Basic[6] Centre which is the centre of solid matter.[7] *Kundalinī Shakti* is Consciousness, Bliss and Play.[8] Hence in matter too there is an infinite reservoir of Bliss[2] and Play.[3] And part of this fund is patent, kinetic also,

---

[1] Chit. [2] Ānanda. [3] Līlā. [4] Bhūta.

[5] Kundalinī. [6] Mūlādhāra.

[7] Kshiti-Tattva. See "Serpent Power".

[8] Chinmayī, Ānandamayī and Līlāmayī.

though matter may commonly present to us an appearance of absolute lack of spontaneity or freedom. Ascending the series, we come to plants and animals and, then, to man. The lowest type of life, say the amœba, is noticeably characterized by play.[1] Its behaviour as a whole is unforeseeable, incalculable; though it may be only approximately so. Its behaviour generally conforms to that of the type: but every individual speck of protoplasm has a life of its own too; its idiosyncrasy; its play, and therefore, its Self. It has its own slightly, and often unnoticeably peculiar "curve" of life which generally or abstractedly conforms to the general equation of the curve representing the life of the species. It has its "personal equation". A crystal, which grows according to a definite geometrical pattern, has an idiosyncrasy of its own; its own eccentricities; its own play. Deterministic physical explanations are always ultimately faced with a residuum or margin of eccentricities, which, as it is pursued, recedes and recedes like the chased horizon, but never completely vanishes.

In man, *Māyā*, in the form of subtle tendencies[2] and gross embodiment of tendencies (*i.e.*, the physical body, senses, etc.,) imposes limitations or conditions on his essential being and activity which are Joy[3] and Play.[1] But through all limitations his essential freedom vents itself. In all his actions, however much determined, he is a free agent,[4] whether his freedom may be vented through spontaneity or through volition. His essential freedom is never altogether suppressed; his "empirical determinism" is never absolutely complete. In man we may, however, have grades of freedom. Accordingly, we have three

---

[1] Līlā. [2] Sangskāras. [3] Ānanda.

[4] A Karttā, a līlāmaya. The psycho-physical which is a manifestation of the Power of Ātman is determined but the Ātman itself is ever free (nityamukta).

orders of Man: *Pashu*, *Vīra* and *Divya*.[1] The first is in *Pāsha* or bonds[2] (never absolutely so, however), that is subject to the veil;[3] the second is a "hero"[4] who is active to free himself from them that is to lift the veil;[5] the third is a man in whom the *pāsha* has become so light or slender[6] that he is practically a master of himself.[7] The object of ritual and yoga practice[8] is to gain complete mastery over the limiting and conditioning Principle or *Māyā*.[3] The object attained is Self-Rule.[7] It is the consummation of what Kant and other Western thinkers have conceived as the Autonomy of the Self or "Practical Reason".

We have briefly reviewed the ladder by ascending and descending. Now, let us return to our block of stone. *A priori* argument has been given to show that the essential mark of the Self (*i.e.*, play)[9] should be recognisable in it also. *Ahalyā*, the wife of the *Rishi Gotama*, was according to the Shāstra transformed into a stone for a sin she had unwittingly committed. The contact of *Shrī Rāmachandra's* lotus feet retransformed her into her human shape. This, either way, could not be stated to be possible if stone and man were considered to be essentially unlike

---

[1] See for explanation of these terms "Shakti and Shākta".

[2] Hence called Pashu.

[3] He is subject to the veiling factor of the Psycho-physical Principle as Prakriti or Māyā.

[4] Vīra.

[5] In whom the Rajas guna in the Psycho-physical Principle is active to suppress veiling and to present consciousness.

[6] His bond then being mainly that of Sattva-guna.

[7] Svarājyasiddhi. Chhāndogya, VII, 25, 2; also Brih. in some places.

[8] Sādhanā.

[9] Līlā.

each other ; if, for example, Self which is in the latter were not really, though in a less developed form, given in the former. Similarly, when in worship it is sought to "dematerialize" a piece of stone, and evoke in it *Chit*, Life[1] and Mind,[2] success can be had only because, in reality, it is so. By practice[3] man only breaks the bonds of his own ignorance and non-realization, and dematerializes that which, chiefly with reference to his veiling *tendencies*,[4] has appeared as dead, senseless, Selfless "matter". By *veiling tendency*[4] we mean a specific form of limiting tendency which is both caused and presupposed by a particular type of practical living[5] in the world. This ignorance[6] is often spoken of in the *Shāstra* as a cave,[7] sometimes as night,[8] and occasionally as sleep.[9] When the Lord of the Veil veils Himself, the veiling, in that aspect, is called yoga sleep. In relation to finite Selves, who are not complete masters of their ignorance[6] or "sleep,"[9] the veil is an Obstructing Power.[10]

As in the vedic parable *Indra* or *Āditya*, led by *ushā* (Dawn), first hears the lowing of the cows in the cave, and then proceeds to liberate them; so the Self of the aspirant[11] directed by the dawning perception of Truth,[12] first hears, so to say, the call of the Self shut up in the cave of "Matter," and then recognises that Matter is only another form[13] of *Sachchidānanda*, as it were solid masses afloat in the unbounded sea of Being-Consciousness and Joy[14] as Shrī Rāmakrishna Paramahangsa used to say. In fact the cosmic Cause evolves matter through and after Mind.[15]

---

[1] Prāna. [2] Manas. [3] Sādhanā.

[4] Avidyā-sangskāra. [5] Vyavahāra. [6] Avidyā. [7] Guhā. [8] Rātri.

[9] Nidrā. For example, we hear of the yoga-nidrā of Vishnu (The "All-pervasive") in the first Māhātmya of Shrī Chandī.

[10] Nirodha-Shakti. [11] Sādhaka. [12] Tattva-drishti.

[13] Vigraha. [14] Sachchidānanda. [15] Buddhi, Ahangkāra, etc.

which must as an effect involve its cause though in a subtle[1] form. The same operation of "spiritualizing" matter is more systematically tried in *Kundalinī yoga*. *Kundalinī Shakti* or latent causal Power at rest which is at the Radical Centre[2]—the centre of solidity[3]—is the embodiment of all the 36 modes of Reality-Power,[4] the synthesis of all forms of Power,[5] knowing, willing, acting,[6] and the Synthesis of all units of "Sounds".[7] The *Svayambhu-Linga* in the Radical Centre round which Shakti or Power has coiled herself up in "three coils and a half," is the Self or *Ātman* in the Principle of solid matter which is sheathed by the coils of the "Serpent Power" here immanent in Matter in its grossest form.[8] All this signifies that Matter really involves Self or *Ātman* and the Power whereby this Self is sheathed is really Perfect Power, though "asleep". It is not, therefore, merely what the physicist would recognise as Physical Force or Energy. Mind as *Buddhi* and other forms are all there in it. As the Basal Centre has its *Linga* or Self, so have the other Centres[9] in which other forms of Matter and Mind[10] are represented. The Self of the *Yogī* so acts on these Centres that what is coiled up in them becomes uncoiled, what is latent patent. Thus the Material Tattvas are successively "spiritualized," and are ultimately cast as offerings into the "Fire of Supreme Consciousness and Bliss" in highest realization.

An atom of matter, according to this conception, is not dead, inert, insensate and selfless. In it the Effulgent

---

[1] Sūkshma. [2] Mūlādhāra chakra.

[3] The Prithivī or "earth" Centre. [4] Sarva-tattva-rūpinī.

[5] Sarva-shakti-svarūpinī

[6] Jnānashakti, Ichchhāshakti and Kriyāshakti.

[7] Sarva-varna-mayī. As to Shabda, see "Serpent Power".

[8] Prithivī. [9] Chakra.

[10] Prithivī, Ap, Tejas, Vāyu, Vyoma, Antahkarana.

Person of whom the *Chhandogya* says that He is possessed of golden hair and a golden beard and so forth (who can be seen in the "Sun,"[1] also, on a smaller scale, in the pupil of one's eyes,) is in disguise, a disguise due partly at least to the necessity of having to deal with it in specific pragmatic relations of enjoyment and suffering,[2] and, therefore, would not exist in, and as, this particular disguise if man's unseen result of Karma,[3] were, or could be made, different. The disguise is relative to the conditions of present practice[4] which set down certain limitations to the functioning of the instruments of apprehension and thinking in man. If one could apprehend the fourth dimension, for instance, a stone would not be to him what it is to us. So again, if one could exercise subtle vision,[5] one might see or hear the actual dance of the particles in a stone—a dance which though it may conform generally to a measure and law[6] might be seen as not wholly determined or bound by it, but as the expression[7] of Joy,[8] even as man's own voluntary actions are so admittedly. This stone, too, has its unseen Karma[3] by which its position and state in the cosmic system are determined relatively to those of other objects. Irrespectively of other objects, therefore, it is not what it appears to be: a block of stone. It is the Whole.[9] This is its *Kaivalya*—that is, its being apart from specific relations to other beings in a stressing cosmic system. Even in actual relations, it is not relatively to one class of objects what it may be relatively to another class.[10] So long as a thing is a member of the cosmic stress-system, it is a certain thing relatively to man who "is his own measure". Man thus thinks that, relatively to the stone,

---

[1] Āditya-mandala. Chhāndogya, I, VI. [2] *i.e.*, of Bhoga.
[3] Adrishta. [4] Vyavahāra. [5] Divya-drishti.
[6] Chhandah. [7] Līlā. [8] Ānanda.
[9] Pūrna. [10] See *Post*.

he is the knower or enjoyer,[1] whilst the stone is known and enjoyed[2] only. But this is veiled thinking. The stone is, according to its unseen karma[3] a knower and enjoyer also. In the case of the sculptor and the stone we have "enjoying" in both, though, in accordance with his unseen *Karma*, the fact may be patent and pronounced in the former, and, in accordance with its *Karma*,[3] it may be latent and hidden in the latter. All that we have a right to say is this however that it is latent and hidden in the latter relatively to our *Karma*[3] or to that of others who are, or are conceived by us to be, constituted and "cosmically situated" similarly to us. It need not necessarily be so, relatively to other constitutions and cosmic situations.

Explanation by an Universal "Over-soul" and Reservoir of Power will not materially affect the position stated above. *Chit-shakti* in evolving as the World of Forms, divides itself, so to say, into a double line of manifestation —cosmic and micro-cosmic. Thus there are, on one hand, Universal Life,[4] and individual, finite lives, on the other.[5] The Universal is the causal ground of the individual or particular. The individual thus arises out of the Universal, and in dissolution[6] is dissolved in it again. The Universal is therefore not simply the aggregate of the particulars. Thus *Hiranyagarbha*[7] is not merely the sum of individual lives[7] and minds.[8] It is their beginning and end. And co-existing with them, it controls them and lies at the back of them as an inexhaustible fund of vital and mentative power. It is also their connecting and pervading "medium" like ether of material bodies. Its control,

[1] Jnātā and Bhoktā.

[2] Jneya and bhogya. [3] And Adrishta.

[4] Prāna. [5] Antahkarana. [6] Laya. [7] Prānas.

[8] Manas. See the "Garland of Letters" where these relations are explained, and particularly, the diagrams.

however, is not determination. And an individual Centre by "closing the circuit" between itself and the Universal Self, can draw upon that general fund of power. In that case, cosmic power flows on into the individual and fills it, just as, on the physical plane, electricity may, through conductors, flow from one body into another and saturate it. As in matter, flow presupposes difference of level, pressure or potential, so in life and mind, flow implies that one object is relatively greater or fuller in power than another. But the lesser thing, though actually or apparently lesser, must have potential capacity, so that it may contain currents of life more than what it ordinarily does contain. That is, even in the case of actual conduction of cosmic power into a finite Centre, we must presuppose that the latter has potential capacity greater than its actual or seeming capacity; which means that though, practically and seemingly, it is finite and small, yet really and potentially, it is great. And since there can be set no limit to what a "finite" Centre can contain of the Power of the Cosmic Self flowing on into it, we must presuppose that its capacity is potentially indefinitely great or infinite.

Hence in order that Cosmic Power in a large measure may flow into it, its potential capacity must to that extent be kinetized. Otherwise, a well remaining a well will never contain the sea. To contain it it must be sea itself. And it can become the sea because really, though not "in ordinary use," it is the sea. Hence the position that a finite thing, even though material, is merely an empirical[1] form in which the Measureless[2] and Whole[3] appears as Little[4] and Imperfect,[5] and sectional, is not affected by the view that a finite thing's accession to power (physical, vital

[1] Vyavahārika. [2] Bhūmā. [3] Pūrna. [4] Alpa.

[5] Apūrna. The "disguise" is variously referred to in the Ups.

or mental) is due to the conduction into it of Power from a Cosmic Reservoir. We have seen that such conduction and expansion and filling of the Little is possible, because under the action of the Cosmic Power it can be, more or less nearly, assimilated to the state of the latter; and that it can be so assimilated because potentially it is identical with or similar to the Cosmic Power. In fact, while turning a "finite" face to other centres and in world-experience[1], it must be conceived as turning an infinite face also to the Infinite Self.

Or the position may be stated thus: It is the Universal Self[2] who, whilst remaining as such, finitizes itself by veiling into a plurality of finite selves; the Universal thus appears in two forms—as Universal and as Particulars which are really the Universal but variously self-veiling. The finite centre's drawing the current of Universal Life really therefore means the Patent and Manifest Universal removing the veil It has put on in, and as, the finite particular. It is really Infinity discovering Infinity in the midst of pragmatic limitations created by Itself. The conduction or "flow" view, therefore, instead of shewing that the little is little, shows that the little is great, the finite infinite. Greatness is not merely "thrust upon" it by an extraneous Agency; it is "born" great, and therefore naturally "achieves," or is made to achieve, greatness. That Mind and Life[3] are given in a block of stone is a position which from this view of things remains unshaken.

But, as on the material plane, we have induction of vital and mental power also, which directly suggests that a "small" thing has a great capacity. In conduction power actually flows from a source to a receiver, and the amount

---

[1] Vyavahāra. [3] In Prāna, Manas, etc.

[2] As Buddhi, Ahangkāra, Manas, Prāna.

added to the latter is subtracted from the former. In induction, a charged body by its "influence" evokes a corresponding charge in another body. There is no actual give and take. In induction Power in the two bodies is of the same sign; in conduction Power disposes itself in opposite poles in the two bodies. Suppose we take two bodies X and Y of which the former is charged with positive electricity. Now, what happens if Y be brought close to it (but not in contact)? Suppose the faces which X and Y turn to each be A and C respectively, and their respective "backs" B and D. Then, the charge of X will so act upon the neutral condition of Y as to polarize it into a positive charge and a negative charge, and of these, the negative one, which is opposite to the positive charge on A, will settle on C. That is, the two bodies will have their confronting faces, A and C, charged with electricity with opposite signs. Induction, therefore, may be said to reverse the "sign" of power in the influenced body relatively to the influencing body.

Now, consider a stone again. Relatively to the results of previous Karma[1] and the common experience[2] of Self-conscious Man, the direction of Power in a stone is downward:[3] from the evolution of mind, to that of gross matter (in which the former as causal is involved), the curve of Power is a descending one. Man-principle represents an ascending current of power as compared with the Matter-principle. This difference of direction can be symbolized by a difference of sign. Now, in ordinary relation, when a man faces a stone, we have this upwardly-directed Power and this downwardly-directed Power facing each other. The former means evolving, unfolding Power; the latter means involved, folded-up Power. The former gives unfolded,

---

[1] Adrishta. [2] Vyavahāra. [3] It is adhah-srotah.

manifest, patent being; the latter folded-up, unmanifest, latent being. Hence, commonly, a man facing a stone means a self-conscious being facing a thing in which Self and so forth are folded up, latent. Thus the stone appears as neutral, inert. But suppose the man is able to "influence" the stone in the manner before described. The influencing will mean the reversing of the direction of sign of the Power in the stone, that is, making it an ascending instead of a descending current, unfolded, instead of folded, evolved instead of involved. That is to say, Self, Mind [1] and Life [2] so long involved in it relatively to the man, will be evolved relatively to him. This change implies, as before explained, a change of Karma [3] of the one relatively to that of the other.

This is Induction in the higher planes which descends, with a special form and name, on the plane of matter. Man's spiritual effort may be through conduction or through induction ("vicarious action") or through both. Some forms of it lay stress on the one, and other forms on the other. The method of Prayer is mainly one of conduction (in which Divine Power flows on into the devotee); the method of *Bhūtā-Buddhi* or *Kundalinī yoga* is mainly one of induction.[4] But we must not actually separate the one from the other. Every act of perception requires both induction and conduction of Power. And whether it be conduction or it be induction, it has been shown that according to Vedānta a block of stone or a lump of earth, however it may pose itself relatively, to the "potential worths" [3] of other things, is really and potentially the Universal Self, Life and Mind in a certain form of self-limitation; being so, it is always really Bliss [5] and Play [6]

[1] Antahkarana. [2] Prāna. [3] And Adrishta.

[4] See "Serpent Power," "The Philosophical Basis of Kundalinī yoga".

[5] Ānandamaya. [6] Līlāmaya.

as the Self is (for it is none other than the Universal Self); it can be made to appear as a blissful and playful [1] Self only if we can make our "attitude" [2] different and appropriate in relation to it.

The gross view of Matter was the ignorance or nescience of nineteenth-century science, but the present dynamical conception of matter (with which the Indian Doctrine of Power agrees) has gone a considerable way in paving the path for the acceptance of the Vedāntic view above explained. The atom is said to be no longer a "hard billiard-ball" but a sort of miniature universe, with a practically incalculable fund of energy; [3] it ordinarily conserves itself but is, in radio-activity, transforming and evolving; the aspect of Power as *evolving matter*, and that as *dissolving* matter are also perhaps already recognisable in it. Motions and masses in it are calculable only abstractly (that is, after some limitation of the data), but not concretely. Determinism or the "rule of formula" can never be completely established in its domestic or "foreign" life. The Principle of Relativity has also been an upsetter of the old bases of calculation. Hence Physics may be supposed to have indicated already that it is a magazine of Power which creates, evolves, conserves and destroys (thus indicating play [4] in all its phases); that it has a system of domestic economy; that it has its own idiosyncrasy; its own "memory," and so on. These indications are, if anything, suggestive of a Self in the atom doing play [4] out of Joy [5] appearing as subject to conditions. What Physics covers or tries to cover by its mathematical formulæ and equations, is an abstract atom representing some only of the conditions; the real concrete atom exceeds

[1] Ānandamaya, lilāmaya.

[2] See *post*. for further explanation of Adrishta and Karma.

[3] See "Matter". [4] Līlā. [5] Ānanda.

these formulæ and equations, and must ever exceed them, because its essence, its driving force is Power which is Joy[1] which expresses itself in spontaneity, freedom and play. Clear-sighted Physicists have long recognized that the nineteenth-century atom is conceptual, abstract, but they must now also recognise that the twentieth-century atom, corpuscle and so forth are no less conceptual in so far as they are supposed to be exactly coverable by differential equations. But the real atom is also slowly disentangling itself from those physico-mathematical bonds.[2] The Self in it has now spoken; evidence of play[3] in it can no longer be mistaken. All this is not to say that the Self in the atom is actually a thinker, a logician, or a judge. A block of stone does not think and judge (by means of categories) its states as we think and judge ours. But this does not affect the position that it has its Self, its experience (however veiled relatively to us) of Joy,[1] and its Play[3] (however determined its behaviour may appear to our abstract calculation).

Thus all the three issues raised with regard to it have been decided according to Shāstric principles. A block of stone is *Sachchidānanda* or Being Consciousness Bliss veiling itself in a particular manner, but never so veiling as to make its essential nature completely suppressed. Its Self, its Joy[1] may be ordinarily hidden from our practical cognisance which is cognisance within certain narrow, pragmatic limits only.

We began with the *Māyā-vāda* definition of Real as that which is common,[4] not limited by Time and Space, or without exception.[5] Enquiry has shown that of all the

[1] Ānanda.

[2] The dynamical view is a long step already taken towards the "dematerialization" of matter. And "Psychic Research" is furnishing corroborative evidence. See *Post*.

[3] Līlā. [4] Sāmānya. [5] Avyabhichārī.

infinitely varied objects of experience the common, the invariable element is Being Consciousness Bliss or *Sat-Chit-Ānanda*. This, therefore, is the lasting Real; the forms and names not being invariable are "unreal" in the sense of being transient. The fundamental importance of the conception of Experience as being essentially *Sachchidānanda* (especially the last)[1] has justified a detailed examination of the matter.

But, as in the other case, *Māyā-vāda*, in thus defining the essence of Reality and Experience, has drawn the veil over, and therefore hidden, something. That essence of experience alone is not Perfect Experience—the Whole.[2] Unless we add to it Power to change or evolve as varied Name and Form,[3] we have "Fact-section" only, not the "Fact". The Real is not the Essence only which is massive Consciousness as Chit,[4] and Bliss,[5] but the Power also by which Joy[5] appears as full activity or play. The Whole[2] is Bliss[5] in itself, as well as Power to manifest as play.[6] One aspect apart from the other is but a fraction.[7]

In conceiving the Whole[2] as Reality (or "Fact"), we must beware of two possible abstractions. To restrict the Fact to the changeless and universal element of experience alone is one abstraction. The other is to restrict it to a sort of statical, unmoving "perfectness". All the *Shāstras* (Vedas as well as Shākta and Advaita Shaiva[8] Tantras) agree in maintaining that there is a transcendental state (immanent in ordinary experience also) of *Chit* which is

---

[1] The fundamentality of Ānanda is especially treated in Taittrīya-Up. (Brigu.-vallī); see also Brahma Sūtra, I, 1, 12.

[2] Pūrna. [3] Nāma and Rūpa.

[4] "Vijnānaghana," etc., as Brihadāranyaka-Up. (IV, 5, 13; III, 9, 28; II, 4, 12, etc.)

[5] Ānanda. [6] Līlā. [7] Kalā.

[8] The Advaita or non-dual position is alone dealt with.

pure,[1] unveiled,[2] stainless,[3] undivided,[4] quiescent[5] and without a second;[6] that this is changeless and abiding while all forms change, appear and disappear; that this is the Substance, Ground and Root of all world-manifestation; and that liberation[7] can be had by realizing this *Sachchidānanda*. *Māyā-vāda* may be justified not only in emphasizing this transcendental aspect of *Chit*, but also (as one method and to some extent,) in concentrating the *sādhaka's* thought on this aspect, since without realizing this aspect there is no liberation,[7] and, since according to this method, this aspect should be realized transcendentally first, and then immanently in the varied experiences of the world. That is, *Chit* must first be recognised as differentiated from name and form,[8] and then, as identical with the Power evolving them.[9] With this supreme object[10] in view, *Māyā-vāda* defines the transcendental and unchanging aspect as Reality, and the reverse as neither real nor unreal. Let us let alone the unreal, and concentrate our thought on the Real, because that is unchanging, pure, massive *Sachchidānanda*, the realization of which is liberation,[7]—this is what *Māyā-vāda* in fact says. Now, assuming the truth of non-dualism no objection can be taken to this as one method of realizing the supreme goal by those suited to this Path. Our interest is naturally in name and form[11]; to transfer it to Pure *Sachchidānanda*, we must provisionally discard, and belittle name and form.[11] We have to be persuaded that our interest should lie in Pure *Chit* and not in the forms. And this persuasion is attempted while the Vedantist declares the former as real and the

---

[1] Shuddha. [2] Nirlepa. [3] Niranjana. [4] Akhanda.
[5] Shānta. [6] Advitīya. [7] Mukti.
[8] Nāma and Rūpa. Expressed by "So'ham".
[9] Expressed by "Sarvo'smi". [10] Paramārtha.
[11] Nāma-rūpa or the psycho-physical.

latter neither real nor unreal. From its standpoint *Māyā-vāda* may be right.[1] But still it should be observed that in this we have attempted to define the undefinable, offered as Real that which is an aspect (however fundamental) of the Concrete Whole. Such defining and offering are necessary for the realization of the object in view; but still when it[2] comes to be a question of *living* the full and undivided Reality, we must be careful to recognise that *Chit* as Reality is unchanging, but it is *also* Power to change as the world of name and form[3]; that *Chit* is not Ether-consciousness[4] only, but is also Power in Play[5] manifesting as the world; that *Chit* as Ether[4] only is not Joy[6] but *Chit* in play[5] also is Joy.[6] We have no right to draw a line and say that the Real is here and not there. The Whole and Full is the Fact. Hence the *Upanishat* or real name of the *Brahman* is The Reality of Reality.[7]

Nor must we look upon the Fact as a statical, unmoving, "eternally realized" perfectness. That is another abstraction. There may be an aspect of experience in which everything stands manifested in the fullness of its relations to all other things. There is nothing unmanifest, unrealized in regard to such Experience. Here knowing[8] and so forth are eternal.[9] Nothing being here unknown and unrealized, this experience does not evolve. Many western as also Indian thinkers,[10] have conceived such a level of eternally and perfectly realized experience.[10] It also represents the 26th *Tattva* (Principle), *viz.*, *Īshvara*, of the

---

[1] *i.e.*, in view of the Paramārtha.
[2] Pūrna and Akhanda.
[3] Namā-rūpa or the psycho-physical.
[4] Chidākāsha.
[5] Chid-vilāsa.
[6] Ānanda.
[7] Brih.-Up., II, 1, 20; Maitri-Up., VI, 32 (Ka).
[8] Jnāna.
[9] Nitya.
[10] Cf. the doctrines of Rāmānujāchāryya, Madhvāchāryya, Vallabhāchāryya, Nimvāchāryya and others.

Yoga System.[1] He is the knower of all generals[2] and of all particulars.[3] His sound-predicate[4] is the *Mahāmantra Om.*[5] Man's experience has generally been conceived as "a gradual and partial reproduction" of that Spiritual Principle. We do not know, and cannot relate ourselves to, a thing in the completeness of its relations. Hence we know more and more; will and act to place that thing in other and yet other relations to ourselves.

That Consciousness as *Chit*, in evolving by its Power of the world of names and forms, shows a perfect and realized Form (the Supreme Form)[6] and an unending series of less and less perfect and less realized forms, yet remaining as it is in itself always and everywhere, whilst veiling and limiting itself variously as it descends from the Supreme Form and Name[7] to the lower levels, is a position which is assured by the very nature of evolution itself. Evolution means this. A Supreme Form or Ideal, as actual Reality, involves or folds itself up progressively by its veiling and finitizing Power; but the Supreme Form possesses supreme *elasticity*[8] (as the imperfect forms, material or otherwise, possess their own elasticities by which when strained they stress to regain their own forms; whereby in and through all strained, that is veiled and finitized, forms, it again tends to regain its Supreme Form). This is Cosmic Elasticity and it is at the root of Evolution. It is analysable into two factors—a downward or forward sweep and an upward or backward sweep; an outgoing current and a return current[9]; an ejection and an absorption. One of the

[1] Pātanjala-Sūtra—concept of Īshvara.

[2] Sarvajna. [3] Sarva-vit. [4] Vāchaka

[5] "Tasya vāchakah pranavah"—Pātanjala-Sūtra. [6] Īshvara.

[7] The Supreme Shabda-Artha-Pratyaya, which is the Lord Īshvara.

[8] See post for further explanation.

[9] Pravritti and Nivritti Mārga.

Shāstric symbols is the Divine Tortoise[1] who projects and withdraws His limbs, and Who is described as having borne on His back the *Vedas* (*i.e.*, the highest form of Experience together with all sounds[2]) in the "Causal Waters" during Dissolution. The movement of the Divine Tortoise is the symbol of Cosmic Elasticity by which finite forms, etc., are projected from the Supreme Form (representing the "strains"), and are again withdrawn into it. The factors of the Cosmic Elasticity are concurrent, but one factor may have a cyclic or rhythmic ascendency over the other factor. That is, in the cyclic life of the world the two factors appear alternately as the dominant and the recessive respectively. This being the meaning of evolution, we must hold that the Supreme Form as actual Reality is at the root of the process; and that it is a partial and incorrect view to say, with many of the western evolutionists, that the very lowest and simplest forms only are at the start, and that the higher and more complex forms are progressively evolved, with occasional reversions to lower forms, the tendency being on the whole towards the realization of perfect forms which perhaps cannot be realized under existing circumstances in finite time. This gives us a side view and a distorted view of the matter. The Supreme Form[3] and the higher Forms[4] are in the beginning as actual realities, who supervise, as *Chit-Shaktis* or Controlling Principles, the downward sweep which gradually involves the higher forms as well as the upward sweep which gradually evolves them. The Supreme Form or

[1] Kūrma. [2] Shabdas. [3] Īshvara.

[4] Such as the Prajāpatis, Mānasa-putras, Manus. It is interesting to note that practically all ancient traditions make History start with Manu. India, Manu; Egypt, Manes or M'na; Crete, Minos; Lydia, Manes; Phrygia, Manis; German, Mannus; and so on.

Īshvara[1] is thus given in the process not merely as an unrealized, infinitely distant Cosmic Ideal, but as a Reality present in, and controlling, the whole cosmic process.[2]

But the Supreme Form must not be offered as being alone the Reality. It is an aspect or Form of Reality, as Pure *Chidākāsha* is an aspect. The Full Reality[3] or "Fact" is *Chit* which, while remaining by its Power the Pure Ether which is *Sachchidānanda* or *Shiva*, yet evolves by its Power, the World-Mother, as the world of forms. The Supreme Form,[4] involves Itself into lower and lower forms and also evolves these again into higher and higher forms until in dissolution they are withdrawn into Itself to be projected again during creation. *Being-Consciousness-Bliss as both Power to Be* and *to Become or evolve is therefore the Reality-Whole.*[5] Time, Space and Causality are born in its womb;[6] that is, in itself It is *Mahākālī*, which means not only that *Mahākāla* or *Infinite* Time is the Power, but that She "stands upon" *Mahākāla* who, as the symbol depicts, is "at Her feet". She is the Mother as also the Consort of *Mahākāla*—a truth which is now understood. She produces Time, and having produced, plays with, and as, Time. Such play is Her play,[7] Her love-joying.[8] She is the Supreme Principle[9] evolving as, and transcending, the 36 Tattvas or Stages of involution

[1] In the scheme of "36 Tattvas" Īshvara-tattva is given a special meaning.

[2] The doctrine therefore does not favour any theory of "God in the Making." Shruti very often uses the epithets "sarvādhyaksha," etc., meaning that He is the Supreme Lord, Overseer, etc.

[3] Pūrna. [4] Īshvara.

[5] Pūrna (Parama-Kalā). This fundamental doctrine is evidenced by the association of Shiva-Shakti on all planes and their unity. They are never, even in dissolution, apart from one another.

[6] Kāla-Shakti is one of the Kanchukas. Chit as Power becomes in evolution Kāla-Shakti.

[7] Līlā. [8] Ramanānanda. [9] Pūrna-Tattva.

and evolution. The Pure[1] *Chit* of *Māyā-vāda* and also the eternal Whole with attributes[2] are both Her aspects: She is both above the factors[3] of the radical psycho-physical potential[4] and their support,[5] and is both without and with attributes constituted of such Factors.[6] She is the Supreme without aspects, as well as with aspects.[7] We cannot define Her by anyone of Her aspects. In Herself She is the Whole which manifests as the Universe of Parts existent within It.

---

[1] Nirguna.

[2] Nitya-Pūrna-guna-vishishta. The Chit of Vishishtādvaita, for instance.

[3] Gunātīta. [4] Prakriti Shakti. [5] Gunāshraya.

[6] Gunamayī. [7] Nishkala as well as Sakala.

CHAPTER VII

CONSCIOUSNESS[1] AND UNCONSCIOUSNESS[2]

In the previous Chapter we have dealt with *Chit* as Reality. But, whether tacitly or explicitly, we have, throughout the discussion, proceeded on the basis that there is no *Achit*[3] or unconsciousness, no "thing" independent of Consciousness. We must now briefly examine that basis. The previous discussion has already sufficiently prepared the ground for such examination.

Unconsciousness[3] may mean three things: (1) Objects known by Consciousness and yet believed to exist by their own right outside of Consciousness, *e.g.*, a block of stone we now see or touch; (2) objects believed to exist by their own right of which we have no consciousness at all; and (3) anything which is, or can be, made an object of knowing,[4] and which therefore can be distinguished from the "I" or subject or principle of knowing[5] as "This".[6] The second class of objects may be of two kinds: (*a*) Objects which, though themselves conscious, are yet outside and independent of our consciousness; and (*b*) objects which are outside and independent of our consciousness and are believed to be unconscious in themselves, *e.g.*, unknown material objects. Now Vedānta does not recognise the first two classes (1 and 2), as unconsciousness[3], though,

[1] Chit. [2] Achit is 'not Chit'. [3] Achit or Jada.
[4] *i.e.*, Jneya. [5] Aham, Jnāta. [6] Idam.

pragmatically, it may sometimes call them so. There is nothing outside and independent of Consciousness as such; nothing existing by a right which is not the supreme right of Consciousness-Being; hence there is no unconsciousness[1] in the first two senses. Consciousness should not, however, be taken to mean veiled, individualized Consciousness which means Consciousness so limiting itself as to have other "consciousnesses" and things existing outside its or their limits. Thus a block of stone even while it is being seen and touched by a Subject A, is believed to exist independently of A's Consciousness; and that belief is correct, and Realism is justified, in a certain sense. An unknown object, far away in the heavens, or far below in the interior of the earth for instance, may thus really exist outside of the consciousness of A or B. But still it never exists independent of Consciousness as such or Cosmic Consciousness which is the unveiled form or state of Consciousness. Even, with regard to A's consciousness, it is outside and alien in so far as A's consciousness is A's and not B's or C's; that is, in so far as it is veiled consciousness setting up the pragmatic walls of the sub-conscious and unconscious about it. Cosmic Consciousness is Consciousness *minus* these walls and partitions. Every object is in it, and of, it.

Consider an unknown star so far distant that its light neither reaches the eyes nor affects a sensitive photographic plate. It is thus outside of, and alien to, A's consciousness. But what part of it? That it is outside the inner ring of A's consciousness which is the accepted and recognised portion (commonly called the consciousness) is clear. But what about the outlying zone of gradually thickening and darkening sub-consciousness? Many things, not recognised

[1] Jada

in the "broad daylight" ring, can be by means of the "searchlight" discovered in the darker zones—in the realms of "twilight" for instance, which some western psychologists call the "fringe of consciousness". Now, is the unknown star here? In other words, has it really been known without our noticing it—recognising that it has been known? No; the searchlight does not discover it. Has it no place in the semi-conscious and sub-conscious zones then? We can never be sure that it has not.

The universe is an infinite stress-system. All centres, near or distant, are in constant interaction. For instance, if a lump of matter be suddenly created or annihilated now in space thousands of billions of miles away from us, that event will certainly affect the entire stress-system of the universe, of the earth and of A's organism for the matter of that. The effect may be inappreciably small, if the event in question be small, or too far away. But this only means that our sense-organs and perceptive machinery have been so constituted and adjusted that they ordinarily do not record disturbances (sound, heat, light and the like) which do not come within certain limits of intensity, duration, and so forth. But this does not mean either that the distant event has failed to influence our organism and machinery at all, or that, having influenced it, it has not contributed its share to the general, vague, massive feeling, partly semi-conscious and partly sub-conscious, which always clings to and constitutes a sort of "background" of all definite and recognised feelings or perceptions that we may have in life. In fact, it must follow *à priori* from our position in the cosmic stress-system (which has no "watertight compartments") that every move in this cosmic dance must produce a corresponding tremor in the chords of our feeling, and that the "clear notes" which one hears from those chords are always set in a background of half-tones and subtones—a general, massive indiscriminated, unrecognised chorus of notes—to which the movement of any corpuscle anywhere in boundless space must have borne its share. The clear note is gross;[1] this background of sub-notes represents the realm of subtle[2] variously graded. The first with the second is the concrete whole of feeling; it is an abstraction and unreality without the second.

Our searchlight does not commonly reveal everything in this background because it is a pragmatic searchlight, ordinarily so fitted and adjusted as to reveal objects within certain limits only. But by *Yoga* this searchlight can be made to approach as near as possible to perfection.[3] By its means the subtle background of our experiences can be made to come into clear relief. Thus a *yogī* may know by meditation[4] a subtle,[2] obstructed,[5] distant[6] object or event, because it was already in his feeling, though unperceived and unrecognised. To say that he discovers it not by exploring his own experience but by drawing upon a perfect bank of experience which is Cosmic Consciousness is only a different way of stating what has been above formulated. The difference between his own experience and that of the Lord and Mother is a difference of veiling or ignorance only; so that the same act (meditation and so forth) by which he "explores" his own experience and discovers a previously unkown element in it, is also the act by which he lifts the veil drawn over his own knowledge and assimilates his mind to that of the Lord.[7] His

[1] Sthūla. [2] Sūkshma.

[3] This includes what is now cultivated in the West as "X-ray vision" or as Clairvoyance, or "Psychometry," etc.

[4] Dhyāna. [5] Vyavahita. [6] Viprakrishta.

[7] Īshvara and Īshvarī according as we regard the Shiva or Shakti aspect of the Whole.

exploration becomes productive of new discoveries in proportion as this unveiling and assimilation progresses. Finally, when perfect assimilation is effected, his experience becomes the Experience of the Lord [1] which is Perfect *Veda* or *Veda* in the limit to which man's *Vedas* and even those of the *Rishis* are more or less distant or near approximations. To bring oneself in perfect rapport with the Perfect *Veda* is to *become* It.[2] Clairvoyance and like faculties in which things subtle, far distant in time and place, are perceived, is thus the recognition of the unrecognised in our experience, or otherwise stated, the projection on the lighted white screen of the seer's consciousness of the things that are in the Cosmic Consciousness. This being the position, it is clear that things (known or unknown) which are believed to exist objectively to, or independently of, A's consciousness, really do so if A's consciousness be restricted to what he and others accept as such ; but if A's consciousness, including the realms of the semi-conscious, sub-conscious and "unconscious," be so unveiled and lighted as to become identical with Cosmic Consciousness, then there is, or can be, nothing existing independently of it.

A material thing, for instance, is independent of the "normal" consciousness of A, both as regards the primary and the secondary qualities. But does it exist exactly as a copy of A's perception? No. A's cognitive faculty being limited and conditioned by his tendencies [3], he knows a part only of the thing as a whole, and that part too, to some extent in his own way. Even in perception each person

[1] Ishvara and Ishvarī according as we regard the Shiva or Shakti aspect of the Whole.

[2] And so it is said "To know Brahman is to be Brahman (Brahmavid Brahmaiva bhavati)". The kind of "Knowing" is jnāna svarūpa as contrasted with "Knowing in the subject-object relation" or Jnānakriyā.

[3] Sangskāras.

has his idiosyncrasy, his "personal equation". Thus A's perception is not exactly equal to B's; B's not exactly equal to C's. The inspection of the Scientist or the meditation[1] of the *yogī* gives a fuller picture; but these fuller pictures also more or less differ. The question therefore arises: What is the standard perception or the cognition of the thing in the perfectness of its qualities and relations? This standard perception may again relate either to the pure type[2] of the thing, or to *all* the details or particulars in their correlation. The former is the General[3] and the latter the Particulars.[4] Both are cognised by the Standard Mind which is the Lord Who, in respect of the former is called "Knower of all generals,"[5] and in respect of the latter, "Knower of all particulars."[6] Hence what exists really independently of A's normal consciousness is the Standard Thing as cognised by, and as existing in, the Lord.[7]

Common Realism objectifies A's perceptions; they are objective not only as regards their exciting cause or ground, but also as regards their primary and secondary qualities; but not simply in the sectional view which A, by reason of his limited capacities, takes of it, nor in the more or less "coloured" view which A by reason of his idiosyncrasy or special tendencies[8] forms of it. Even the scientist relying on his artificially extended capacities of perception has to neutralize these idiosyncrasies and so forth; hence his real thing is what is perceivable by a "mean or average" observer with the help of "perfect" instruments. Both are ideal conditions. The "average" man does not actually exist; and no earthly workshops can of course turn out "perfect" instruments. For the "mean" man with perfect instruments we substitute the Standard Mind, and though

---

[1] Dhyāna. [2] Jāti or Sāmānya or ākriti.
[3] Tanmātra. [4] Vishesha. [5] Sarvajna.
[6] Sarva-vit. Mundaka-Up., I, 1, 9; II, 2, 7. [7] Īshvara. [8] Sangskāras.

this latter may be beyond mathematical measurement (" Science is measurement "), it is within the possibility of realization, being the unveiled " that which we are in ourselves."[1]

Vedānta thus does not recognise unconsciousness[2] in the first two senses set forth above. Where it uses the term, it does so in the third sense, that is, the *known* represented by " This ".[3] Briefly, according to this conception, Illumination[4] is *Chit* or Consciousness, and that[5] which is made an object of the former or revealing is, as such, object, unconscious. The Mind[6] and the limited Self produced through its operation[7] are thus unconscious because both can be, and are, known as " this ". But, be it noted that, they as well as the so-called Matter are unconscious[8] only in this sense, that as being the object of the conscious Ego they are therefore as such object not conscious. Apart from this sense, and in themselves, they are consciousness.[9] The point is that *Chit*, makes unconsciousness of itself by making an "object" of itself. There is nothing but *Chit*, object or no object. There is even in fact no such thing as seeming or " reflex " consciousness.[10] There is nothing other than *Chit*, lucid or opaque, on which the " Light " of *Chit* can reflect itself, thus making that object to look like something luminous. To say that there is really an unconscious thing,[8] which looks as though it were conscious owing to its association with *Chit*, is Sāngkhyan Dualism, and in Monistic[11] doctrine no relic of that Dualism can be suffered to remain.

Mind[6] is at base really *Chit*, though, pragmatically, it may be called unconscious[8] on account of its being an

---

[1] Svarūpa. [2] Achit, Jada.
[3] Idam. See Shārīraka Bhāshya, Upodghāta.
[4] Prakāsha. [5] Vimarsha. [6] Antahkarana. [7] As Ahangkāra.
[8] Jada. [9] Achit. [10] Chidabhāsa. [11] Advaita.

"object" of knowledge, and its having a varying veil, measure and movement. It never ceases to be other than *Chit*. It is *Chit* limiting and defining itself as Mind as distinguished from Matter,[1] for instance, which is *Chit* limiting and defining itself in Matter.[2] Vedānta does not countenance any essential dualism of Mind and Matter. It maintains an unmoving, unveiled, unmeasured aspect of *Chit* as well as a moving, veiled, measured aspect. The latter is Mind, Matter, Space, Motion and so forth. Hence it does not hesitate to conceive Mind as something having a variable measure (sometimes expanding, sometimes contracting), a variable structure owing to the variable mixing of the three Factors[3] of the Principle of Contraction and a variable movement even in Space (as in Perception, and so forth).[4] It is really *Chit* moving in *Chit*, existing in *Chit* and functioning in *Chit*. If there be Extension, Inertia, Movement, Impenetrability, etc. (the usual marks of Matter) in the world, it is because *Chit* has so defined itself as to be extended, inert, mobile, impenetrable and so forth. Western philosophers sometimes look askance at thought-movement and so forth, because they hold to the disparity of Mind and Matter. And, usually, they do not distinguish between Mind and Consciousness. Consciousness as such does not come and go, but Mind as psychic process does.

There has been, both in India and elsewhere, much controversy about the question whether there may be "unconscious ideation" or unconscious experience. It seems hardly open to doubt, however, that many commonplaces of experience as well as many "abnormal," extraordinary and "occult" experiences cannot be satisfactorily

---

[1] Antahkaranāvachchhinna-chaitanya.

[2] Prameyāvachchhinna-chaitanya. As Vedānta-paribhāshā defines.

[3] Shvetāshvatara, Up., III, 18; Brih.-Up., IV, 3, 7: Chhānd.-Up., VIII, 6, 5.

[4] Guna.

accounted for at all except by maintaining that there is a "normal" or "threshold" line of consciousness in man in respect of which his curve of experience is partly above and partly below. Habit, Memory, Instinctive thinking and action, dreaming which have been said to involve repressed, unsatisfied desires, and the like, as also many "uncommon" experiences presuppose a continuous curve of experience part of which is "subliminal," and which, therefore, like a floating ice-berg is not all that it looks. The explanation by "cerebral vestiges," without having recourse to subliminal depths, is not sufficient and cannot cover all cases. The brain may not be a necessary organ of the mind, and in so far as it is an organ, its stresses may correspond to, run parallel to, without wholly causing, the stresses of the mind. Vedânta not being afraid of Matter, is not, therefore, afraid of the brain. It is prepared to maintain a real interaction between the brain and the mind; which is not simply a parallelism between psychosis and neurosis. But still the mind may have a life larger than, and in some cases, and to a certain degree, independent of the brain. The "cerebralist," on the other hand, makes the life of the brain larger than, and independent of, that of the mind. Thus brain-activities may go on without there being accompanying mental states; and brain-vestiges may remain without there being actual mental "seeds," and tendencies.[1]

A stronger position is that mental states, after their intensities or interest sink below a certain "mark," persist as subliminal forms and stresses which are tendencies,[1] and when these tendencies press themselves beyond a certain mark, they again become "conscious" presentations.

---

[1] Sangskâras. See Chap. on Consciousness and Brain, P.N.M.'s Introduction to Vedânta Philosophy.

Between a presentation and a "tendency," the difference is really one of degree; the latter is a veiled or subtle kind of presentation. That certain "mark" is approximately determined by the needs and interests of "normal" life—it slightly varies with different people, and can be varied considerably by hypnosis, trance, *yoga*, etc. Thus a man searching into the subliminal depths of his consciousness may "see" the subtle presentations.[1] The transition from "normal" consciousness to "unconsciousness" is not abrupt—there are different shades according to degrees of veiling. The so-called "sub-conscious" and "unconscious" are only modes of consciousness which cannot be restricted to what little may be practically accepted in the indefinable vastness of actual personal experience. So one may not be prepared to admit the sub-conscious and unconscious as orders of experience different from the conscious. They are the veiled, ignored, non-accepted, unnoticed zones in consciousness itself. Thus the Shāstra takes up a position which is not either that of the "cerebralist" who would confine experience to "normal" consciousness only and explain memory, habit and so forth by brain-vestiges or brain-dispositions, or that of the common type of the philosopher of the Unconscious who, while admitting experiences below the threshold line, regards such experiences as really sub-conscious, thus setting the threshold line as the boundary of consciousness itself (his consciousness being, therefore, not other than "normal," pragmatic consciousness which is but a section of actual consciousness). As the cerebralist in the Vedāntic view commits the mistake of regarding mental life (or experience) as a structure raised on the wider and more enduring basis of cerebral life, so the "sub-conscious thinker" is in error in regarding consciousness as a structure raised on the wider, deeper and

[1] See Pātanjala Sūtra.

more abiding basis of sub-conscious experience. Consciousness as *Chit* is the basis, and there is no other. *Chit* is not "normal" or pragmatic only.

In the *Sāngkhya* Philosophy, experience,[1] being a mode of the Psycho-Physical Principle[2] (which is unconscious,[3]) is also unconscious;[3] and it is only when the Unconscious "reflects" itself on, or catches the "reflection" of the Conscious[4], that it becomes conscious experience. Thus experience has two forms—conscious and unconscious, of which the former is a reflex or imposed form. This apparently comes near to the position of the western "subconscious thinker," but, fundamentally, it is a different position inasmuch as its consciousness is not a variable "accident" of experience only, but an independent Principle existing by its own right. Thus though experience may be conscious or unconscious (as the western sub-conscious thinker holds), yet Consciousness is neither a proprium nor an accident of anything other than itself. It is eternal,[5] changeless, pure, though it may variously reflect the character and complexion of the mind[6] with which it may be associated.[7]

This position is only a "stopping short" of the final position which is taken up by Vedānta. Analysing experience we find Illumination[8] and illuminated[9]; *Chit* which reveals and the "Stress" which is revealed. Experience as joining together these two aspects is the Fact; each is an abstraction considered by itself. Now, *Sāngkhya* makes a substance of each of the two abstractions. The underlying

[1] Buddhi-vyāpāra.

[2] Prakriti which is a Real independent of Consciousness as the Selves or Purushas.

[3] Achit. Sāmkhya-Kārikā, 11.

[4] Pūrusha which is Chit.

[5] Nitya.

[6] Buddhi, etc.

[7] See Volumes on "Reality" and "Mind".

[8] Prakāsha.

[9] Vimarshā.

principle of this procedure is this: Illumination[1] cannot make an "object" of itself; on the other hand, an "object" cannot be its own revealer[2] or cogniser. In the Vedāntic view it is a plausible principle without being a valid one; and if man did not normally deal with pragmatic Fact-sections or abstractions, he would have discovered that the principle is invalid.

The *Bhatta*[3] School of interpretation in the *Pūrva-mīmangsā* (of Jaimini) also proceeded upon this principle and conceived the *Ātman* as possessing a dual character—being conscious in one part, and unconscious in another. The *Ātman* was compared to a glowworm which now shines and now does not. *Atman* was *chit* as knower[2] and *achit* as known, as object,[4]: *chit* as seer[5] and *achit* as seen.[6] *Sāngkhya*, as we have seen, stows apart what are thus juxtaposed and made to co-exist in one and the same substance. Vedānta identifies in essence the Illuminator[2] and the Illuminated[4]; the *Bhatta* school differentiates them and places them side by side like the two seeds in a grain of gram; *Sāngkhya* takes them quite asunder. The first is for non-difference;[7] the second for difference, non-difference[8]; the third for difference.[9] The invalidity of the second and third positions lies in this: the revealer[2] does not make a revealed[4] of itself; nor does the revealed[4] become its own revealer.[2] It is *Chit* simply which by Its Power is the Revealer[2] as well as becomes the Revealed.[4] By its power, or rather, as Power.[10] It is thus polarised.

[1] Prakāsha. [2] Prakāshaka.

[3] See Shloka-vārttika (Shūnya-vāda, Ātmavāda) of Kumārila-Bhatta.

[4] Prakāshya. [5] Drishi. [6] Drishya.

[7] Abheda. [8] Bhedābheda. [9] Bheda.

[10] Commonly we speak of the Power of Consciousness but Power is in itself Consciousness. And so the Devī or Mother-Power is Chidrūpinī.

The *Prabhākara* school of Pūrva-Mīmāngsā, as also the Nyāya-Vaisheshika School, makes the *Ātman* unconscious[1] in itself, its consciousness[2] being a separable property which is existent in it only when certain conditions are fulfilled, and which is non-existent otherwise. Just as a leaf may be the support of a particular tint of colour which may not always exist in it, so the *Ātman* is the support of the quality of consciousness.[3] In dreamless slumber, for example, there is (it is supposed) no consciousness as evidenced by the subsequent recollection—"I was asleep; I knew nothing." This, however. is a mistake. "I knew nothing" means of course "I knew nothing in particular". During slumber there is this positive knowledge of knowing nothing in particular, and also, as the *Shruti* maintains, a veiled consciousness of amorphic Bliss.[4] As regards the general position that *Ātman* is unconscious,[1] and becomes conscious only conditionally, that is when linked up with mind and its object, we need observe merely this that in this position *Chit* is recognised only as "normal or pragmatic" consciousness which is a section only; that this pragmatic consciousness, which is one of "interesting" particulars, is mistaken for consciousness as such, so that when in slumber particulars or forms do not exist, it is thought that consciousness as such also does not exist. Not perceiving that the essence of Substance-Energy is *Chit*, it wrongly makes an attribute[5] of *Chit* which sometimes inheres and sometimes does not in a Substance[6] which in itself is different

---

[1] Achit. [2] Chaitanya. [3] Jnāna or Chaitanya.

[4] Ānanda or Sukham. Māndūkya, Up., I, 5. It is said in the sūtra "Happily I slept and knew nothing. That there was bliss is shown by the recollection of it on waking. For there can only be remembrance of that of which there has been experience (anubhava)".

[5] Guna. [6] Dravya.

from its attribute,[1] and is unconscious[2] when the attribute[3] does not exist in it.[4]

But is the essence of Substance-Energy *Chit*? Cannot *Chit* be an attribute[1] only? It need not be an "epiphenomenon" a "by-product," as the Materialists and *Lokayatas* (followers of Chārvāka) say, of Matter. It may not either be a separable phenomenon like the consciousness[5] of the First Standard *Ātman*. But should we not regard it as a phenomenon still—as distinguished from the Noumenon or Thing-in-Itself? Even the *Yogāchāra Bauddha* to whom the universe (subjective and objective) is merely a beginningless succession of transient[6] "pulses" of experience,[7] as modern psychologists might call them, and various grouping or clustering together of such pulses[8]; who breaks up the apparently continuous flow of "Self"-consciousness into a series of rapidly succeeding but discrete apperceptions (perceptions of Self or "I"), and distinguishes this series[8] from the series of object-perceptions[9] (in the "mind" or outside it)[9];—even he would not make these pulses of experience, succeeding one another and grouping together, the Substance or Reality as many western Empiricists have done. No "thing" exists of course as other than the knowing[7] (this is denial of Realism); but even the knowing does not "exist"—that is, the knowing[7] is of, and in, the Void.[10] The *Vaibhāshika* and *Sautrāntika Bauddhas* believed in things independent of experience (the latter making them directly perceived,[11]

---

[1] Guna. [2] Achit. [3] Chit-Guna.

[4] In Sāngkhya-Vedānta, Ātmā is Nitya-Chaitanya; in Nyāya-Vaisheshika, it is Āgantuka-Chaitanya.

[5] Jnāna. [6] Kshanika. [7] Vijnāna.

[8] Ālaya-vijnāna. [9] Pravritti-vijnāna.

[10] Shūnya. [11] Pratyaksha.

the former making them indirectly or inferentially known); but here also, the Basis of things is not *Chit* but the Void.[1]

But what is it really? What constitutes the essence of Thinghood? Consider again a block of stone. It is seen, touched, pressed, lifted, pushed and pulled, and so on. We have just a group of "experiences" succeeding one another—the experience[2] as above explained. Is it merely the aggregate of these actual experiences and certain others that may be possible? Either it is or it is not. If it is, then the experiences[3] coming and going in a "medium" or "ether" or *Chit*, make that block of stone nothing but a structure of experiencing[3] raised upon the basis of *Chit*. Reflection will show that the succeeding "pulses" of feeling require at least two permanent Principles: a self-distinguishing Subject called the "witness"[4] which notes the pulses as coming and going, as before and after, as related in this way or that, and which therefore must not itself come and go, be past and future, be related in this way or that. To know for instance that A, B, C have succeeded one another, there must be a Knower who has remained above the succession so as to correlate them according to a certain temporal scheme. He must abide and witness, and distinguish himself from the changing phenomena. This "I"[5] or Witness cannot itself be broken into rapidly succeeding pulses of "I" feeling;[6] for, who knows and says that the "I" feelings are succeeding? We require a Self behind these fleeting "selves". Who, again, remembers that when C is, A and B are no more but that they

---

[1] See Sarva-darshana-sanggraha. [2] Vijnāna. [3] Vijnānas.

[4] Sākshi Chaitanya. Mundaka-Up., III. 1. 1; Shvetāshvatara-Up., IV. 6.

[5] Aham. [6] Aham-pratyaya.

were before?[1] To say that the Series[2] knows and remembers itself, is to forget that what actually exists as experience[3] at any moment is not a series but a particular experience[3] and that the series does not, and cannot, exist as series except to a Witness who is not in, and of, the series. To say again that the last term of the series, that is C, as an actual experience[3] remembers, sums up and judges the past experience,[3] is to assume that past and non-existing experience[3] can yet exist in a manner in the present pulse, C; that C can somehow involve a thought of B and A which are no more.

But suppose this assumption is correct; C does remember and judge A and B. But what is this C—this so-called present "pulse"? If we do not pragmatize and ignore the given whole of experience, we shall see that C is not a pulse at all, but the indefinable, alogical universe of experience, (*i.e.*, Fact) which, in order to suit our practice and our theory, we are cutting up into "pulses" coming and going, judging and remembering, and so on. Experience is an indefinable universe in which we accept certain aspects or sections only, and in which those sections are correlated by us or by our tendencies[4] temporally, spatially and causally, thus giving us thoughts and things succeeding one another in time, co-existing with one another in space, and causally affecting one another. "Pulses" are thus born of "ignorance". In fact we have the continuum of experience; and this continuum, which in an alogical way whilst remaining such continuum, yet, as *Chit*, variously stresses into correlated forms. This *Chit* as Continuum is at the back

---

[1] In other words who is responsible for Smriti, Pratyabhignā, Anuvyavasāya, etc.?

[2] Vijnāna-santāna. [3] Vijnāna. [4] Sangskāra.

of all pulses, and all experiences[1] which Buddhistic Philosophy has often looked up to as the great Void. Hence the fleeting-states or pulses to be known and remembered as such require not only a permanent Witness[2] but a permanent Continuum also.[3]

Of these two the latter is the more fundamental; because while the Witness is indispensable to experience treated as a logical order (*i.e.*, in the thinking and reviewing of experience), the latter is indispensable to experience both as logical and as alogical. As a matter of fact, in intuitive, as distinguished from thinking and judging, life, the Self as "Subject" is often in abeyance; the Subject-witness presupposes a thing or object witnessed—that is, a polarity.[4] In non-polar[5] experience the Subject-witness as witness therefore need not exist.

Thus we cannot according to Vedānta do without *Chit* as a substantive background, even if we agree to regard a block of stone as a cluster of actual and possible "sensations". Sensations are the outcome of a threefold ignorance and abstraction. Sensations are abstractions from perceptions which are relatively more concrete; perceptions are abstractions from the entire universe of experience at a given moment; and the universe of experience at a given moment is a temporal cross-section and abstraction of the real "Fact" which is *Chit* as Power stressing and constituting as such an indefinable, alogical Whole involving Time, Space, and so forth.

But let us, in the alternative, regard the stone as not an aggregate of actual and possible sensations, but as the objective ground and cause of sensations (as Realism holds). But how can we be sure that the "objective ground" really exists? We firmly believe that it does, but evidently the

[1] Vijnānas. [2] Sākshi Chaitanya. [3] Chidākāsha.
[4] Dvaita. [5] Advaita.

belief also is a part of our experience and thought, and, therefore, cannot carry us beyond to anything outside and independent of experience and thought.[1] But then why should we believe that which is not the fact? And there are marks which indicate that the belief is well-grounded. Perceptions and "objective experiences" by reason of their independence of our wish and insistence on our attention, and so forth, constitute an altogether different order pointing to an objective order of realities. Their relative permanence, independence in being and becoming, resistance and insistence, objectification and localization, vividness and interest, and the like are the important distinguishing marks, of which the first four are the most important.

We may concede, without further discussion, that if Solipsism and Subjectivism cannot explain away these marks or explain them satisfactorily, on the other hand it is difficult to make an out-and-out Subjectivist answer any outside knocks or calls once he has bolted all his doors and windows and locked himself in.

So a block of stone is there permanently, unlike a feeling or idea in the mind; it is there though we may wish it away; it is and changes according to its own laws; it resists our movement and will; it thrusts itself upon our mind when the senses and attention are near and not otherwise engaged; it is more vivid and interesting than a corresponding image in the mind; and so on. Hence it exists by its own right. It does; but where and how? Its existence is, in some essential respects, independent of the particular Centre's experience and thought; but can it exist independently of Experience or *Chit* as such? No. It exists and is a mode of Perfect *Chit* in the fulness of its relations, which a limited Centre knows gradually and partially—that is,

---

[1] As was argued by the Vijnāna-vādins.

accepting in part but ignoring as a whole. The ignored realms are the realms of the "objective"; every imperfect perception is an act of partial owning; perfect perception is perfect owning in which the distinction between subjective and objective, as we have it, disappears. But why should not a thing exist apart from Experience, imperfect or perfect.

This, for long, has been a point of dispute between the so-called "Idealists" and "Realists". Vedānta is Idealism in so far as it makes Being or *Sat* identical with Consciousness,[1] and that, in its essence, the same as Bliss.[2] Vedānta is Realism in so far as it makes objects or things independent of a specialized Subject's modes of consciousness: a thing is not thus in the Mind, it is actually outside it. Matter is thus every whit as real as Mind. Both, however, are in, and of, *Chit*.

These following grounds are offered by Vedānta as the main lines of proof:

(*a*) No rational theory of perception is possible without postulating essential identity between the Self and Matter. Perception is an act of "owning," and there can be no owning where the object is absolutely foreign to the Subject. Attempts to explain the "agreement" between "Chit" and "Matter" by the theories of Occasional Cause, Pre-established Harmony, Parallelism and Materialism have led either to an evasion of the real problem, or to failure to solve it (as in the case of gross Materialism). In the Indian view the only possible explanation is by a doctrine which makes Spirit or Consciousness in the sense of *Chit* (and not in the sense of Mind[3]) the ground as well as the activity of both Mind and Matter. Such fundamental identity between Mind and Matter being given, we can well conceive a direct interaction between the two; as also their

[1] Chit. [2] Ānanda. [3] Antahkarana.

operation according to certain fundamental laws which apply to Matter as well as to Mind.[1] Thus Mind[1] being acted on by Matter through the senses *reacts* by going out to where Matter is, "envelops" it and makes a "mental double" of it in Space;[2] we can conceive even the assimilation of one to the other, and the transformation (in part, generally) of one into the other. It is, therefore, not Materialism to assert that the mind[1] moves, expands or contracts like matter; and that the one kind of Substance-Energy is convertible into the other.[3] The difference between Mind and Matter is this that whilst the Root-Substance-Energy (*Chit*), appearing or evolving as Mind[1], appears in a comparatively subtler form and operates according to laws which restrict to a lesser extent its essential nature[4] (indicated in Play[5]), it appears in a grosser or cruder (*i.e.*, less elastic and dynamic) form as Matter, and operates according to the laws which restrict to a greater extent its Being-Consciousness-Bliss. The latter form and the latter operation being only less perfect (as regards expression and dynamic "coefficient") than the former, the difference between Mind and Matter is a difference in degree and "stage of evolution" only; so that Matter is comparatively "rigid" or "dense" Mind, and the Laws of Matter are comparatively "stereotyped," inelastic forms of the Laws of Mind.

(*b*) The action of Will on Matter (directly or through Matter organised as the brain) is inexplicable without such essential identity being given. Causation or activity in its

---

[1] Antahkarana.

[2] See the Vedānta view of Perception described in "Power as Mind". See also P.N.M.'s "Introduction to Vedānta Philosophy".

[3] Cf. Chhāndogya-Up., VI, 5, 1, etc., describing how the "finest elements" of the food eaten go to constitute "Manas," etc.

[4] Being (Sat), Consciousness (Chit), Bliss (Ānanda). [5] Līlā.

fundamental nature is not easily understood; still it is easier to conceive causation or interaction between two similar forms of Substance-Energy than between dissimilar forms. Modern scientific explanations of the interaction between Mind and Brain tend either (1) to deny all causal activity to Consciousness (making the chain of physical causation a "closed curve," like that of the evolution of the radical Psychophysical Potential[1] in the Sāngkhyan doctrine which though denying direct action of the consciousness[2] on such Potential,[1] yet granted the existence of a kind of "catalytic action"), or (2) to "parallelism" which, in its turn, tends either to Materialism or to Spiritualism.

(*c*) To these ordinary psychic phenomena must now be added others[3] which many investigators in the West have recognised and called *Parapsychic*[4] that is, mental facts, well established, which cannot be explained by the known laws of Physiology and Psychology. These phenomena, now investigated under the three heads of *hypnotoidal*, *magnetoidal* and *spiritoidal*,[5] seem to point to the essential affinity between Mind and Matter, and between Vital Force and each of the other two—an affinity which shows Matter-Energy, Vital Energy and Thought-Energy in an ascending order of dynamism,[6] and, therefore, of fundamentality.

Telepathy or Thought-transference, "Psychometry" (which Dr. Maxwell[7] defines as "the faculty possessed by certain persons of placing themselves in relation, either

---

[1] Prakriti. [2] Purusha.

[3] For long studied and experimented upon in India.

[4] Prof. Emile Boirac, La Psychologie inconnue.

[5] Bhūta-Shakti, Prāna Shakti, Mānasī Shakti. [6] Shakti.

[7] Quoted by Maurice Maeterlinck in his "The Unknown Guest" (p. 49), 3rd. Ed.

spontaneously or, for the most part, through the intermediary of some object, with unknown and often very distant things and people"), "Levitation" (or the lifting of material objects in the air without touching or handling them), "Materialization" (or the condensation of "Psychic forces" into apparent grossness), "Exteriorization" (or the projection out of the body of the motor and sensitive forces), "Dissociation" (or the act of separating certain psychical elements from the body through psycholgical methods and processes), "Astral Projection" (or the act of projecting by the action of the will, consciously or unconsciously, the human "double"), and many other phenomena, now under serious investigation in the West, require for their explanation a basis which cannot be supplied by the "orthodox" views on Spirit, Life and Matter (making each separate from the others and each being regarded as consisting of discrete units only). If Spirit and Matter be ontologically or substantially distinct, it cannot be understood or even imagined how a person touching a material object (say, a flower or a sheet of paper) may leave "the impress of his personality" on it, which that object may bear for an indefinite length of time, and which makes it possible for a "medium" to "read" the whole history of that person, and of others connected with him, by merely handling the object once touched by him. It is supposed that the object touched by a person becomes "impregnated with his fluid" (or, as Dr. Osty[1] says, "the object can latently register the human personalities which have touched it"). But what is this human "fluid," and how can a "material" object be impregnated with it, and carry it for an indefinite length of time? And how can the "register" thus kept by the object be deciphered again by a proper Subject? The

[1] Author of *Lucidité et intuition*.

Dualistic view of Mind and Matter fails to go to the root of the matter in trying to answer these questions. A sheet of paper so touched may be likened to a gramophone record where a whole musical composition lies latently registered; but there the forces making the "register" are physical forces, and the mechanism by which that record may be deciphered is also a physical mechanism. We have not, therefore, to leave the physical plane at any step. But the system of ideas (conscious and subconscious), thoughts, feelings, desires, and so forth, of a person which constitute his personality are not physical forces; and these are the first link of the causal chain; at the other end of the chain we have the "latent register" in the sheet of paper touched; the act of touching is an intermediate link in the chain, and it means a vital motor activity. In this case, it appears that Vital Force[1] negotiates between "Soul"[2] and Matter[3] (*viz.*, the sheet of paper). Assuming such Power[4] is established, how can this be understood from a dualistic or pluralistic position?

Then, again, in what is now called "Psycho dynamism"—exemplified in such phenomena as levitation, materialization and the like—we must admit an essential identity between the forces which constitute matter and those which constitute the *psyche* or soul: the moment which we see at the outer end (*e.g.*, in the table raised in the air) presupposes at the other and inner end also something which is analogous to movement. And if that which is at the two ends are each capable of movement, it is reasonable to suppose that they are similar, substantially and dynamically—that is, as being and as energy.

---

[1] Prāna. [2] Antahkarana. [3] Jada.

[4] In India generically described as *Siddhi*. A considerable portion of the Tantras deals with these supernormal faculties. This so-called "Magic" is an extension of normal faculty and natural.

These "parapsychic" or metapsychic (often called "occult") facts as well as the facts of common psychology require for their explanation a basis, deeper and wider than what we have above indicated. They presuppose not merely affinity between Spirit and Life and between Life and Matter (1) as regards substance, and (2) as regards dynamic operation; they presuppose at their very root a universal Spiritual Stuff or Substance-Energy which, while evolving as a system of correlated Spirit-centres, Life-centres and Matter-centres remains as the Mother Energy-Stuff, sustaining, nourishing and connecting all its numberless evolutes. The Mother Substance-Energy does not cease to be Itself in evolving as an infinite system of centres: the centres would not be centres if it were so; and, no unfoldment of the centres and no interaction among them would be possible if it were so. The Mother Substance-Energy perpetually abides as the universal background of sustenance and evolution and interaction for every centre, whether "material" or otherwise. Behind and overlapping the "Self" of man, the cell of a plant and the "sphere" of a material corpuscle, there is, therefore, the unbounded and unfathomed Being-Energy or *Mahāmāyā* which has evolved those centres, and which remains as an infinite reservoir of energy of all these centres to draw upon in their being as well as in their becoming or evolving. The part of the energy which a material or a living centre ordinarily stands for and uses, constitutes, from the standpoint of that particular centre, its kinetic energy. The infinite reservoir at the back or root of its being is, for all common purposes, latent, dormant. And this infinite dynamic potential has been called *Kundalinī Shakti*, (or, cosmically speaking, *Mahā-kundalinī Shakti*,) in the Shākta Tantras of the *Āgama Shāstra*. Thus conceived, not only the human body, but every form of centre (say, an atom of Hydrogen) must have *Kundalinī Shakti* given at the "heart" or base of its being, its radical centre.[1]

Not to speak of parapsychic or occult phenomena, even such a commonplace as an act of perception or volition, cannot be probed to the root without revealing the background of the Mother Substance-Energy in which and of which the perceiving agency and the object perceived are both imbedded and interlinked centres; which makes it possible for the energy of the one to pass to the other, and "assimilate" that other to itself (which is the essence of perception).

In the case "psychometry" through an intermediary object (for example, a sheet of paper touched by a person not now present), the suggestion put forward by Dr. Osty is probably well-founded: "This object has no other function than to allow the medium's sensitiveness to distinguish a definite force from among the innumerable forces that assail it." The obvious implication, in the words of Maurice Maeterlinck,[2] is this: "It seems more and more certain that, as the cells of an immense organism, we are connected with everything that exists by an inextricable network of vibrations, waves, influences or nameless, numberless and uninterrupted fluids. Nearly always, in nearly all men, everything carried along by these invisible wires falls into the depths of the unconscious and passes unperceived, which does not mean that it remains inactive. But sometimes an exceptional circumstance . . . suddenly reveals to us, by the vibrations and the undeniable action of one of these wires, the existence of the infinite network."

The infinite network we have (following Shākta Vedāntism) otherwise expressed as the Universal Stress-system

---

[1] Mūlādhāra Chakra. [2] The Unknown Guest.

in which all objects, spiritual or "material," great or small, are centres. A material atom, an organic cell, a Self[1] or Person thus represents a definite but not isolated strain-and-stress-centre.

But this strain-and-stress centre must be in, and of, something. That something-in-itself must be unbounded, unfathomable Being.[2] It must be Power (*Shakti* manifesting as Soul-Energy, Vital Energy and Matter Energy, since the essence of everything is in its dynamism.[3] And this Power must be fundamental in relation to Thought-Energy, Vital-Energy and Matter-Energy.

And that fundamental Power is *Chit*, an untranslatable word, commonly translated as Consciousness. The so-called *Achit* or Unconscious, arises from a pragmatic limitation of *Chit*, from the veiling or ignoring of *Chit* by itself, thus concealing its essential nature of Being-Consciousness and Bliss. (*a*) All objects must be necessarily known and conceived in terms of "modes" of consciousness, or to express it more rigidly, as particular strain-forms in Consciousness; the opposite is conceivable. This, however, does not mean that things must be known as subjective "representations" or ideas. (*b*) All objects at the root are Power; and Power must be known and conceived as Consciousness-Power (such as we experience in volition, attention, mental effort and the like); the opposite is, in reality, inconceivable. "Blind" physical energy, "unconscious" vital or mentative force have been supposed to exist and work; but they cannot be actually conceived as other than Consciousness-Power. Blind and unconscious forces are born of veiling and abstraction. (*c*) Perception and volition involve a belief in the Not-Self existing by its own right; the Subject perceiving

[1] Jīva. [2] Bhūman.

[3] In Shākta doctrine Power or Shakti in the ultimate Real of which the Universe is the manifestation.

requires at the other "pole" an independent Object perceived; and the agent acting requires not only a patient acted upon, but an independent agent reacting. This is Realism, and it is perfectly valid. But Realism does *not* require that the Not-Self and the independent agent must be essentially different from, or dissimilar to, the Self or Conscious Power operating in, and as, ourselves. On the contrary, if we could lay aside the pragmatic attitude which we commonly take in our actions and perceptions, we should discover that the actual implication of our realistic belief is that the external agent is a centre of Consciousness-Power such as we are ourselves. It is our practical attitude in relation to them which makes some of them appear to be, or present themselves to us, as unintelligent, unconscious, blind—in fact, as devoid of Consciousness[1] and Bliss[2] and its expression, Play.[3] Commonly we are *not* interested in taking them as forms of Consciousness-Power,[4] as incarnations of Bliss[2] and as capable of Play.[3] In relation to our practice,[5] and therefore factor conditioning karma[6] which underlies it, they have put on a veil and a disguise. This pragmatic view of things has naturally affected Science and Philosophy in a way which they have not found it easy to shake off.

To Vedāntism, and the *Shākta* form of it in particular every object down to the material particle is a Divinity or *Devatā*, which means that it is a form of Conscious-Power, whose being is Joy and whose life or activity is Play.[3] A particular thing, A, by virtue of its position in the Stress-system[6] in relation to another thing, B, may behave as though it were devoid of Consciousness, Bliss and Play (*i.e.*, free, spontaneous action); but this does not mean

---

[1] Chit. [2] Ānanda. [3] Līlā. [4] Chit-Shakti.
[5] Vyavahāra. [6] Adrishta which stands for past karma.

either that A is in itself (that is, irrespectively of its relation to B in the Stress-system) devoid of these, *or* that it is necessarily devoid of them in relation to a third centre, say, C. C may recognise it as *Devatā* while B does not. Whether A will manifest itself as Consciousness,[1] Bliss[2] and Play[3] or not, will, in fact, depend upon two co-efficients or determinants: its past action[4]—assigning its place in the cosmic stress-system, in Space, Time and Causal chain, and tending to hold it there[5]; and its play[3]—changing or tending to change its place in the cosmic stress-system, therefore tending to move and evolve it.[6] Now, A's position[4] can be regarded from three points of view: (1) A's position considered in relation to a Perfect Centre, that is, its position as it is in the cosmic stress-system as a whole; (2) its position in relation to its own point of view (therefore, more or less limited or restricted); and (3) its position in relation to B, C, D, and others. It is obvious that the position[4] in relation to A, B, C, D, etc., are different. So that while to A, B, D and others, A's being appears as "dead," "inert" and "material," it is possible that to C, it may appear as Life, Mind, Consciousness and Bliss including Play.[7] C, therefore, may have a truer and deeper intuition of its being.

Adrishta[8] is static power in the sense that though it may also move things, it moves them in a fixed, determined line; Play[3] is dynamic power in the sense that it tends to

---

[1] Chit. [2] Ānanda.

[3] Līlā. [4] Adrishta determining present condition. See Text *post*.

[5] This in its statical aspect is Dik Shakti.

[6] Kāla Shakti of which that which moves things on or the vital urge is a component.

[7] Prānamaya, Manomaya, Vijnānamaya and Ānandamaya (including Līlāmaya).

[8] Compare it with "Niyati," one of the 36 Tattvas (See "Garland of Letters"—The Tattvas).

make things depart from any line that may have been predetermined for them by the total assemblage of conditions. It implies, therefore, freedom, or power transcending the causal chain of necessity. Every object in creation possesses the power, since it is an incarnation of the Supreme Power which is Being, Consciousness, Bliss and Play.[1] The result, accordingly is, that the world does not move in an absolutely fixed line; and the so-called causal chain of necessity is an outcome of abstract analysis of physical and *quasi*-physical science.

In its actual manifestations, that Power has, however, chosen to subject itself to varying limitations, or as it has been often put, clothed itself with "sheaths"[2] of varying density. This is a precondition of the evolution of a world of infinitely varied forms, or as we have put it, a system of countless strain-and-stress centres. There would be no such world of varied forms if the Fundamental Power were to remain undifferentiated and undivided, or else, divided as a system of undifferentiated points only.

Evolution and history have become possible because the Power has manifested itself as Centres. A Centre is, Cosmic Power or Potency condensed into a point[3] in a certain stage of evolution: it therefore presupposes a relative disposition or ratio of latency and patency of the Perfect Potency,[3] and readiness to create, whose evolute it is. Thus in a given centre, A, the ratio of latency and patency of Power may be different from that in another centre, B. Apart from this ratio, A = B = Bindu = Perfect Power. It is the ratio which constitutes the difference. The ratio may be otherwise expressed as the ratio of determination[4] and freedom.[5] In every object these two factors co-operate. Now, centres may be arranged

---

[1] Sachchidānandamayī and Līlāmayī. [2] Kosha or Kanchuka.
[3] Bindu. See *ante*. [4] Adrishta. [5] Līlā. Or Karma.

in order of evolution or progress according as the latter factor prevails over the former; in other words, according as freedom or self-determination prevails over "other determination". Centres are higher in which spontaneous activity[1] is more manifested, and determination[2] less insistent. Matter, Life and Mind constitute, from this standpoint, an hierarchy, because the co-efficient of free play[1] is more and more manifested as we pass from the first to the second, and from the second to the third. The "matter" of Physical Science appears to be wholly determined without the least suggestion of freedom:[1] but this is only an approximate truth. According to Vedānta freedom to act[1] must be there in it because the free *Chit* is its essence. The very smallness of the atom seems to be a strength instead of a weakness: its energies are vast, and its atomic motions incredibly rapid. It also is a world. If its behaviour seems restrained and uniform and lacking in self-conscious direction, it is not because it is in fact unconscious mechanism but because the *Chit* which is its essence has freely so determined to present itself. Whatever be the form it takes, self-determination is free determination.

Moreover, a lump of matter, with reference to our pragmatic attitude and factor conditioning action,[2] appears as (approximately) dead, inert and determined; but we are not permitted to generalize and say that it must be so (1) to itself, or (2) to other beings whose attitudes, tendencies[2] and factor conditioning action[2] are markedly different. To the Seer[3] for instance, its common crust of inertness

[1] Līlā.

[2] Adrishta. This determines the psycho-physical subject to freedom of choice of the essentially free self.

[3] Tattva-darshī or Sūkshmadarshī who unlike the Sthūladarshī, sees the subtle nature of things.

may break away revealing it as consciousness[1] instead of earthiness.[2]

Every centre is, therefore, *Bindu* subject to the varying ratio of determination[3] and freedom.[4] It does not appear as Perfect Being and Power (which *Bindu* is in absolute condensation) because of its special relative disposition of determination[3] and freedom.[4] It is this which constitutes the difference between an atom of Hydrogen and an amoeboid cell and the soul of a Shangkara. If we take into account both what is latent and what is patent, what is actual and what is possible, then the first = the second = the third = Perfect Being and Power. Not only does Perfect Being and Power lie at the root and background of all things, but all things are, in the complete view (as distinguished from the partial and pragmatic view which we commonly take), Perfect Being and Power—that is, *Brahman*. It is owing to man's pragmatic veiling and "ignorance" (determined by his action[5] and position in the cosmic scheme,[3]) that they appear and behave as finite, circumscribed specific objects.

Brahman, or *Shiva* (or in Its dynamic aspect, *Shakti*) thus works the greatest of all miracles which is this: while evolving as the world of infinitely diversified names and forms, It does not suffer Its own immensity, fullness and perfectness to be narrowed and whittled down in the process. Its immensity and infinity inalienably abides in, and through, all things, great or small: particular, finite things being only the practical ignorance of that Immensity and Infinity.

That Immensity and Infinity has two aspects: the infinite[6] aspect, and the infinitesimal[7] aspect. The former

---

[1] Chinmaya. [2] Mrinmaya. [3] Adrishta.
[4] Karma as Lilā. [5] Karma.
[6] Virāt or Mahat. [7] Kshudra or Anu.

is the aspect of infinite expansion, diffusion and manifestation[1] the latter is the aspect of infinite or ultimate condensation.[2] Now, *any* finite Centre, apart from its ratio of determination[3] and freedom[4] (which does not allow its recognising and accepting its being in all its dimensions), involves Power both in the infinite and the infinitesimal aspects above explained. It is *Brahman* which is greater than the great,[5] and smaller than the smallest.[6]

The infinitesimal is not infinitely small in respect of Being or Potency: it is infinitely small in the sense of not being further divisible into more elementary dynamic components (hence called "*Bindu*" or "Point"). It is called "small" also because of its appearing to us as subtle and condensed[7] and unmanifest.[2] In reality, however, it is, as we have seen, Perfect Being and Power.[8] And, if we call condensed Power "Potency," then it is Perfect Potency.[9] The electric corpuscle or "vortex-ring" in ether which builds the chemical atom, the nucleus of the germ or seed of the animal and plant, are approximate representatives and compounded forms of the true Dynamic Point or "Bindu". It is the condition of Consciousness-Power operating to create and evolve: because, whether on the whole or in

---

[1] Abhivyakti. [2] Avyakta. [3] Adrishta.

[4] Karma. [5] Mahato mahīyān.

[6] Anoranīyān. Shvetāshvatara, III, 20. Metapsychically the first is the Ether of Consciousness and the second Bindu. Physically the first is the Ether and the second the atoms of matter in it. Those who, like many of the present-day Relativists, discard the Ether, may substitute Space-Time Continuum.

[7] Sūkshma.

[8] It is not in itself subject to the Spatial and Temporal Orders, but involves them. It is, in one aspect, connected with the Space-Time Continuum out of which our relative spaces and times are evolved. See for discussion of this question P.N.M.'s "Introduction to Vedānta Philosophy" (1928).

[9] It is also Perfect Readiness to create or evolve. See *ante*.

detail, there is no creative process without Power massing itself[1] into Points. Diffusion is the condition of dissolution[2] as concentration is that of creation.[3]

Matter, Life and Mind are the threefold manifestation of Mother-Power. Centres of each are centres (in the sense above explained) of the Mother-Power as a whole. In the Matter-aspect, the Mother-Power is Ether,[4] a matter-particle is, therefore, a strain-centre in Ether, which means and implies that it is a centre at and through which the stress-system of Ether operates in a given manner. In the life-aspect, and Mother-Power is *Prāna* or *Āditya* in the sense these terms are understood in the Upanishads.[5] A particular living cell is a centre of this Vital Power,[6] which as the Maitri-Upanishad explains, is not summed up by the apparent solar energy, but diffused throughout the universe. In the mind-aspect, the Power is Cosmic Mind which in the Vedānta is called *Hiranyagarbha*. An individual Self is a centre at and through which the Cosmic Mind operates in a given manner; which does not exclude determination and freedom for the individual, because the individual is the Cosmic-Mind, accepting its infinity being and potency only in part, and operating in a specific manner.

Sound,[7] Object[8] and Thought or Idea[9] are another threefold manifestation of Mother-Power. That Power in its Sound aspect is the most generic and fundamental "Sound" whose "approximate acoustic equivalent" is what

---

[1] "Chidghana" Ghanībhūtā Shakti. [2] Laya. [3] Srishti.

[4] Ākāsha. Or Space-Time Continuum. For a particular modern presentation of this concept in relation to Deity one may instance the speculations of Prof. Alexander and others in the West.

[5] See Maitri-Up. in particular.

[6] Prānashakti or Āditya-Shakti.

[7] Shabda. [8] Artha.

[9] Pratyaya. See "Garland of Letters" as to these terms.

is heard by gross ears as the *Mantra, Om.*[1] All particular "Sounds"[2] are particular modes and manifestation of *Om.* In the object-aspect, Power is the Cosmic Form or Order—the relative disposition or configuration of the elements of the world-system. Any particular object is and represents the Cosmic Order[3] in a particular way. It is no wonder, therefore, that a material atom is "a miniature universe": everything, structurally and dynamically considered, must be so. Each body is a "little universe".[4] So that a "Seer" can see "folded up" in every object the whole Cosmos; and he who is competent, can evolve all things out of everything.[5] The dynamic graph or the diagram of forces by which anything (say, a magnet) can be represented—the picture of the constituent forces—is called the *Yantra* of that thing. And though of course each particular object must have its own peculiar *Yantra* (as also *Mantra*), it is to be observed that its *Yantra* must only be a modification or particular form of the *Mahāyantra,*[6] (analogous to the *Mahāmantra, Om*) which stands for the Cosmos as a whole. In the thought-aspect, every object, even a grain of matter, must be a mode of Cosmic Consciousness-Power (with Its three components of Power as Will, Knowledge and Action[7]) which is the essence of both its peculiar being and dynamism. Every being—since it

---

[1] See "Garland of Letters".

[2] Vishesha Shabda.

[3] Virāt or Vishva-rūpa.

[4] Kshudra brahmānda.

[5] "Sarva-smādeva sarva-samudbhavah. A Version of the Hermetic doctrine relative to the Macrocosm and Microcosm (Mahā brahmānda and Kshudra brahmānda) is given in the Vishvasāra Tantra as follows: "What is here is elsewhere. What is not here is nowhere. (Yadihāsti tad anyatra Yannehāsti na tat kvachit.)

[6] Study the famous Shrīyantra of the Devī, Tripura-Sundarī which sums up all Tattvas and their evolution; and also, other yantras. See Tantrarāja Tantra, Introduction; and Kāmakalāvilāsa.

[7] Ichchhā-Shakti, Jnāna-Shakti and Kriyā-Shakti.

is a mode of Cosmic Consciousness-Power, that is, uncircumscribed Consciousness-Power—must in the Vedāntic view involve, whether latently or patently, Consciousness-Power in its threefold division; that is to say, even a grain of matter must involve Power as Knowledge, Will and action[1] though these may appear to be latent in relation to man's present condition. And if what is latent and what is patent, what it veils and what it reveals, be added, then, in a grain of matter we must have as its stock the Whole as Consciousness-Power.

This last aspect of Power (*viz.*, Consciousness) is the fundamental aspect of which Sound[2] and its meaning[3] are side-aspects or derivates. Because while all things and processes (including sound[2] and meaning[3]) are sustained in, reducible to, and perceived and conceived in terms of, Consciousness, there is nothing else which can be conceived as the sustainer of Consciousness, nothing else to which Consciousness itself can be reduced, and nothing else in terms of which Consciousness itself must be known. Consciousness, therefore, is the basis of all being and all power. It being given, a thing is; it being not given, a thing is not. Things being given, it is; things not being given, it still is; which is Pure Experience, which the Buddhistic systems called *Shūnya*, the Void.[4] Further, it being given, all else can be perceived and conceived; whilst, its not being given, can neither be perceived nor conceived. We do sometimes conceive "unconsciousness" in ourselves, or in matter; but this is abstract, pragmatic, symbolic and approximate thinking. Concretely and really, the "unconsciousness" in us or in matter is simply not the sort and

[1] Ichchhā-Shakti, Jnāna-Shakti and Kriyā-Shakti.

[2] Shabda. [3] Artha.

[4] Shūnya. The term is also used in Hinduism not always in the sense of nihilism but of indetermination of being.

tone of consciousness which we have, in practice, learnt to accept as "our conscious life," extended over a narrow area, and expressed in certain pragmatic responses and signs. Beyond that area, and in default of those signs and responses, we "see" nothing but unconsciousness.[1]

The Subconscious Mind, or the "Subliminal Consciousness" is now requisitioned to explain many common psychic as well as many "parapsychic" phenomena. Like an iceberg floating in water, "nine-tenths" of mental life is said to lie submerged in subconsciousness. "It (subconsciousness) has been likened to an immense block of which our personality is but a diminutive facet; to an iceberg of which we see a few glistening prisms that represent our life, while nine-tenths of the enormous mass remain buried in the shadows of the sea. According to Sir Oliver Lodge, it is that part of our being that has not become incarnate; according to Gustave Le Bon, it is the 'condensed' soul of our ancestors, which is true, beyond a doubt, but only a part of the truth, for we find in it also the soul of the future and probably of many other forces which are not necessarily human. William James saw in it a diffuse cosmic consciousness and the chance intrusion into our scientifically-organized world of remnants and vestiges of primordial chaos. Here are a number of images striving to give us an idea of a reality so vast that we are unable to grasp it."[2]

Psychometry, "X-ray vision," and "mediumistic phenomena" generally, would seem to require not only that a subconscious background of our "conscious life" exists, but that it must be credited with potentialities of knowing and acting which exceed the limits of man's common intelligence and will, and which, therefore, in that way and to

---

[1] Achit.

[2] Maurice Maeterlinck, The Unknown Guest, p. 321 (3rd. Ed.).

that extent, should rather be called Super-consciousness. It may be that the so-called subconsciousness is really cosmic consciousness—all-seeing, all-knowing and all-powerful—hidden from our ordinary conscious life by a pragmatic veil which, when "accidentally" lifted, gives us what the Psychic Research Societies of the West are now studying as "occult" phenomena; and, when lifted by suitable practical methods,[1] give the higher psychic powers[2] and vision[3] to which every individual can attain (since, Supreme Spirit[4] being connected with every individual spirit, psychic powers, and so forth cannot be an exclusive possession), provided he cares to train himself properly in accordance with those methods.

Hindu Systems of Philosophy, and the Vedānta in particular, have recognised this Supreme Spirit[4] of which, and in which, all particular Spirits[5] are; and Vedānta has held that a particular Spirit[5] is the Supreme Spirit, separated by a veil of practical "ignorance" or non-acceptance; so that it realizes itself as the Supreme Soul, in knowledge and in power, in proportion as, by effort[1] it can raise the "veil" between itself and its Prototype. The veil gone, it is, and realizes itself as, the Whole.[6] This consummation can be made available to all who care to go through the necessary discipline. Revelation is not merely a past historic fact. It is a present possibility.

In the West "the laboratory methods" applied to the study of these phenomena have produced admirable results so far as the testing, recording and ordering of facts are concerned. But hypotheses such as will explain them are still vague, hesitating and unsatisfactory,[7] and there seems

---

[1] Sādhanā. [2] Siddhi. [3] Sūkshma-drishti.

[4] Paramātmā. [5] Jīvātmā.

[6] Pūrna-Brahmaiva bhavati.

[7] The Unknown Guest, by M. Maeterlinck, p. 259.

to be as yet little suggestion of courses of systematic discipline by which one who is not "by nature" a medium, and so forth, may develop the higher psychic potentialities, and with perseverance, may even, ultimately, bring them to perfection.

M. Ernest Bozzano, whose article in the *Annales des Sciences Psychiques* (September, 1906), M. Maeterlinck cites (The Unknown Guest, 3rd Ed., p. 324) says: "It does not seem that it is possible to cultivate or develop them (occult faculties) systematically. The Hindu races in particular, who for thousands of years have been devoting themselves to the study of these manifestations, have arrived at nothing but a better knowledge of the empirical methods calculated to produce them in individuals already endowed with these supernormal faculties." The Hindu position however is that it is possible to cultivate and develop these "faculties" systematically, and bring them to perfection; that it is possible to arrive at a knowledge of the Principles, not merely of the "empirical" methods (which, therefore, are not purely empirical); and that, the methods can be applied, and if properly applied and pursued, success can be attained, by all individuals.

In India, the Vedāntic doctrine has afforded a wide and firm basis for the understanding of our common as well as "occult" experiences, and that doctrine is clear in its main outlines. On the practical side, too, the Indian genius has been remarkable for the courses of *Sādhanā* or discipline it has evolved, suited to the varying temperament and competency[1] of men, leading by steps to the highest stages of realization—"I am the Whole."[2] Human personalities alone are not in, and of, the Supreme Spirit, but all things conceal beneath their apparent cramped existences mines

---

[1] Adhikāra. [2] Pūrno'ham, Brahmāsmi, Sarvo'smi.

of unbounded subliminal Power (which is ultimately Consciousness-Power). The so-called "instincts" (*e.g.*, the instinct of direction) of animals, particularly of ants, bees and many insects, show this unsuspected Power at work, and doing things which man's intelligence cannot, in some cases, do at all, and in others, do but haltingly and imperfectly. It has been claimed that the famous Elberfeld horses in Germany trained by Krall proved two things—first, that rationality is, ordinarily, only dormant in the lower animals, or passes unobserved; second, that even animals can, acting under proper circumstances and stimuli, perform wonderful intellectual feats, particularly in the domain of abstract numbers which human intelligence, has so long regarded as peculiarly its own. For instance, an Elberfeld horse could extract the fourth root of a number of six figures (involving in actual calculation 31 operations), in five or six seconds, "that is to say, during the brief, careless glance which he gives at the black-board on which the problem is inscribed, as though the answer came to him intuitively and instantaneously."[1]

The "lower" animal has his share in the occult phenomena also. M. Ernest Bazzano[2] has collected 69 cases of telepathy, presentiments and hallucinations of sight or hearing in which the main parts are played by animals. The Hindu scriptures are replete with stories in which, not only Animals, but "Stocks and Stones"[3] also, are shown as possessing a Consciousness, ordinarily latent in them, but becoming patent under certain relative circumstances

[1] The Unknown Guest, p. 259, by M. Maeterlinck.

[2] In an article on Les Perceptions Physiques des animaux (Annales des sciences psychiques, August, 1905).

[3] To the upper and lower fire-producing sticks (Arani) which in Rigveda appear in the role of two lovers (X, 95), male and female are called Ūrbashī and Purūavāh (Yajurveda Mādhyandinī c. 5, Kandikā 2).

of Kārmic condition. The substance of these myths is in accord with the fundamental position of Hindu Thought, which holds that *Chit* and the Vital Principle (really one) not only pervade all creation, but that all objects are forms and modes of *Chit*, both substantially and dynamically.

As regards these stories it is to be observed that a careful study of the so-called "earlier" as well as "later" *Shāstras* shows that, behind the veil of its sensuous manifestation, every object was believed to be a mode of *Chit-Shakti* technically called "Presiding Deity".[1] Every object is, therefore, naturally addressed as a *Devatā* or Divinity or Consciousness-Power, and the *Sādhaka* is taught to bring himself into "living" contact with the Power embodied in them, and to make that Power available for the furtherance of his desired ends.[2]

In fact, according to Vedāntic conceptions, all things or centres, though essentially they are Being-Consciousness-Bliss,[3] present varied aspects to one another by virtue of their varying action and factor conditioning it. Hence, a given thing, A, may seem and behave, for all practical purposes, as totally or partially "dead" and "unconscious," in relation to B, or even to itself. Now, this "unconsciousness" is only consciousness veiled or ignored and such veiling has degrees.

Man's own "unconsciousness" and "subconsciousness" are thus veiled, unaccepted, unrecognised forms of Consciousness itself. Or if we are likely to create confusion by using the word "Consciousness" (which is used in a limited and pragmatic sense in the West) we must employ the Vedāntic term *Chit* itself which means the Reality-Whole. We should then say that "unconsciousness" and "subconsciousness" are modes of *Chit*.

---

[1] Abhimāninī Devatā.

[2] Purushārt

[3] Sachchidānanda.

It has been shown in previous chapters that man's Experience is really a Universe; that for practical reasons he ignores the immensity of experience, and seizes upon particular features only which happen to interest him, and thus carves a portion out of the Infinite Given, and regards this portion alone as his consciousness of the moment. In reality, no bounds can be set to the Given which is the alogical Whole, and, is therefore, all-inclusive: It is *Brahman* and the Immense.[1] Dynamically, it must be so: since men are centres in an infinite Stress-system, the stress (which is the basis of its experience) of a given centre must involve, and be connected with, the entire system. As the forces producing experience cannot be in themselves hedged round, so experience cannot be hedged round. If we hedge it round, it is because our tendencies[2] and factor conditioning[3] action do not require the whole. This limiting is due to the so-called ignorance.[4]

Conversely, by knowledge[5] (chiefly, "spiritual" intuition or "vision"), the limits of the given experience can (it is claimed) be indefinitely pushed back, and the whole Universe, past, present and future, can be "discovered" in it; since it *is* the Universe. Sub-consciousness, in that consummation reached by degrees, becomes Super-Consciousness and Perfect Consciousness.

---

[1] Bhûman; both terms have the same meaning.

[2] Avidyâ.

[3] Vidyâ. Both Vidyâ and Avidyâ are Powers of the one Divine Mother. By the first she frees, by the second as Cosmic Mâya, she binds, that is, involves herself as Consciousness in Mind and Matter. The being of the centre thus produced is a form of Avidyâ.

[4] Bhûman; both terms have the same meaning.

CHAPTER VIII

CHIT AND "CENTRES"

WITH the aid of the explanations given in the foregoing sections, we can attempt to formulate an approximate idea of *Chit*—approximate because *Chit* as the Whole[1] is alogical, and therefore, indefinable.[2] It can be thought about and defined only in aspects or sections.[2] Now, *Chit* is the Reality-Power which is fundamentally the Consciousness in us, but which as such is infinitely larger than what is commonly and pragmatically accepted as our "conscious life"; stretching over, and remaining as, the realms of the "sub-conscious" and "unconscious"; evolving and manifesting as Vital Power and Forms,[3] and as Material Power and Forms;[4] in other words, evolving and manifesting as the Universe which we regard and treat in Time, Space and Causality (which does not mean that these are only Forms of Thought), but which has an aspect transcending these categories also.[5]

Further, *Chit* in evolving and manifesting as this universe of multifarious forms, in some of which its essential nature as Consciousness and Joy seems to be veiled or even reversed,[6] never ceases to the Perfect Reality-Power that it is. That is, *Chit* as Perfect Being-Consciousness-Bliss[7]—(*a*) becomes the World of finite forms; (*b*) is

---

[1] Pûrna.

[2] Avâng manasa gochara.

[3] Prâna-Shakti.

[4] Bhûta-Shakti.

[5] Rig-veda and Atharva-veda, Purusha Sûkta; Shvetâshvatara-Up., III, 14, 15, 16.

[6] Vâdhita.

[7] Sat, Chit, Ânanda.

immanent in the World of finite forms; and (c) is transcendent in relation to the World of finite forms. It never ceases to be (b) and (c) in being (a).

The unchanged Perfect-Reality-Power, as underlying, and yet distinguished from, the changing world-forms, has, again, two aspects: (1) the absolutely great,[1] diffuse and undifferentiated aspect which is the Ether of Consciousness[2] and (2) the absolutely small[3] condensed, "potentized" aspect which is *Bindu* of which "Self," living "Germ," material "Atom" or corpuscle are lower forms and evolutes. As the Perfect Continuum[2] has a tendency to evolve as a series of Lower Continua in which it still remains immanent (and also, transcendent), so the Perfect Dynamic Point[4] has a tendency to evolve as a series of Lower "Centres," and yet remain as the "Point" at the base of them all: it is thus, "the Centre of all centres". It is also transcendent in this sense that a given Centre, say, a material atom or a living cell, ordinarily manifests and draws upon a part of its infinite dynamism or potency.

As the Ether of Consciousness[2] is the direction of Unity and Undifferentiation, so the Point[4] is the direction of Plurality and Heterogeneity. That is, *Chit*, in having to become many and varied, must begin as *Bindu*, so that *Bindu* is the start of the creative and evolutionary process as the result of the Desire "may I be many".[5] *Bindu* contains within itself "seeds" of multiplicity, illustrated by the desire of the Self to multiply or reproduce itself in generation and creation by the vital impetus in the "cells" towards cell-division and multiplication; by radioactivity and other phenomena showing how matter continually

---

[1] Paramamahat

[2] Chidâkâsha.

[3] Parama-anu.

[4] Bindu.

[5] Vahu syâng prajâ-yeya.

tends to split and rebuild itself into new kinds of matter starting, as physicists now generally believe, from one fundamental kind of matter. By reason of this fundamental tendency to multiplicity, we have the Prime Bindu[1] splitting into a multiplicity of Points[2] which become the starting nuclei of the world of correlated centres.

Chit, which is immense Power, condenses itself into the *Bindu* for purposes of creative evolution. By this operation, as *we* must think, magnitude or "field" of being is infinitely contracted, but Power is infinitely massed—which is infinite Potency and Readiness.[3] *Bindu,* therefore in our conception, is the "Limit" of strain (*i.e.*, change of dimensions), as also the "Limit" of Stress (*i.e.*, power involved in the change of dimension, *e.g.*, in a rubber ball pressed by the hand, or in a stretched bowstring; and also the power by which it tends to regain its natural dimensions or form). "Limit" means here "the ultimate point or extent beyond which we cannot go". So that *Bindu* is the ultimate point of Power beyond which a thing or energy cannot be contracted and condensed (*i.e.*, strained)—perfect condensation or compactness; it is also Perfect Stress in the sense that it is endowed with perfect Power to regain its original Form, *i.e.*, *Brahman* as immense kinetic, manifest Power. In a limited way, this is illustrated by a germ or seed, when, by its inherent power, it tends to grow into an animal or a plant. Bindu's inherent power to evolve may be otherwise expressed by saying that *Bindu* possesses Perfect elasticity. Ordinary centres have imperfect strains and stresses (for practical purposes), so that their elasticities too are imperfect.

---

[1] Parama-Bindu as Supreme Self.

[2] Bindus or limited selves (Jīva or Purusha).

[3] Uchchhūnāvasthā.

As *Bindu* is at the base or "heart"[1] of all cosmic Centres, its elasticity is the basis of the differing elasticities of different centres on account of which they grow, tend to push back and outgrow their constraints, and gradually evolve towards perfection. The reason of cosmic stressing and evolution is, therefore, given in the elasticity of the *Bindu* which must "swell".[2]

Thus we have a fundamental cycle or "circuit" involved in the very fact of creation: *Brahman* as the Kinetic Immense infinitely strains (*i.e.*, condenses) into *Brahman* as Immense Potential (which is *Bindu*); this Immense Potential by reason of its perfect Elasticity swells into Immense Kinetic or Manifest again. Here we have cyclic movement which requires that (1) the cosmos as a system of centres must have cyclic life; and (2) individual centres and groups of centres (*e.g.*, species of animals, communities, nations and so forth), must have cyclic life too. The factor of Bliss and Play[3] ensures, however, that this cyclic life is not a mere mechanical spinning round and round in an eternally fixed groove.

---

[1] Shakti or Power is called the "Heart of the Supreme Lord" (*hridayam Parameshituh*).

[2] A state called Uchchhūnāvasthā. It is interesting to note how this idea of "swelling" and dynamic, rhythmic expansion and contraction (Sangkocha-vikāsha) of Bindu is coming to be recognised recently as essentially the idea of the Atom, which is a representation of Bindu in the material plane: "According to Bohr, the emission of light from an atom is not a single process but takes place in two distinct stages. The first stage is the energising of the atom, in other words, its passing over from a normal or non-luminous condition into a new state of higher energy content. The second stage is the return of the atom to a condition of lower energy accompanied by the emission of light . . ." From the Presidential Address, Indian Science Congress, 1928. Whatever the explanation of the phenomenon be, the phenomenon itself (*viz.*, the expansion and contraction of the energy-content of the Atom) now appears to be established.

[3] Ānanda-and-Līlā.

Elasticity, as we have seen, involves both Strain[1] and Stress.[2] The correlate "pole" of the illumined[3] is illuminator.[4] The latter (or *Shiva*) "projects" out of Itself Its own creative Power (with which It is in indivisible unity): this Primary action is the illumined;[3] then, the latter reacts on the former[4] by "reflecting itself on it," *i.e.*, by making itself an Object of Illumination or Consciousness. Thus arises the Supreme Cosmic Self-Consciousness or Supreme Self[5] which is the state of Supreme *Bindu*.[6] From this last, by multiplication, correlation and co-ordination, the World (often compared to an *Ashvattha* Tree) sprouts into manifestation. In the plane of Mind, the *Bindu* is represented (perfectly in the case of the Lord, but approximately in our case) by the Ego or Self; in the plane of Life, it is represented by the "cell-nucleus" (which is also "Self" veiled); and in the plane of Matter, it is represented by the "central electric charge" (as known to physicists so far)—which is "Self" still further veiled. Self, therefore, is—and according to the Cosmic plan above explained, must be—in every form of being. Modern Physiologists generally restrict consciousness to the cortex of the brain; so that actions of the sub-cerebral centres are sub-conscious or unconscious. But from the premises which have been submitted, and also from other scientific and *quasi*-scientific considerations which we have previously partly stated, it should on a Vedāntic view follow—(1) that Consciousness and Self cannot be restricted to the life of the cerebrum; (2) that all Centres of the organism (down to

---

[1] Sangkocha.

[2] Vikāsha-Shakti. According to Shāstra, Sangkocha-Shakti + Vikāsha-Shakti = Vimarsha-Shakti. Elsewhere we have used "Stress" in the sense of Power acting and reacting in *all* its phases; *e.g.*, in the conception of the World as a Stress-system.

[3] Vimārsha. [4] Prakāsha. [5] Para-ahantā. [6] Para-Bindu.

the cells or even their elements) must have their own consciousnesses and selves, which are, generally, "ejective," (in the sense in which William James used the word)[1] in relation to central consciousness and our ordinary self; and (3) that these selves, though they may be mutually ejective, co-operate for the purposes of the enjoyment and action[2] of the organism[3] The Body (gross and subtle) is thus a corporation of *Devatās* or Divinities. What is true in this case, is true in the case of all Things constituted. There is no unconsciousness, or unconsciousness appearing as consciousness[4] to be controlled only by *Chit*. *Chit* is both the Material and Efficient Cause.

As we have seen, the appearance of *Bindu* and its derivate, Centres, implies Power operating as a contracting Force.[5] The result of such contraction is called *Kanchuka* or envelope.[6] Diversity of Centres imply divergent working of such envelope[7]; a higher Centre is that in which the constraint[7] is comparatively more relaxed. *Parameshvara* or Supreme Self is the Lord of such constraints.[7] In point of relaxation these constitute an ascending order of higher and higher Centres. Its operative arrangement in a given Centre constitutes its system of "sheaths". All Centres have "sheaths". In man, their operative arrangment is given by the system of the "five sheaths".[8] According to another scheme, the arrangement is represented by

---

[1] Principles of Psychology, Vol. 1. [2] Bhoga and Karma.

[3] Or the Pindābhimānī Self or Jīva.

[4] Achit and no Chidābhāsa. As in Sāngkhya and Māyāvāda.

[5] Sangkocha.

[6] See "The Garland of Letters"—"Kanchukas" in which Māyā is the Primordial Kanchuka, referred to before.

[7] Kanchuka.

[8] "Annamaya," etc., of Vedānta: see in particular, Taitirīya-Up.

the "seven planes"[1]; according to another, it is the "seven Centres".[2] Planes, sheaths and so forth are, however, not peculiar to human constitution; they are involved in all things, though, possibly, in varying degree "folded up".

The World shows Centres in different stages of growth: they appear to constitute an hierarchy from "dead" matter to the highest Spirit. It both means and requires that their positions in the cosmic dynamic system are different, and their actions or *karmas*, that is, more or less spontaneous activities by which those positions are sought to be altered, are different. *Adrishta* is often substituted by its equivalent, *Sangskāra* ("tendency" or "predisposition"), and *Karma* by its expression, *Bhoga* (enjoyment of Pleasure and Pain, etc.). *Bhoga*, is the expression of *Karma*, because *Adrishta*, though apparently a factor conditioning *Karma*, and therefore *Bhoga*, is itself the result of previous *Karma*. At the root, we can have nothing but *Chit* "elaborating" its Bliss by Play; no particular Centre can, therefore, have its action absolutely determined. Practically, however, *Adrishta* and *Karma* constitute what is called "cyclic causation" in which the latter is conditioned by certain pre-existent tendencies. Two Centres, A and B, are different; because, their *Adrishta* and *Karma* are different; these latter are different because the elasticities of A, B have been different; that is, A's power to modify its strains has been different from that of B. And, in our temporal thinking, there is no absolute beginning in time of these differences in the elasticities of Centres: in *Laya* or "Cosmic Sleep" these differences must be imagined as still persisting as "seeds".

---

[1] Loka. See "The Serpent Power" for explanation of these matters.

[2] Chakra of the spinal column (merudanda).

Differences are infinitely various, yet Centres may be grouped together as Matter, as Life and as Mind. We have seen that there is, in a certain sense. an antithesis between *Adrishta* as presently determined condition and *Karma* which essays to change and master it; and that *Karma* is essentially the expression of *Joy* and *Play*.[1] Now Matter is that in which *Adrishta* predominates, and *Karma*, from man's standpoint at least, in the sense of autonomous action, is almost completely disguised. Mind (as Self-Consciousness and Self-determination) is that in which *Karma* predominates. Life, in the plants and animals, regarded from Man's standpoint again, lies midway between these two. In fact, the greater its co-efficient of *Karma*, involving control of *Adrishta*, and the greater, therefore, its manifestation of Joy and Play,[1] the higher is the place of a Centre or group of Centres in the Scheme of Beings.

Matter moves, but its "career" is traced in almost (it cannot be absolute) fixed curves and expressed in nearly fixed rounds or routines, covered by the physicist's formulæ and equations. The "life-curve" comes to be less and less fixed as we proceed from Matter to the lower forms of Life, and from these to the higher forms; because the factor of *Karma* more and more asserts itself. The lowest forms of life seem to be endowed with power of spontaneous action: Life is seen to seize upon the atoms of C, H, N, O, build by means of these materials the cell of protoplasm, which it then proceeds to differentiate and integrate with a view to reproduce a certain species or kind. This power of construction for an end is even more marked in the activities of the Self working through, and as, Mind,[2] This power, which is natural in man, can be developed by self-discipline and development,[3] so that the limited self may progressively

[1] Ānanda and Līlā. [2] Antaḥkaraṇa. [3] Sādhanā.

become controller and creator of wider and wider phases of creation, until at last it becomes identified with [1] the Supreme Creator and Controller [2] Himself.[3] Shāstra, therefore, holds—*first*, that any Centre, by appropriate *Karma*, can raise itself to the level of the Highest Centre, because it carries, as manifestation of Power [4] the potentiality of the Immense or *Brahman*; *secondly*, that *Manu*, *Daksha* and other Higher Powers who preside over what are called their respective jurisdictions,[5] are Centres who have attained their high altitude by *Karma*; and *thirdly*, that aspects of the world-process, as a whole presided over by the Supreme Centre, are presided over by "deputies" in detail—an arrangement which, while ensuring the rational direction of the creative process, does not annul the possibility of *Karma* on the part of subordinate Centres. *Karma*, implying freedom, is the "birthright" of every Centre; it is not "delegated"; it cannot, therefore, be taken away. On the other hand, evolution does not proceed on a footing of "fortuitous modifications" and "chance conglomerations". It is a directed and "supervised" process.

If the world-process were to proceed on purely mechanistic and deterministic lines, its curve of history would be absolutely and eternally fixed: things and processes would go on spinning in eternally fixed cycles. On the other hand, if *Karma* were to work absolutely independently of *Adrishta*, (*i.e.*, the total assemblage of conditions), the curve would most likely be a "whimsical" one, not amenable to law and

---

[1] Sāyujya-siddhi.

[2] Prajāpati or the Lord.

[3] In fact, Manu and others, who are credited with having started and presided over different aspects of creative evolution, are Centres who by disciplined fervour (*tapasyā*) have raised themselves to their high level of creative efficiency.

[4] Bindu- Shakti. [5] Adhikāra.

order. As a matter of fact, the curve has reference to collective *Adrishta* as well as to collective *Karma*; so that the world-process, though generally cyclic, moves to change also. And, in order that such movement may on the whole be towards betterment or "progress," collective *Karma* must include *Karma* by some Higher Centres who know the road to real betterment and are competent to direct the *Karma* of others, without compulsion, to and along that road. This shows the place of *Manu* and others in the economy of world evolution.[1] The *Karma* of Centres makes the curve of history not a mere cycle, which, *Adrishta* left alone, would make it. The control of Higher Centres makes the curve, so to say, *spiraline*,[2] that is, one in which the movement of rotation is combined with a movement of upward (and, from man's limited point of view, sometimes downward) translation. But for this control, the *Karma* of ordinary Centres—not generally characterized by any clear and sure intuition of the True, Good and Beautiful—would, in the resultant, be either mutually destructive (truths and falsities, good and evil intentions neutralizing one another), or be precarious and unsteady (that is, not steadily making for an ideal).

From man's pragmatic point of view, the Cosmic Spiral[3] is generally hidden as a whole, and manifest only in parts, sections or aspects. He, therefore, sees now upward phases, and now downward phases—in his own life-history, in the history of groups, and, as he thinks, in the history of the world as a whole. Hence there is both progress and

---

[1] This Indian Doctrine appears to be represented in Theosophy by its teaching regarding the "Masters".

[2] See "Garland of Letters".

[3] The Six Centres through which the "Serpent Power" (itself "spiraline") ascends to the highest, are seen to be arranged spirally, shewing the Cosmic Plan of Movement and, possibly, also Constitution.

"reversion" (or degeneracy) in the career of a Centre or a group of Centres. In the complete view, all such upward and downward phases are seen to be "elements" of the continuous World-Spiraline Movement.

The Spiral, as we have seen, combines translation with rotation, the former being due to *Karma*, especially those by the Higher Centres. Any *Karma* done affects, therefore, the aspect of translation; both as regards magnitude and duration. A good and wise *Karma* contributes to upward translation or progress[1] being greater and more rapid; a bad and foolish act tends to make it less and delayed. By ignorance and sin man falls. This fall may, in the long run, raise him, through repentance and expiation, after several births if not in the same birth, higher than where he had been before he fell.[2] This shows that there is progress even through falls and lapses. But the path would assuredly be both straightened and shortened if man could, at the critical moment, develop Power or *Shakti*, in knowledge and will, so as not to fall. Hence the spiraline (or cosmically progressive) nature of the world-curve does not warrant that any Centre should merely drift in order to reach the highest point. Since the current is towards the highest end, it could reach it by drifting along the current; but it could not reach it, even in that prodigious age which is called *Kalpa* (counted in thousands of billions of human years), but, so far as man can see in nothing short of infinite time; and, during that unending course, it would have to pass through countless ups and downs spelling untold miseries. In order to cut short this protracted career, in fact, in order to dissociate himself from the mazes

---

[1] Abhyudaya.

[2] The Kulārnava Tantra says that man should learn to raise himself by that which causes his fall through abuse of natural function.

of the Spiral, "the Wandering"[1] itself, man must be up and doing, and be a devotee and striver or *Sadhaka*, and "tap" the potentiality of infinite knowledge and power and bliss which is contained in his being.

Any discipline[2] which is calculated to straighten and shorten its career in the Spiral is called the *Dharma* or Law of Form (incompletely translated as Religion) of a given Centre; by following it, its "lifts" are assured and multiplied, and its "falls" prevented and minimized. The result is called progress.[3] When, ultimately, the Centre, by realizing itself as the whole Consciousness-Power,[4] can dissociate itself from the Spiral itself, having no further need of specialized effort and movement, the consummation reached is called Liberation.[5]

Where the co-efficient of *Karma* is, practically, very small, as in the case of the Matter-centres, *Dharma* is Power as Law summing up and describing the routine of their behaviour. In the case of higher centres, there is no "routine" strictly so called; so that *Dharma* is Power as Law ("regulative" or "normative" without being binding) relative to the conservation[6] of those Centres essentially as such, as well as to the progress and liberation[7] (in the senses above explained) of them.

It has been seen that voluntary control of evolutionary movement especially by the higher Centres (from Man upwards) is not only possible, but it exists. We have to consolidate and intensify this control—which is *Sādhanā*. In this process, intellect, feeling and will are at work to

---

[1] Sangsāra. [2] Sādhana. [3] Abhyudaya.

[4] Pūrna, Chit-Shakti. [5] Nihshreyasa or Moksha or Mukti.

[6] Sthiti. Dharma comes from the root Dhri "to maintain."

[7] Abhyudaya and Nihshreyasa.

prepare the aspirant for *Yoga*[1] directed for the attainment of the Supreme End.[2] This *Yoga* effects the transformation of the "Little Self"[3] into the "Supreme Self"[4] by removing the veil of ignorance[5] which alone separates the one from the other; the Yogī leaves behind his "little" intellect, feeling and will, as tools of practical deliberation and selection (therefore, tools that limit, dissect and define), in entering into the realm of the super-consciousness,[6] and Alogical. All forms of *Yoga* agree in placing the Supreme Experience beyond the reach of "Mind" and "Speech". In the last stages, therefore, the Method is Intuition and Ecstasy.[7] The enveloping[8] and thus limiting powers which confine a Centre to its "little sphere" of pragmatic life must be removed in order that it can realize itself as *All.* In the progress of this liberating process, the Centre subsumes and extends its control over the elements of matter.[9]

Essentially and dynamically the same, Matter-centres, Life-centres and Mind-centres are not only correlated in the Cosmos, but are interchangeable; that is, a Matter-centre can, under proper conditions, "transmute" not only into another kind of matter, but into life and mind; and *vice versa.* Any Centre, in its beginningless career, may have, therefore, passed through all these forms, which means that "sheaths" and "instruments" of the imperishable *Chit* have only varied.

Since *Chit-Shakti*, which is the essence of all centres both as regards being and as regards evolving impetus, is

[1] This term is commonly used to denote both result as unity and the process which achieves it.

[2] It is often unknown that Yoga may be done to achieve any end but Yoga simply ordinarily denotes a "spiritual" process and end.

[3] Jīvātman. [4] Paramātman. [5] Avidyā.

[6] Pūrna. Chit-Svarūpa. [7] Samādhi. [8] Kanchuka.

[9] Bhūtajaya.

imperishable, it follows that all centres, considered as modes of Being-Energy, are so. The particular *forms* ("sheaths" and "instruments") of the centres are continuously changing, however, according to the varying ratios of their *Karma* and *Adhrishta.* Even during what is called a single "lease of life" or birth, the sheaths and instruments of a centre are changing from moment to moment; and what is called the "personal identity" of a centre is only pragmatic identity which, strictly speaking, is not identity. This is true not only of "Selves" and living organisms, but also of material corpuscles which physics has now discovered to be "systems" (and even the Electron, being of finite mass and energy, ought to be so). But in the midst of all this continuous flux, a centre has its endurance or persistence assured in two important respects: (*a*) a centre is in reality the whole Being-Consciousness-Bliss Power, and as such is absolutely imperishable; and (*b*) that Power wills to evolve and "live" as a particular centre; so that this "will" is the "seed" and "root" of that particular centre manifestation; and this seed also is (conditionally) imperishable, that is, as long as the Basic Will lasts. From the latter position it follows that the seed and principle of a given centre must persist through cycles of creation and dissolution, being variously evolved during the former and involved or latent during the latter. The seed of a centre is not destroyed through all these changes of condition—of sheaths and instruments: the "will" of *Brahman* to be and become such centre remaining all through. A centre ceases to be such when it realizes itself as the Whole; therefore, when the Basic Will of *Chit* to be and become *this* particular centre goes, and therefore the root of this particular manifestation "dies".

Of the "sheaths" and "instruments" of a Centre, all are not susceptible to change and disintegration to the same degree. The principle which determines susceptibility to change and disintegration is this: A form of Power which evolves (integrates and organises) another form, and controls the latter when evolved, is more persistent than the latter, *e.g.*, Vital Power which evolves protoplasm out of C, H, N, O, and elaborates this into a living organism, is more persistent than the "material vehicle" so organised and controlled by it; so that, it will persist after the material body has disintegrated. The Self (represented by *Ahangkāra* or "I-making" Principle) which, according to the views here explained, evolves and controls vehicles or sheaths subtler than the gross body, and, through these subtler vehicles the gross body also, is more persistent than all its vehicles, subtle or gross. Power as *Bindu* is the most fundamental form of Power in relation to the evolution of centres; hence, *Bindu* must persist even after centre has disintegrated in *all other* forms. Finally, Consciousness-Power as Whole or Perfect Experience is absolute persistence, since It evolves the *Bindu* itself and involves it again.

So that we have an hierarchy of persistent forms, having at the bottom material vehicles or bodies, and at the top, *Bindu*, if we exclude the Whole which is absolute persistence. The subtle forms of Power are thus more "vital" and enduring than those that are relatively gross.

The death of the physical body does not, according to this view, mean the death of Life and Soul and Spirit. Death separates the subtle vehicle of a Centre from its gross vehicle, and, though these may continuously change by *Karma*, yet they are relatively persistent (*i.e.*, do not disintegrate) through countless births, till by realization, the Centre transcends its own limited self, and becomes merged in the Perfect Whole itself which is absolute deathlessness.

Whether Power as a Centre does or does not evolve and provide itself with a sensuous material vehicle depends on its *Karma* (and *Adrishta*). Its existence as such Centre does *not* depend upon its having evolved a gross material vehicle; so that, it may exist with or without (as the case may be) of a gross vehicle having been evolved and associated with it. Thus Centres may be incarnate or embodied, disincarnate or disembodied.

In its beginningless career a Centre may describe its curve of life according to the "equation" of its varying *Karma* on a board which is infinite Space and Time. And this curve may exhibit it in all possible positions—now embodied, now disembodied; now a "god" now a material thing; now a man, now an amœba. In its passage it meets with no "forbidden tracts" and "reserved compartments". Fulfilling the *Kārmic* conditions, it can become anything from a Creator of the worlds down to a blade of grass or particle of dust. And we have seen that all these Centre-Forms are essentially transmutable into one another, all being in essence Consciousness-Power. Of these countless forms, the Human form possesses some advantages in respect of further evolution; since, this form has a mixed experience of pleasure and pain, good and evil acting as an incentive to betterment, and self-consciousness and self-determination to a requisite degree to think out a path and take to it.

Since the curve is described by *Karma*, we may say that a Centre in its ages-long career ever becomes what it *chooses* to become. It is a Centre of Power the essence of which is Joy and Freedom. Its "littleness" as well as its "greatness" are due to its action—its bondage and liberation; its degeneration and progress. An individual Centre may enter, when the ratio of its collective *Karma* and *Adrishta* so requires it, a given and relatively fixed line of character-attitude in the world which is called a Type, Kind, Species, Race or Caste; but by *Karma* again it can leave that line, and pass into another, higher or lower; and by suitable spiritual effort, in can assimilate itself to the *Summum Genus* which is *Chit* as Whole and Perfect. This consummation is *Yoga* or " Union "

The *Shākta* Doctrine thus makes *every* Centre a Magazine of free and undying Power—essentially Perfect, but pragmatically limited, that is, veiled and ignored.

CHAPTER IX

CHIT AND ITS INVOLUTION

THE study of Perfect Experience has necessarily to start on the basis of man's own experience, and it is no false "anthropomorphic" metaphysic which models the Cosmos essentially on the lines discoverable in himself. In metaphysic no more ultimate and surer basis can be thought of. "What is here is there".[1] Apart from spiritual intuition giving direct apprehension of the Reality-Power, what is open to logical thinking is, first, to attempt a faithful rendering and analysis of man's own consciousness (so far as this may be possible), and thereupon form an idea of the Reality-Power as manifesting in and through ourselves; and then, secondly, to extend and apply this conception of Reality to the interpretation of Life, Matter and the World-system generally. Now, the conception of Reality thus extended either suits (*i.e.*, explains) the World-Order, or does not suit it. If it does not suit, the inference is not that metaphysical enquiry has failed because it has started at the wrong end (*i.e.*, the Self and its experience), but that there has been superficiality or other defect in the rendering and analysis of Self-experience, so that, the premises being vicious have vitiated the conclusions. In fact, the enquiry, to be final, has, according to this doctrine, to be started at one end only, and that end is the Self. We may indeed begin with Life or with Matter or with Force; but

---

[1] Yadihâsti tad anyatra, *ante*.

the enquiry will yield results neither intelligible nor final, till it be tested, revised, supplemented and understood by an enquiry into the experience of the Self. That experience is the ultimate and unquestioned "Fact"; everything else has to make good its title by its bearing upon that Fact; apart from such reference, actual or possible, atoms, ethers, forces and the rest, howsoever perfectly they may be expressed by mathematical formulæ, are nothing else than abstract ideas "without local habitation and name".

It is in man's self that he touches the foundations of the view that Reality is ultimately Consciousness as *Chit* which by its own Power makes an object of itself, and elaborates this object into a world of correlated Centres of Matter, Life and Mind; and that in such elaboration *Chit* does not suffer its essence, that is, Being-Consciousness-Bliss[1] to be either abrogated or changed. That is so in man's own experience: *Chit* becoming varied experience and yet remaining Pure *Chit* always.

It is, again, in his own experience that man must find the key to discover the meaning of the Cosmic Principles called *Tattvas.* Principle is one and it is *Chit*: but it has different phases and aspects of world-manifestation, such as unveiled and veiled; alogical and logical; extra-temporal and temporal; and so on. With reference to such phases, and in describing and explaining them, we have one Principle "evolving" as many. The Philosophy of Shākta Vedāntism and Shaiva non-dualism is the enunciation and statement of the mutual relationships of what are called the Thirty-six *Tattvas.*[2]

[1] Sat-Chit-Ānanda.

[2] See "Shakti and Shākta" and "Garland of Letters" (Ch. on Tattvas), in which the evolution of the "Principles," from the psychological as well as mantra standpoint, has been dealt with, and authorities cited.

Now, the Principles, in their broad outlines, can be discovered in normal experience, and, in detail, can be known and verified by *yoga*, or supernormal experience, which is not an absolutely new order of experience, but is experience more unveiled, more fully recognised and "accepted" than man's normal, pragmatic experience.

Experience is an alogical, undefined Universe. It *is* Pure Consciousness, but is not only that: it has a varied content. It is subjective, but is so only when, and in so far as, it as been "dissected" by a logical operation. It involves all categories or Forms of Thought, but, in its fullness, is not covered by any of them. It is pragmatic, that is, having reference to practical ends, but is so, only as considered as a "section," not as the complete "Fact". Correct intuition will not even allow our saying that "*Chit* is in us"; the fact is that we, as centres of specific action and reaction, are in *Chit* which by its Power appears as such centres.

Man for the sake of the ends of his pragmatic life, disowns his Self which is *Chit*. But suppose he essays to be it. Then it is, and is recognised as, Alogical, the Whole[1] beyond the six Limitations,[2] and transcending all categories, though involving them. It is so, and is so recognised or intuited, if man is able to completely withdraw the Veil,[3] and so, do away with all pragmatic limitations, even what is called "central reference".

Now, what is the import of the revelation of this Experience?

(1) Since it is unveiled and free from all limitations, it may be called both Pure and Perfect. It is the Whole[1] and absolutely pure.[4]

[1] Pûrna. [2] Kanchukas.

[3] *i.e.*, Mâyâ of which the other five Kanchukas—Niyati, Kâla, etc., are born. See "Garland of Letters" ("Kanchukas") in which the matter is explained, and authorities are cited. [4] Shuddha.

(2) Since it is alogical and indefinable, it cannot be called a *Tattva* which means Reality-Power defined in a particular way, that is, as regards a phase or aspect. It is therefore beyond [1] (though involving) all (*i.e.*, 36) *Tattvas.*

(3) It is Being, Consciousness, Bliss,[2] but the aspects are not "sundered" or thought apart. It is the manifesting Principle [3] as well as object and manifestation,[4] *Chit* as well as Power, but these are in indistinguishable unity. Something reveals and something is revealed, but there is no logical separation of the one from the other. It is *Parā Samvit* or *Chit* which is Perfect Experience of which the Ether of Consciousness [5] is an undistinguished phase.

Suppose, now, we proceed to think about this alogical Whole of Experience. We ask ourselves: What is it? What is there in it? We see that it is Consciousness stressing as a universe of experience. This is the fullest account we can render of the Fact. We see also that Consciousness and Its Stress or Power is one and not two, though we think them apart. Consciousness, in our review, is the Manifesting Principle,[6] and Its stressing is the content or object of manifestation.[7] But the former is also Power, and the latter is also manifestation (since it is abstraction to say that manifestation is one thing and its "content" or object is another; and though it may be possible in *yoga* to have experience as Pure Manifestation without any special content,[8] in that case, Manifestation becomes its own content; and in other cases where there is special content,[8] this latter as manifested is the indivisible concrete fact which abstraction splits into manifestation *and* manifested). Hence *Shiva-tattva* and *Shakti-tattva*

---

[1] Tattvātita. [2] Sat-Chit-Ānanda. [3] Prakāsha.
[4] Vimarsha; Antarlīna-vimarsha. [5] Chidākāsha.
[6] Prakāsha, called Shiva-tattva.
[7] Vimarsha, called Shakti-tattva. [8] Vishesha.

are one. And yet now, from the standpoint of our thinking, manifestation[1] and manifested[2] exist like two seeds contained in a grain of gram.[3] It is also pure[4] because though our thinking has now distinguished the indistinguishable and thought about the alogical and unthinkable, (1) it has not yet set apart one aspect from the other aspect and looked upon them as distinct Principles (*i.e.*, there is as yet no duality), (2) nor has it yet hedged round and veiled the Complete Fact, accepting parts only and rejecting or ignoring others.

The manifested[2] is the fact of Consciousness being a content or object and making a content or object of itself. (This is depicted in the symbolism of the *Kāmakalāvilāsa*[5] as the reflection of the Self in a mirror).

Suppose next, we essay to give to ourselves a summary statement of the illumining-illumined, this *Shiva-Shakti* experience. What is the most general category under which we may (approximately of course) subsume the experience? By what name may we call it, though absolutely unnamable it be?

The category which most nearly subsumes and expresses the whole of man's experience is—"I" (*Aham*). This "I" should, however, be distinguished from what is pragmatically known and used as "I" which is but a comparatively limited section of experience, referred to a centre, *i.e.*, Ego, and sharply contrasted with a vaster non-ego or not-self, known and used as "*Idam*" or "This". What it may be asked is all this manifestation as experience? And the first

---

[1] Prakāsha.

[2] Vimarsha.

[3] Chanaka.

[4] Shuddha Tattva.

[5] A work by a Shaiva author on the great Shree Yantra of the Divine Mother Mahā-tripura-Sundarī.

and most comprehensive answer is—It is "I".[1] In this, Consciousness or Manifestation makes a content or object of Itself—the Primary Object. And since we have called this fact the illumined,[2] the Primary Object may be called the I-experience.[3] Its logical correlate is, of course, "This,"[4] but in the primary stage, the This is as yet latent, implicit: we know and describe our entire Being-Experience as "I," and nothing but that. In pragmatic thought, "I" is Subject in relation to "This" as Object; but in this primary representation of Experience, "I" as concrete consciousness makes an object of itself, as, relatively speaking, in the pragmatic sphere also, we sometimes make an object of "I" or Ego. And since in the primary presentation, "I" is all-inclusive, leaving no margin for a correlate "This," Power as *Vimarsha*, in so far as it functions to present this latter, may be supposed to be *negative*.[5]

Shiva-tattva is then the presentation (primary in the logical line, but approximate and secondary in relation to *Parā-Samvit* which is alogical) of Experience as an exclusive "I," the associate *Shakti-tattva* so operating as not to present the other logical pole—"Idam" or "This". It is "pure" in the sense that though experience is not here partitioned into "I" and "This," the Whole (with nothing veiled or subtracted) is thought of as "I". The province of "This" not being rejected, is covered by the all-inclusive concept, "I".

Next, in the seamless experience thus intuited as "I," a seam or fissure is seen to appear—the Polarity of I[6] and This,[7] but the latter "Pole" is as yet, very faintly or

---

[1] Not to be confounded with empiric or Pragmatic Ego or Self; it is Transcendental Self, whose object is the universe as itself and not as in the case of the limited self as non-self.

[2] Vimarsha. [3] Aham-vimarsha. [4] Idam-vimarsha.

[5] Nishedha-rūpa. [6] Aham. [7] Idam.

hazily, folded up with the "I". There is as yet (1) no clear differentiation or projection of the latter Pole;[1] and (2) no distinct blossoming[2] of it. The 'This'[1] is faintly perceived by the 'I'[3] as part of the one Self, the emphasis being therefore on the "I" side of experience.[4] There is representation of, and warrant for, this in man's own ordinary experience. This second logical stage is called *Sadāshiva-Tattva*. It is the stage of the subject relation.[5] The This is however here the self and not non-self, in which the stress is on the first. It is also pure[6] (approximately so, when compared with *Parā-Samvit* or the alogical *Whole*), in the sense that, though polarity is here introduced, experience is still intuited as a whole and not in this aspect or that only. The limitations (*Māyā* and "her progeny" contracting experience) have not yet commenced to exist and operate.

An appeal to normal experience will show that when the above stage has been reached, attention or regard swings from "Fact conceived as I" to "Fact conceived as This". This, evidently, is not the Fact (*i.e.*, the Universe of Experience) becoming veiled in one "section" or aspect, and revealed in another. The Fact as a whole was there (approximately, because we were logically operating on the alogical) in the state of I-emphasis,[7] as it is now in the state of This-emphasis.[8] But of the two polar concepts, "I" and "This," the former was emphatic in the first, and latter emphatic in the second. The emphasis or regard

---

[1] Idam.

[2] Sphutatvam. Yogamuni says the function of Power is to negate (Nishedha-vyāpāra-rūpā shaktiḥ). This is said as regards Shakti-Tattva specifically so called; is applicable to all forms of Shakti.

[3] Ahaṁ.

[4] "Garland of Letters," p. 94.

[5] Aham-Idam-Vimarsha.

[6] Shuddha.

[7] Aham-Vimarsha.

[8] Idam-Vimarsha.

plays between these poles. The same complete "Universe" is differently regarded (*viz.*, as "I" and as "This") in the two cases. The Universe has not been sectioned yet, and has not been laid upon any "basis"[1] other than consciousness. There is as yet no double framework, one for the Self and the other for the Not-Self. This is *Īshvara-tattva.* It also is pure.[2]

Then, as a preliminary to the "disruption" of the Universe of Experience into Self and Not-Self, *Purusha* and *Prakriti,* thought of as independent of each other, we have a state of experience in which the "Universe," still remaining (approximately) entire and still regarded as laid upon the one[3] non-dual basis of Consciousness, is conceived both as 'I' and 'This,'[4] the emphasis being laid on both. In normal experience, too, the like of this is seen when man's "Fact" is equally and indifferently regarded as "I" and "This". "I" and "This" here are not the "I" and "This" of ordinary pragmatic thought which refers to different "sections" of experience, and, in the case of external perception, lays them upon a dual and independent basis (*e.g.*, Mind and Matter).

This is *Sadvidyā* or *Shuddhavidyā Tattva.* It is also pure[2] and the last of the pure Tattvas.[5]

After this the operation of *Māyā,*[6] *Kanchukas* and duality[7] begins, concealing and limiting the dimensions of the Universe, and sharply dividing it into Self[8] and Not-Self,[9] setting them up as independent Principles. Commencing from this stage, their reign extends over the evolution

---

[1] Adhikarana.

[2] Shuddha.

[3] Advaita.

[4] Aham and Idam.

[5] Shuddha Tattvas.

[6] See "Shakti and Shākta" and "Garland of Letters"—Māyā Tattva.

[7] Dvaita.

[8] Purusha.

[9] Prakriti.

of the lower *Tattvas* ;[1] and we have, further, the emergence of the order of Time and that of Space, which prior to this were not evolved.

Broadly speaking, then, we have two aspects and two stages in the second aspect: (1) the aspect as Alogical Whole; and (2) that of the transcendentally[2] logical *Shiva-Shakti-tattva* and its unmanifested[3] stages down to *Sadvidya-tattvā*; and (3) the empirical pragmatic manifested stage of the Psycho-physical Potential[4] down to solid matter.[5] The Sāngkhyan Prakriti is one, but in Advaita Shaiva philosophy, many. Between (2) and (3) there is a transitional, dual-non-dual[6] or difference-and-not-difference[7] stage during which *Māyā* (the Principle of Difference),[8] the five ("Sheaths")[9] and *Purusha* or the individual self are evolved.

The main outlines of the order of stages of Cosmic Evolution,[10] are, as indeed they must be, traceable in the evolution of man's own experience, if he essays to uplift, as far as possible, the Veil hiding from his pragmatic eye, the real and total content and import of his life and existence. The more he removes the veil, the larger and deeper become the content and import of *Chit* operating in, and as, himself. The question, evidently, is: What is that content and that import of *Chit* in the "limit," that is, when the veil has been completely uplifted? That "limit" is Consciousness as It is in Itself or *Parā-Samvit*. The main "lines" of the evolution of the microcosm are also,

---

[1] Called Shuddhāshuddha and Ashuddha.

[2] "Transcendental" logic, because the categories here dealt with are the transcendental Aham and Idam, and not pragmatic, empirical Self and Not-Self, Subject and Object.

[3] Adrishtasrishti. [4] Prakriti. [5] Prithivī.

[6] Advaita-dvaita. [7] Bhedābheda.

[8] Bhedabuddhi. [9] Kanchuka. [10] Tattva.

in the "limit," the lines of the evolution of the macrocosm. Those "lines," are: (*a*) A neutral, undifferentiated, non-polarized condition (the Alogical); (*b*) a condition of potential differentiation or polarization, in which, the Substance still remaining undivided, there is emphasis on one "pole" or on the other (the condition of Fundamental Movement);[1] and (*c*) the condition of actual dissociation of the poles, and resultant splitting up of the non-dual Substance into dual and Manifold. The Supreme Point[2] must be implicit in the second stage, since we cannot have "poles," potential or differentiated, and stressing upon and between them, without Power focussing itself into a Point.[3] *Bindu* is manifestly operative in the third or differentiating and multiplying stage.

Now, Matter (believed to be constituted by Positive and Negative charges of electricity) may be, and by some has been, conceived as evolving from the Mother Stuff (*e.g.*, Ether) substantially in the manner described in (*a*), (*b*) and (*c*)—a neutral state; a potentially polar (but undissociated) stressing state; and a dissociated (though configurated), stressing state of electrons and protons constituting an atom of Matter. The non-nucleated protoplasm; the nucleated protoplasm in which the sex-difference is still implicit; the organised plant or animal tissue in which the sexes gradually dissociate themselves (in some plants, for example, though the sexes are dissociated, they are still parts of the same organism); these prove the "lines" or stages in vital evolution. Or, without reference to sex-difference, we might trace the "lines" more simply thus: first, non-nucleated protoplasm in which the nucleus may be implicit; second, the nucleated protoplasm often

---

[1] Of Spanda, Para Shabdā or Para-Nāda.

[2] Para Bindu.

[3] Chidghana.

involving another nucleus within itself, stressing, under the conditions of nutrition, etc., to "divide" itself; third, the divided cell of protoplasm, each with its own independent nucleus. In experience, too, knowledge begins with an undifferentiated state; evolves the poles (first associated and co-substantial) of "I" and "This"; dissociates the poles and makes independent substances of them. The study of even a common act of perception, if not allowed to be swayed and cramped by pragmatic considerations, will show that this is so. Man's experience has three broad forms. Cognition, Feeling-attitude and Volition; each is, or tends to become, polar; thus cognition is of this object or of that; feeling is either pleasure or pain; volition is either attractive or repulsive.[1] Now, intuition is relied on to show that a neutral, non-polar condition is the basis and background of each of these three pairs of poles. Cognition of this or that is based upon, and branches off from, a generic cognition;[2] pleasure and pain are based upon, and shoot out from, a "mother-stuff" of feeling which is veiled bliss;[3] and attraction and repulsion[1] presuppose, and may reveal, a placid background of quiescence.[4]

So the "lines" of the Grand Cosmic Evolution, as traced before, are repeated in the details of creation.

And, all that exists, all whether as Mind, Life and Matter, are forms and products of the one fundamental Substance-Power which is *Chit-Shakti*, or unlimited Being-Consciousness as Power which is also Bliss.

---

[1] Râga or Dvesha.
[2] Sâmânya jnâna.
[3] Ânanda.
[4] Shântabhâva.

CHAPTER X

RETROSPECT AND CONCLUSION

THERE is no finality in human science, and its conclusions are, and are apt to remain, for the most part dubious. Yet, the results and hypotheses of science in the domains of Matter, Life and Mind (including what are called "para-psychic phenomena") as they now stand, and also regard being had to what they now point to, appear to be not antagonistic to the principles of *Shākta Vedāntism*; nay, they appear, so far as they go, to fit in with those principles. The modern dynamic view of the constitution of Matter—a view that has tended to dematerialise Matter; a view that sees in the atoms of Matter a vast magazine of Power; a view that is faced with a residual element of the inexplicable in all its mechanistic explanations; a view that sees in radio-activity the drafting of new and practically inexhaustible energy into the hither-to-supposed close-ed and constant realm of physical energies;—already shows that Physical Science has taken vast strides towards the *Shākta* position which (*a*) makes Power to be the essence of everything; (*b*) makes Power in reality immeasurable in everything and in the universe for the matter of that; and (*c*) makes the "Dynamic Point" the Perfect Magazine of Power (hence making the "atom" also a vast magazine). As regards the further and higher view of *Vedānta* that this Power manifesting as Matter is essentially Consciousness-Power which is measureless Joy expressed in unrestricted Play, Physical Science has, as such, nothing to say at present; but if one were logically to work out what is now implicit in its position, and imagine the promise contained therein fulfilled, particularly in consonance with the results and promises of Biological and Psychical Sciences, one might feel that Science has, unconsciously, taken even a longer stride than one would imagine towards the final position of *Shākta* Vedāntism. To see this, the results and indications of one Science should not be reviewed by themselves alone; but they should be correlated to, co-ordinated with those of the Sister Sciences—because, Science is one. As it is, Physical Science within her own province has steadily, and now very closely, approached the ideal of unification and correlation. She has tended more and more to reduce all kinds of Matter to one kind, and all forms of Energy to one kind; and has, further, tended to reduce Matter and Energy to a Common Root. So that the physical universe has now become a universe of Stress-systems, not of gross stresses only but subtle stresses (as evidenced by X and other invisible rays, and the Hertzian waves of the wireless among other things), not limited and calculable but practically unlimited and incalculable (as evidenced by radio-activity), not forming a "closed curve" but in subtle and constant action and reaction with other kinds of forces—vital and psychic.

The Vital and Psychic Sciences, in their turn, are helping this grand unification and the universal linking up of forces and phenomena. Though the "living molecule" is now even a greater mystery than it ever was, the gulf between the living and the non-living is steadily narrowing rather than widening, and already there are indicators of the characteristic responses of the living being, in a veiled way, discoverable in the so-called non-living matter; and, within the province of the living itself, the supposed absolute difference between plant life and animal life is in the course of being gradually effaced, not of being accentuated. Evolution is now sought to be explained less and less on mechanistic lines or in terms of "fortuitous modifications," and more and more in terms of an "original impetus," free and not determined, given in the constitution of things and at the root of phenomena to change and evolve (a position from which one can have a vision of Vedāntic Joy and Play—the basic factors of world-evolution and involution). And Biologists, no less than Physicists, are now on the way to perceiving that the path of world-evolution is not traced by an "upward movement" only, but that it is a curve showing rhythms and cycles—making the world's history one of evolution and involution and then evolution again.

Within the living organism itself Biology, so long content to explain its phenomena on quasi-mechanistic lines in terms of nerve-stimulation, cell-disturbance, and so forth, has now unexpectedly stumbled upon a new and mysterious factor whose action on the organism is found to be more profoundly "vital" than that of any other known agency: the mysterious glands ("pituitary," "pineal," "thyroid," "adrenal," "interistial") and their mysterious secretions ("hormones"). Descartes, it is true, had suggested the pineal gland as the "bridge" between the Mind and Matter in us; but he was never taken seriously until quite recently.

Correspondence between Science and *Shākta* Doctrine should be understood in the full depth of its import. It shows that as in radio-activity Science has discovered the physical atom to be a magazine of Power whereby its constitution as well as its "evolution" (or transmutation) is determined, so in the case of the cells of these glands and their subtle secretions (analogous to the radiations of the radio-active atom) she has now discovered a magazine of Power and its workings whereby the constitution of the body and its growth, etc., are regulated. In Physics she has discovered the vast potency and efficiency of the smallest thing—the atom, and of its unseen emanations; in Biology she has discovered the wonderful potency and efficiency of the smallest constituents of the gland and of their subtle secretions. Apparently the smallest is thus being perceived to be really and dynamically the greatest—a perception which is preparing the way for a final recognition of the "Dynamic Point" of the *Shākta* Doctrine, which is "smaller than the smallest and greater than the greatest".

As regards the position that Consciousness merely accompanies and "lights up" some of the processes of the nervous system (*viz.*, the cerebral processes), it has been shown before that the actual evidence before us does not warrant the conclusion (1) that Consciousness is simply an onlooker and revealer exercising no causal influence on the cortical phenomena which by themselves form a "closed curve"; and (2) that Consciousness as such, that is as distinguished from that part of it which is pragmatically accepted as *the* Consciousness, is limited to the cerebral centres and lines only, not having anything to do with other centres which are commonly taken as subconscious or unconscious. On the contrary, on two grounds at least Consciousness must be believed to possess causal efficiency (not merely as a directing force or "switcher" but as a supplier of new energy)[1] over the whole range of man's

[1] As the physical doctrine of Conservation of Matter and Energy has now ceased to be looked upon as an "axiom" or "first principle" in view of radio-activity and the dynamic and evolutionary view of Matter, the fact that Consciousness is a supplier of new energy is no challenge to an "established" law of Matter and Energy.

nervous mechanism: *(a)* the fact that a very slight stimulus (*e.g.*, the reading of a line of a message that a beloved friend is seriously ill) provokes an enormous and complicated response (in emotion, idea and action) out of all proportion to the physical nature and intensity of the provoking cause; and *(b)* the fact that the activity of every nerve-centre whether in the cerebrum or in the spinal cord, is in the nature of an overflow of energy and selective operation (suggesting, therefore, Joy, Play and Choice). Besides these, there is also the indisputable evidence of self-consciousness showing Consciousness—to be an ever-active operative Power—not merely in the so-called "motor" phenomena of conscious experience as attending, striving and willing, but also in what are called the "sensory," cognitive and affective phenomena—knowing, imagining, thinking and feeling. Consciousness as operative Power is a matter of direct and constant experience.

Mental Science, in dealing with ordinary psychic and the "parapsychic" phenomena, is steadily veering round to a position whence one can have not a very distant view of the ultimate truth as held in Shākta Vedāntism. Mental Science is coming to recognise (1) that ordinary, pragmatic consciousness is only a part of a large Consciousness which it now calls "Sub-consciousness"; (2) that this larger Consciousness is not only a Power but the Power which seems to contain within itself the whole mystery and wonder of Life and existence; (3) that this larger Consciousness is one in which all individual pragmatic consciousnesses "live, move and have their being"; that it is to the individual Centres what the Ether is believed by many to be in relation to the strain-and-stress centres in it; (4) that to this larger Consciousness, Matter and Force are not alien, but they seem to be its evolutes, products and dependents; and finally, (5) that Time and Space also are not alien to, and independent of, it; that these are its own ways of representing itself to the centres involved in it. The fourth point is being steadily established by the accumulation of phenomena collected under the general heading, "psychodynamism"; and the fifth by the phenomena of "psychometry," "X-ray vision," and so forth, in which spatial determinations such as "here and there," "near and distant," as well as temporal determinations such as "now and then," "past and future" all appear to be, not only "in the melting pot," but meeting in a "Point".

Referring to certain genuine cases of pre-vision of the future (Dr. Maxwell's, Professor Flournoy's, Mrs. Verrall's . . .) M. Mæterlinck writes . . . "Under the erroneous idea we form of the past and the present, a new verity is living and moving, eager to come to light. The efforts of that verity . . . strike to the very roots of history. We soon lose all inclination to doubt. We penetrate into another world and come to a stop all out of countenance. We no longer know where we stand; before and after overlap and mingle, we no longer distinguish the insidious and factitious but indispensable line which separates the years that have gone by from the years that are to come. . . . We discover with uneasiness that time, on which we based our whole existence, itself no longer exists . . . it alters its position no more than space, of which it is doubtless but the incomprehensible reflex. It reigns in the centre of every event; and every event is fixed in its centre; and all that comes and all that goes passes from end to end of our little life without moving by a hair's breadth around its motionless pivot . . . yesterday, recently, formerly, erstwhile, after, before, to-morrow, soon, never, later fall like childish masks, whereas to-day and always cover with their united shadows the idea which we form in the end of a duration which has no subdivisions, no breaks and no stages, which is pulseless, motionless and boundless."

The "to-day and always" without subdivisions and breaks and stages is rather the "now and always"—showing Duration[1] in the aspect of "Point" (now) and in that of boundless "Continuum" (always); that is to say Duration which has no beginning and no end and breaks is also wholly condensed into a "Point," and this latter aspect is referred to above as the "centre of every event" or phenomenon, "its motionless pivot". But though the centre or pivot is "motionless" in this sense that the whole of Duration or History is condensed into, and as, it (so that to be at the centre is also to be and have the whole), it is also dynamic in the sense that the centre or "Point" does expand as a sphere, and an ever-widening sphere, which is the Experience of Duration—the beginningless and endless History with past, present and future. If the "Point" were to remain statical, there would be no experience of Duration or History as it actually is (involving past and future); on the other hand, if Duration or History were not wholly condensed into, and given in and as, the Point, the pre-existence of the future in the present, and therefore, foreknowledge of the future (either Divine or human—that of the "seer") would not be possible; but since this is said to be not only possible but is, already to some extent, a fact, so it is claimed, perfect foreknowledge and perfect recollection must be believed to be possible also; and that is possible only if the Future and the Past in their entireness co-exist and meet at a Point.

The same reasoning will apply to Space also. If the "X-ray vision" with respect to a spatially remote thing or event be a fact, then, we must believe that Space too, like

[1] This is Parakāla, or supreme Time, as opposed to Kāla which only comes in "with moon and sun".

Time, has the twofold aspect of "here and everywhere"[1] —the former aspect (here) containing as a "Point" the whole of Space regarded as a boundless "Continuum" ("everywhere"). And the "Point" is dynamic in the sense above explained.

The Dynamic Point, as we have seen, occupies a very prominent place in the Shâkta-Vedânta: It is the Consciousness-Power regarded as Perfect Potency to envolve; and It is also a Perfect Universe in the sense that whatever is to evolve as the world in Time, Space and Causal concatenation, is contained in the *Bindu* which is the seed of everything. It is thus the centre of every being and every event: the centre "swells"[2] into every being and every event, and every being and every event is reabsorbed, folded up into the centre. Time, Space and Causality are "forms" or modes of such "swelling" and "shrinking"[3] of the Dynamic Point. Hence to be consciously in touch with the *Bindu* is to know whatever exists or goes on in the spatial, temporal and causal scheme of the universe.

The possibility of foreknowledge (perfect or partial) does not, however, require that the world-order is unalterably fixed and determined leaving no margin for free play. The world is a free play;[4] every being is an incarnation of Joy; and every act and event is a play out of Joy. Joy and Play are the "birthright" even of the so-called material thing, and, there is no reason to suppose that it has entirely forfeited that right. Actions are, more of less, free or

[1] *Cf.* the verse (before quoted in Vishvasâra-tantra): "What is here is everywhere, and what is not here is nowhere."

[2] Uchchhûnatâ.

[3] Sangkochaprasara. *Cf.* The modern dynamic view of the Atom as outlined by Bohr and others, and the Quantum Theory of Radiation (the "Compton Effect" in particular).

[4] *Cf.* the saying of Dionysius—"He, the very cause of all things, becomes ecstatic, moves out of Himself, by the abundance of His loving Goodness," etc.

undetermined in every instance. No foreknowledge of them is, therefore, possible if, and so long as, we take actions and events in the ordinary temporal way—arranging them according to the scheme of past, present and future: what is not yet determined cannot now be known. But in the Dynamic Point where all times and spaces meet (in an alogical and unthinkable way), what is not yet co-exists with what has been and what is. So that there the undetermined future co-exists with the determined past, and with the present determining itself. Here, therefore, foreknowledge of a still undetermined future becomes possible, because here Time itself is annulled or transcended. A "seer" placing himself in rapport with this "Point"-Universe may, therefore, (it is said) "see" exactly how a person "will" act or an event "will" happen, though the acting and the happening are, wholly or partly, free and undetermined.

This "mystic sense" is, of course, inexplicable. But we may suppose that the seer may, after seeing the free and undetermined act in the timeless and spaceless Point, decipher his mystic knowledge back into temporal and spatial terms, and predict that so-and-so will act thus or do this at that particular moment and that at that particular place. The case is, in a way, analogous to the "deciphering" by the motion of the machine itself of a gramophone record where a song is given and inscribed in co-existent scratches back into the singing of the song in which the notes succeed one another. The analogy, however, is partial, because, though the record contains an order of succession transformed into an order of co-existence, it is not the "Point" transcending both Time and Space; and so what the machine does is apparently to retranslate a song already determined and spatially inscribed into a rehearsal of the song in the usual temporal way.

Whilst the *Sangkhyan* Doctrine makes the evolution of the world a process of actual change of the Root Principle, and *Māyāvāda* makes it one of seeming change of *Brahman*, the *Shākta* Doctrine combines the two views recognising in each a partial truth. The Root changes as the evolving world, and yet, It changelessly abides—an insoluble logical contradiction for which, however, man has, in his own experience, sufficient warrant. The corollaries to this Principle of Evolution are important:

(1) Pure and Perfect Consciousness, in evolving by Its own Power as finite and particular consciousnesses (*i.e.*, consciousness of varying modes, degrees and limits), does never cease to be Pure and Perfect Consciousness; so that, restricted consciousness, "sub-consciousness" and "unconsciousness" are imbedded in a never-failing background of Pure and Perfect Consciousness.

(2) Consciousness as Pure and Perfect Bliss-Joy and Freedom-Play remains as such, never ceases to be other than Itself, though, as finite centres, It evolves as infinitely varied pleasures and pains, actions and their determining conditions. Just as in the first case, the Universe regarded as Experience is not merely the sum total of restricted, particularised consciousness, subconsciousness and unconsciousness, but is like an unbounded sphere of Pure and Perfect Consciousness within which these are included as smaller spheres, so also in the second case, Pure and Perfect Bliss-Joy and Freedom-Play is not the sum total of the particular pleasures and pains, actions and conditions of the particular centres, but, (*a*) includes these and is immanent (as an unfailing background) in these, and (*b*) exceeds these as Pure and Perfect Bliss.

(3) Its condensation as the Dynamic Point does not efface the immensity of Its Being-Power; hence, the Point = the whole *Brahman* or *Shiva-Shakti*.

(4) The Point also, in actually "swelling" and "shrinking" (as evolution and involution of the world), does not cease to be the Perfect *Bindu.*[1]

Each of these corollaries, it will be observed, involves the insoluble logical contradiction above referred to.

In the scheme of 36 Principles outlined in the previous chapter, it has been noted that *Īshvara-tattva* has a place especially assigned to it, and that, considered in that technical sense, it is not the highest category. The highest Category in the logical line is *Shiva-Shakti,* beyond which there is *Para-Samvit* which is alogical, beyond the scheme of Principles, and, therefore, not Itself a Category. It will thus be perceived that what western metaphysic and religion regard as the highest category of Being and Thought (*viz.*, God) cannot be identified with the *Īshvara* in the above scheme: It corresponds rather to *Shiva-Shakti.* The *Shāstra,* however, does not require that the "higher" and "lower" in the above scheme should be taken in a rigid and absolute way, especially in that part of the scheme which shows the evolution of what are called "Pure" Principles. In the domain of the "impure" Principles—where *Māyā* and the Envelopes hold their sway—"higher and lower" as also "before and after," "cause and consequence" have ordinary, pragmatic meanings; but in the realm of Pure Principles, each *is* the Whole with the emphasis of logical representation laid on a special

[1] The fact that Matter and Energy are both of "granular structure," coupled with the fact that Life also is now recognised, (*e.g.*, in Arrheneus' theory of *Cosmozoa* or *Panspermia* which posits "atoms" of Life), as "atomistic," together with the fact that Mind and Soul are widely believed to exist and operate as "atoms" of Energy, shows that the Bindu as such is at the root of all existence and operation. It is now further recognised that both in the creation of "atoms" of matter and their disintegration, enormously concentrated Energy is required; and that high concentration of Energy is required also for the evolution of organic from so-called inorganic matter. Concentrated Power is an approximate representation of Bindu.

aspect (such as "I" or "This"). Hence, *Shiva-Shakti* is also usually spoken of as *Maheshvara-maheshvarī* or as *Parameshvara-Parameshvarī*—usually with the epithets *mahat* (Great) or *Parama* (Supreme) prefixed to the term *Īshvara.*

Now, *Shiva-Shakti* is Being-Consciousness-Bliss. This Supreme Principle veils and finitizes Itself in, and as, the world of finite Centres. As a consequence we have not only different modes of finite being but even so-called "non-being"; different modes of particular consciousnesses but even so-called "unconsciousness"; and different modes of joy and pleasure but also "pains" and "sorrows". Thus also, God who is Pure Act becomes in, and as, the finite Centres actions-and-reactions, conditional actions; Who is Perfect "Energy," becomes in and as, such Centres, mixtures of potential and kinetic power—in which Power is neither wholly kinetic nor wholly potential, and therefore, imperfect energy. But in evolving as all this, the Supreme Principle remains Supreme Being-consciousness-Bliss, Pure Act and Perfect Energy: we have thus an alogical mingling of change and changelessness in the Life of the Perfect Being-Power.

There is much actual pain and sorrow in the world. Since the Supreme Experience of God includes all this, how can it be said that the Supreme Experience is all Bliss? The Supreme Experience (1) sums up all particular pains and sorrows as also all particular pleasures and happinesses, and (2) involves each particular pain or pleasure as such. Now, in the first case, it need not be supposed that the grand total of all pains and pleasures must be a prodigious pain *plus* a prodigious pleasure. As two sets of opposing forces may produce in the resultant not motion this way or that but rest or quiescence; as, again, the sum of all particular sounds is, according to *Mantra-Shâstra,* the *Mahāmantra Om*; as, also, in the realm of colours the synthesis of all the colourbands is white light;—so it may be reasonable to suppose that the grand total of all pleasures and pains is not a dual experience of great pleasure *and* great pain, but a non-dual alogical experience of something which is akin to man's feeling of quiescence. And this feeling of quiescence is imbedded in an undiminished Bliss-Consciousness which, as the *Shāstra* maintains, perpetually abides even while finite Centres of Expression appear in It.

In the latter case, particular pleasures and pains as such enter into the Supreme Experience. But even that does not make that Experience other than an Experience of Bliss-Joy. In the first place, each particular pleasure or pain is not there in Divine experience in a veiled, isolated and disconnected way, but in the fullness of its relation to other feelings and to the whole; and as a particular note, discordant in itself, may not be so when it forms an element of the harmony of a symphony, so a feeling, painful when its relations and background are veiled, may not be so when it is consciously set in its relations to the whole. Hence, Divine Consciousness, though It involves and knows all particular feelings of particular Centres, involves and knows them as "elements" of an infinite whole of Experience, so that their effective tones as veiled and disconnected particulars do not remain when seen as elements of a Grand Harmony which is Divine Life. Pain is feeling of bar or constraint which is created by veiling or ignorance. In Divine Experience there is no ignorance, and therefore, no bar: particulars exist in it but not veiled away from the whole. In such Experience, therefore, there can be no pain as such.

In the second place, the Supreme Being having by His own activity evolved as particular Centres and their particular experiences of pleasure and pain, knows in, and as, such Centres all their pleasures and pains. In fact, their pleasures and pains are His pleasures and pains. Hence, as such Centres, He feels pleasure as pleasure and pain as pain. Therefore, we have four forms: (1) Divine Life as transcendent-immanent Being-Consciousness-Bliss which is unchanged in changing as the varied world—this guarantees a background and "atmosphere" of Bliss-Joy for all particular feelings of whatever kind; (2) Divine Life as the grand total of all particular feelings, which is a Life of Bliss and Quiescence, though the particular constituents may be variously pleasurable or painful; (3) Divine Life as the grand Harmony in which particular feelings without coalescing and neutralizing one another are "seen" in their proper and true relations like the notes of a symphony; and (4) Divine Life as the Life of the particular Centres with their particular pleasures and pains. In the last case, pleasures and pains are "seen" as such, but since the Supreme Being, in becoming a particular Centre, does not (*a*) cease to be Supreme and (*b*) pure Bliss-Consciousness, it follows that the "seeing" of particular pleasures and pains of particular Centres by God means their being reflected on a pure and perfect Bliss-Consciousness, imbedded in an unbounded mass of Pure Joy:[1] It is Infinite Joy and Bliss looking finite pleasures and pains in the face.

Such reflexion of man's pleasures and pains on Cosmic Bliss-Consciousness renders divine compassion and grace possible. And it should be noted that *Shākta Vedānta*, in its practical aspect, is not the Path of Effort and Action[2] only, or the Path of Contemplation and Meditation[3] only, but it also is the Path of Devotion and Love.[4] It is not

[1] Anandā-shraya.
[2] Karma-yoga.
[3] Jnāna-yoga.
[4] Bhakti-yoga.

simply an Art that achieves, a Science that knows, but it is also an Æsthetic awakening in the aspirant of spiritual thirst and feeling, making him love and worship the Divine Mother whose play it is to bind and whose grace it is to liberate. As on the speculative side this doctrine is a synthesis and harmony of partial, and sometimes warring truths, so on the practical side it is a summing up and reconciliation of divergent methods of realisation.

As the Doctrine of Power it looks upon every Centre as a veiled Cosmic Power and makes its emancipation the realization by it that it is the Cosmic Power. Naturally the greatest emphasis is laid on active Effort in the practice of realization. It rightly recognises that complete self-surrender to God and absolute reliance on God's grace is not at all a negative and passive attitude signifying lack of will and power, but it is, really, perfect self-exertion and heroism, and "conquest" of divinity: that if to strive after divinity connotes exertion of Power, surrender to and reliance on divine grace, to the exclusion and inhibition of all little, ordinary self-seekings and self-adjustments, also connotes it. This doctrine lends no countenance to such methods as are really calculated to diminish the efficiency of human will and endeavour, such as really spell lack of vitality. As on the speculative side the essence of Reality is Power, so on the practical side the essence of spiritual endeavour is dynamism.

Accordingly, it is not a cult of false asceticism and excessive mortification of the "flesh". Since all is manifestation of Bliss-Consciousness-Power, and every object of creation, however apparently "lowly" and "insignificant", is an incarnation and magazine of such Power, the highest end of realization cannot be achieved by fleeing from or rejecting the world of objects, but by removing the veil of practical ignorance which has concealed from men their true nature of Bliss-Consciousness-Power. When the veil is removed, the Experience of realization will be of the form "All is *Brahman*"[1] as well as of the form "Thou art It".[2] It is man's use, or rather abuse, that has made things—in reality, "True, good and beautiful"—lowly, bad, ugly, evil and so forth. There are other things, too, which, in man's use, are high, good, beautiful and so forth; but they are finitely and relatively so. To realise "All is *Brahman*," these latter must be perceived to be infinitely and absolutely so—that is, each object must be realized as Mother *Sachchidānanda-mayī* Herself. More essential and more difficult becomes the task when the former objects—lowly, ugly and evil—have to be so realized. And they must be so realized—else, "All is not *Brahman*"—there will be duality of Good and Evil and so forth. Hence, greater emphasis should be laid on this latter task: the aspirant must know that it is ignorant abuse that has made these things evil and ugly and that he can reach his goal of non-dual Perfect Experience only by seeing, realizing the *Brahman* in and through them. This is the true principle of the psycho-physical ritual in the *Shāstra*. It is the effort of the Hero,[3] and not of the ordinary man in his bonds of convention.[4] The purification of the five "tattvas"[5] means or should mean the casting off of their pragmatic sheaths of abuse and ignorance in which they masquerade as lowly and ugly and evil; when these sheaths are cast away, they are as much true, good and beautiful as the Self of the aspirant, and then, they can be assimilated, the result being the Self and the Not-Self assimilated to each other in, and as, the Whole.

---

[1] Sarvang Khalvidang Brahman.

[2] Tattvamasi.

[3] Vīra.

[4] Pashu.

[5] See "Shakti and Shākta," "The Panchatattva."

As to the question whether *Shākta* Doctrine affords a sure and sufficient basis for man's belief in a Personal and Moral God, it may be observed only this that though the Reality-Whole = Perfect Experience = Alogical = beyond all duality such as moral = non-moral, personal = impersonal, and so forth, yet the most fundamental expression of the Supreme Reality-Power is the Supreme "Joy"[1] = Supreme Person = God. God, therefore, is quite secure in this Doctrine, though it does not allow the defining and circumscribing of a Reality which is indefinable and immeasurable. The Supreme Being-Power is a Personal and Moral God, but personality and morality are attributes that do not exhaust the immensity of Supreme Being.

Further, since this Doctrine in solving the world-problem suffers no residue, overt or covert, of duality tore main, since, therefore, according to it, the "lowliest" object is really the Mother who is *Sachchidānanda-mayī* Herself, it follows that physical, moral and æsthetic evil exists only in ignorance and non-acceptance of the Whole, and that in the eyes of him who sees the Whole, the Mother showing Herself in an infinite variety of expression (which finite Centres may know pragmatically as good or bad, true or false, beautiful or ugly and so forth) never goes out of Her Being-essence which is Being-Consciousness-Bliss.

The Cosmos being the theatre of Divine Play provides the arena in which the Centres must interplay and ultimately realise the Divinity playing in, and as, them. The scheme of creation and the principles on which it is run are calculated to lead progressively to the end or purpose of the world-scheme.

As the belief in Universal Power has been the basis of all ancient human faiths, so a body of "mysterious"

[1] See the explanation of Shiva-tattva with its associate Shakti-tattva in the preceding chapter. It is the highest in the "logical line".

rites (called "magical") has been at the basis of all ancient human religious practices. The nature of "magic" has been commonly misunderstood; but modern thought is slowly coming to recognise that it is not "meaningless"; that it is a kind of "primitive science" whereby the primitive man, still in the lower grades of culture, has essayed to propitiate the powers by which he thinks he is encompassed and turn their influence to his own best account. The definition is substantially correct, if we drop the terms by which the cult of magic is thus evaluated as "primitive", "lower", and so forth, and if we drop also the distinction commonly made between magic which is supposed to involve no sense of man's dependence on higher Powers and no element of worship and religion which involves both. *Tāntric* ritual (whether we call it magic or not) is based upon the Science that the World is Power which is the same as the Consciousness-Power in man, that the Cosmic Power can be linked up with Man-Power by worship and other means, giving effectiveness and success to man in the pursuit of his ends, in the world or as liberation therefrom.

This linking up is held to be possible, for at root man's power is the Cosmic Power. The Kulārnava Tantra says that in Shākta doctrine world-enjoyment may be made *Yoga.*[1] Power may be realised in a twofold way; man may wish to remain man, to perfect himself as man, and to have such worldy enjoyment as he may lawfully desire.[2] He then cultivates those powers which are the Mother in Form. Or he may desire to be one with the Formless Mother Herself. This end also may, (according to the system) be achieved on the path of world-enjoyment

---

[1] Bhogo Yogāyate.

[2] In the Purushārtha Dharma or law and morality, is a governing factor both in the case of Kāma and Artha, on the world-path (Pravritti mārga).

provided that it be realised that the individual life is a part of the divine action in nature and not a separate thing to be held and pursued apart for its own sake only. In the Vedas enjoyment is the fruit of sacrifice and the gift of the gods. The higher sacrifice is to the Mother-Power of whom all deities and all men are inferior forms. When this is known and man unifies himself with that Cosmic Power, enjoyment becomes *Yoga* and passage is made to that state in which there is neither sacrifice nor sacrificer. This is the Supreme Experience which is the Mother-Power in Her own formless nature. As the Creatrix of forms the Divine Mother is *Māyā*, and as the produced individual form *Avidyā* (ignorance). As Liberatrix from the ignorance of the forms which are of Her making She is *Mahā-Māyā*.[1] In the Shakti Sūtras of Agastya all is spoken of in terms of Power, which is the essence of Reality as World, and which is the Real, both as God and God-head.[2]

---

[1] Literally, the term means "The Great Measurer". It includes, therefore, Māyā, and is, sometimes, regarded as this latter cosmically considered. In some places, too (*e.g.*, in some of the verses of the Kālikā and Devī Purāna) the term is taken to mean the Veiler even of the Creator, Sustainer and Destroyer of the World. But, fundamentally, She is, according to Shāstra, the Whole Reality-Power, both in Its veiling and revealing, binding and liberating aspect, emphasis being, often, laid on the latter aspect. As the Supreme Veiler She is commonly referred to as Mahā-mohā, and as the Supreme Revealer She is called Mahā-vidyā. In her aspect as Māyā, She is, generally, described as the veiler, creating and drawing the veil over all particular existences; and, according as this veil makes for Bhoga or for Yoga, She is called Bhoga-māyā or Yoga-māyā. For a comprehensive conception of Mahā-māyā, see, in particular, Shri Chandī, Chap. I, 54-87. Verses 55, 56 show Her as the Supreme Veiler, and verse 57 as the Supreme Revealer ("Paramā vidyā"; "mukter Hetu-bhūtā sanātanī"). Verse 58 calls her the Root of the Sangsāra (World) Bond, and, also, the Lord of the Lord of All ("Sarveshvareshvarī").

[2] In Māyāvāda God is only pragmatically real. Though the Shakti-Vāda Brahman has a transcendent aspect, yet it, in such aspect, only, exceeds but does not exclude its aspect as Lord.